Big Ol'!

You' Be da' Man! Without You We'd Be Less + Your Make Us MORE!!

Joe

Cool Hand Lou

*My Fifty Years in Hollywood
and on Broadway*

LOU ANTONIO

McFarland & Company, Inc., Publishers
Jefferson, North Carolina

Unless otherwise noted, all photographs
are from the author's collection.

LIBRARY OF CONGRESS CATALOGUING-IN-PUBLICATION DATA

Names: Antonio, Lou, 1934– author.
Title: Cool hand Lou : my fifty years in Hollywood and on Broadway /
Lou Antonio.
Description: Jefferson, North Carollina : McFarland & Company, Inc.,
Publishers, 2017. | Includes index.
Identifiers: LCCN 2017038140 | ISBN 9781476668154
(softcover : acid free paper) ∞
Subjects: LCSH: Antonio, Lou, 1934– | Actors—United States—Biography. |
Television producers and directors—United States—Biography.
Classification: LCC PN2287.A66 A3 2017 | DDC 791.4302/8092 [B]—dc23
LC record available at https://lccn.loc.gov/2017038140

BRITISH LIBRARY CATALOGUING DATA ARE AVAILABLE

ISBN 978-1-4766-6815-4 (print)
ISBN 978-1-4766-2804-2 (ebook)

Front cover: The author portraying Lord Byron in a 1955 stage production
of the Tennessee Williams play *Camino Real.*

Printed in the United States of America

McFarland & Company, Inc., Publishers
Box 611, Jefferson, North Carolina 28640
www.mcfarlandpub.com

Table of Contents

Preface

In these pages you will meet many of the brave folks who face the realities of trying to make a living out of make-believe. It is also a tempered warning to the unwary innocents and a reminder for the "old pros" never to stop creating and surprising us. Or teaching us.

I learned about theatre and acting from working with Ruth Gordon, Colleen Dewhurst, Lee Strasberg, Zero Mostel, Lonny Chapman, Garson Kanin, Josh Logan, Julie Harris, Elia Kazan.

Roll cameras—There I am at various times and locations directing George C. Scott, Elizabeth Taylor, Stockard Channing, Billy Crystal, Michelle Williams, Art Carney, Lee Remick, and William Shatner shattering the Captain Kirk persona with delight and irreverence. Print, please!

As you'll see, by stirring the past into the present the actors, writers, directors, all performing art contributors constantly elevate their crafts even higher. Careful though, self-congratulation can dampen the burn to learn. Talent can also be like Cyrano's nose, unique and ridiculed. Abandon our fields of battle? Never. As a dying Cyrano intones, "I fight on, I fight … on." As we must.

So please turn off your television, cell phones and unwrap your candy. The Exit Signs are posted there, in your mind. Thank you for coming, and I hope you enjoy our players.

PART ONE

New York, Mostly

1

When You Begin
a Beginning

I was a 12-year-old Little League catcher in Oklahoma City watching a newsreel between a *Flash Gordon* serial chapter and Coming Attractions, when Ted Williams flashed before my eyes in black and white. The swing, the grace, his personality and talent—from that darkened neighborhood movie theater, I wanted to squat behind home plate in Fenway Park. Five years later, a Red Sox scout spotted me in a high school game and told my coach he was interested, to keep in touch. Two games later, I stole home, started to get up, but my right arm didn't want to. It just lay there in the red dust of Oklahoma. Coach Applebee ran to me: "Don't move, Lou, just lay still." He pushed his foot hard to my chest, took my arm by the wrist and pulled. With a pop in my shoulder, and a yelp from me, my arm snapped back into its socket, hanging useless at my side the rest of the day. The orthopedic options were to operate on my shoulder or keep it strapped tightly to my chest for two months. Either way, a 50–50 chance of recovery. At those odds, I chose the sling. For 60 days I fumbled with my left hand writing, eating, doing one particular bathroom necessity rather awkwardly. After my arm was out of the sling, I did pushups and heaved a 12-pound shot put twice a day to strengthen my throwing arm. Fit and strong, I was behind the plate again that summer for Fred Jones Ford, an American Legion team. A guy tried to steal second, I threw, the ball flew from my hand, my shoulder went out of place, the ball bounced off the pitcher's mound and rolled six feet to a stop. My Fenway Park dream died.

Even though coach Applebee shrugged off our injuries with his oft-repeated "Take a chew and forget it," I had to face my withered dream. I could never be a part of baseball. So I took a chew. There had to be more to me than baseball. I just had to find out what it was.

My brother Jim, three years older than I, went to Oklahoma University on a baseball scholarship and enrolled in the drama school. Along with cheering him in baseball, I applauded him in plays! It looked to me like he was having a swell time up there. Since Birdie Tebbetts didn't have to worry any more about my taking his job, I figured I might as well give that play-acting thing a go. That's what big brothers do, set an example. For better or for worse.

In my senior year at Central High, I played a gangster in George M. Cohan's *Seven Keys to Baldpate*, a creaky old mystery that my high school allowed to be performed only if the one "damn" was deleted. Too heavy an expletive for innocent Oklahoma City ears in the '50s. Once I was up there in front of an audience, it was like playing a ball game. Bases loaded, I'm at bat, it's three and two. I tingle with expectation. Every sense was heightened.

It could go either way. Strike out or win the game. Mess up or make the moment. Acting was like sports, every feeling optimized. I'm not only propelled by the sensations, I'm comfortable with them. A ballpark, *swing hard and hope*, a theater, *Androcles and the Lion*, a stadium, *the Detroit Lions*, a coliseum, *Throw 'em to the lions*. It's all entertainment, and heart-pounding.

Having been the editor of my junior and senior high school newspapers, and at age 16 a professional sports reporter for *The Daily Oklahoman and Times*, with a byline, I went to OU on a journalism scholarship. My freshman year I was washing dishes at the Delta Delta Delta sorority house to augment my $400 scholarship. One evening after my kitchen chores, the houseboys who bunked in the basement invited me to join them for a beer with a few of the Delts. The Delts poured me a bootleg bourbon (Oklahoma was a dry state). I wasn't much of a hard liquor guy, but I was having fun. When the whiskey hit me. Wow. I broke into impromptu rhymed couplets. In high school I had been awed by José Ferrer's performance in the film *Cyrano de Bergerac*. The language, his voice, the athleticism, his honor and humor, the sweet romance of it seemed to incorporate elements of Errol Flynn and musical comedy, both of which I was nuts about. All night long, the Tri Delts whooped and clapped and poured.

The attention and laughter of the Delts soiled this 17-year-old's journalistic ambition. My sophomore year I majored in English lit. I started slipping into acting classes to watch what actors did. My first full-length play as an actor at OU was Gertrude Stein's *Yes Is for a Very Young Man*. I got the part only because the play was so far-out, no drama major would try out for it. Set in France during World War II, it concerned a farm family dealing with the Nazi Occupation. My character enters. I say my first line, "Oh, my fingers are cold." I hear a light snicker from some cast members.

"Lou, one more time," says the graduate-student director in cultivated theater tone and diction.

"Oh, my fingers are cold." More snickers.

"Just one more time." More giggles.

After rehearsal I asked the director if my opening line was supposed to be funny. "No," he intoned. "We just wanted to hear our Frenchman actually say 'Oh, mah *faangers* 'er co-uld.'"

Later, on nerve and ignorance and energy, there was O'Neill to play, Anouilh, Molnar, Odets, Saroyan, O'Casey, the Greeks. My favorite was Mercutio in *Romeo and Juliet*. Snickers no more. On my feet, on the boards, learning.

My junior year I switched from English lit (I had an argument with the head of the department) to French. To avoid getting drafted, I had to make the Dean's Honor Roll. With such a strong motivation, I aced it.

One afternoon I was in the drama school library and came across a paper called *Variety*, in which there was a review of a Broadway bound play that had opened in Philadelphia. It received really bad reviews and was going to close there. I went to one of the drama professors. "Mr. Cass, I don't get it, this play got bad reviews and isn't going to Broadway. Can't those Broadway guys just read a play and know if it's any good, if it's gonna be a hit or not? What's the deal, huh?"

A month before graduation, my brother Theo came into town with a graduation gift, a light brown leather suitcase.

For two months, I was Lefty Lou.

"What am I going to do with this, Theo? Where am *I* gonna go?" My only thought of a post-student life was to be astride a motorcycle feeling the winds of America and Mexico. Okay, yes, I was mightily intoxicated from too much *On the Road*. Plus with a looming draft and a Bachelor's in French, what employer would want me? One of the top actors in the Drama Department, Ronnie Claire Edwards, had a suggestion: "Louie, if for nothing else but the fun of it, why don't you try what I've been doing, getting a summer stock job somewhere?"

Harry Scott, me, Judge Springer. My last amateur performance.

Under Ronnie Claire's urging and guidance I shot-gunned some 30 letters and audition tapes to summer stock playhouses. On the tape I was a British cad from *Dial M for Murder* (not a wise accent choice for this Sooner-born, Sooner-bred) and an anguished New York detective in *Detective Story*, another accent oopsie ("Yew ain't nothin' but a whoruh!"). I was offered three jobs! Two Equity companies wrote me to come be an apprentice, meaning paint flats, clean toilets and *maybe* get to carry a spear, or whatever they carried in summer stock. For those glories of Art I was asked to pay them $200! Whereas the White Barn The-ater, a non–Equity company in Terre Haute, Indiana, would pay *me* $45 a week, and provide a round trip train ticket. Plus I was promised *parts*, not spears.

On the train ride to Terre Haute, Theo's shiny suitcase beside me, I couldn't begin to predict what kind of summer I was in for. Here I was, traveling (in more ways than one) into an unfamiliar world. It wasn't a calm and assured young man squirming in that coach chair. If I was stinko, would they send me home? Or worse, what if I was stinko and an audience got a whiff of me? I hadn't a clue as to what this being a *real* actor was all about.

What a summer it turned out to be. Almost all of the actors were from the prestigious Goodman Theatre in Chicago, from which had graduated Geraldine Page, Karl Malden, Harvey Korman, Shelley Berman, and later Joe Mantegna and Linda Hunt. I heard phrases like "the Method," "the Actors Studio," "Meisner." The cast tossed around unfamiliar names

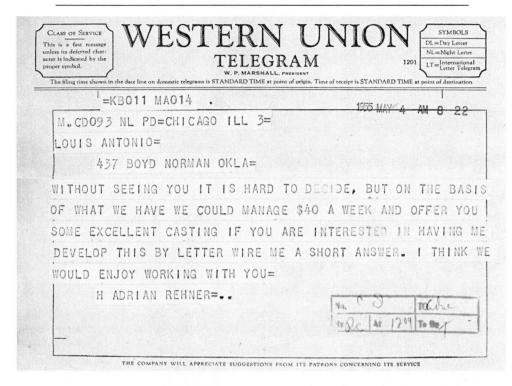

I was hardly in a position to negotiate.

with cool familiarity: "Chuck" (Heston), "Bud" (Brando), "Monty" (Clift), "Lee" (Strasberg). The Chicagoans were hip. I was the greenhorn from Oklahoma who didn't smoke, carried a toothbrush and brushed his teeth after every meal. They could talk endlessly about "the craft" of acting. I could only listen and ask questions. Most of the answers were beyond my minuscule knowledge of acting: "Just find an image and go with it," "An actor is schizophrenic on stage," "Relate to the other actors and with the audience at the same time." Oh, okay. Huh?

My first $45 was for a comedy, F. Hugh Herbert's *The Moon Is Blue* in which two playboys set their sights on a virgin. With white shoe polish in my hair I played the older lech. The three other cast members were Goodmanites. Opening night, my first *as a paid actor*, I was in the middle of a speech and for the first time I listened to myself on stage. I remember thinking, "Hey, I am really sincere here. I'm believing this guy that's me. Or me that's this guy." (I wasn't sure which, and sometimes I'm still not.)

Of the five plays I did that summer, I was assigned mostly older character parts, more white shoe polish, gray penciled lines on my face. The range went from Preacher Haggler in *Dark of the Moon* to the slick producer in *Light Up the Sky*, to A. Rat and Lord Byron in Tennessee Williams' *Camino Real*. As the preacher in *Dark of the Moon* I had to sing a hymn and lead the congregation in song, the congregation being the audience. The producer-director Adrian "Reb" Rehner wanted me to fire up the audience and get them to join in. With fervor and wildly waving arms I got 'em going and stomping and then—oh, pain. My right shoulder came out of place and my arm stuck in midair. "Feelin' the Lawd!" I banged it back into place and did the rest of the performance left-armed.

The Moon Is Blue. **George Spelvin, me standing, Jerry Gordon prone, Jo Jordan kneeling.**

Was that slide into home plate going to shoot down this new adventure too, this acting thing?

The Indiana summer had expanded my Oklahoma upbringing by half. I wasn't at OU any more. The actors were free-thinking and intense and fun. The actresses' sexuality encouraged and enveloped me as none of the "nice girls" back home ever had. I was creating characters, believing the lie, being alone in public, as Stanislavski had said, and gulping approval and kinship from my fellow actors and from the audiences. It was like my dad jumping up when I got a base hit and shouting, "Thatsa my boy!" Is that why this acting got to me? Sigmund, are you listening?

I was 21 years old and had encountered the dedication and open lifestyles of those Big City Actors. In a way, we were like a baseball team, competitive camaraderie yet having to rely on one another to win. Okay, but what if I didn't have the makings of an actor? I'd seen *An American in Paris* 13 times, memorized the map of Paris, spoke college-French, so if acting didn't want me, all right, maybe I'll do the shim sham on the Champs Elysées. Not at all practical, but then how practical is wanting to be an *actor*?

The producer-director of the White Barn, Mr. Rehner, a gentle and knowledgeable man, was a professor of drama at the University of Chicago, and at the end of the season I asked him if he thought I could become a professional actor. I simply didn't know what was required. Rehner leafed through the reviews of the season's plays. "Let's just take a look."

Regarding *Light Up the Sky*: "Mr. Antonio plays his characters from the inside out. He understands them well and he projects that knowledge to his audience."

"Mr. Antonio gave us his southern accent in the first play of the season, his Welsh accent in *The Corn Is Green* and in *Camino Real*, his third play, he read his lines in the role of Lord Byron with Shakespearean overtones. His is one of the most promising talents to appear in Terre Haute."

Mr. Rehner folded the papers and put them aside.

I said, "Yessir, but this is *Terre Haute...*"

"You asked if I thought you could become a professional actor?" I nodded. He said, "Yes."

On the train ride back to Oklahoma City I had a lot on my mind. Was I good enough? Could I make a living at it? What kind of life does an actor have? No Mom and Dad or brothers there to guide me, protecting me, loving me. How and when would I know if I had it in me? Why! *Why* did I want to be an actor!? Questions about myself and my future. And no answers.

* * *

I stood in our small living room with Mom and Dad, two people I was blessed to have as parents. I think of them and thank them for the love and respect they gave their three sons. With only a fifth grade education in the small village of Ano Diminio, Greece, Poppa knew only three words of English when he came to America at age 17, "Yes" and "Thank you." His birth name Antoniou became Antonio when the Ellis Island officials could not pronounce it. Mom and Dad got married as the Depression engulfed our nation. They dished out chicken fried steaks from the two-booth, 18-stool Lafayette Café in Oklahoma City. (He later became known citywide as "Jimmy the Greek, the Chicken Fry King.")

At age nine, I started working at our café. If there were child labor laws in the '30s and '40s, they were either unknown or overlooked. Theo, my oldest brother, worked at the café during the Depression for 25 cents a day, and at the end of the week Poppa would borrow it back, go next door to the pool hall and play dominoes for money. He was good and those dominoes paid for gas, lights and rent.

For 35 cents the customer got a chicken fried steak, a vegetable, spaghetti or mashed potatoes, a side of cole slaw, two slices of white bread and a patty of oleomargarine. Even at that price some of the customers couldn't pay up and would sign "guest checks," settling up later when and if they had the money. One time a customer ran out without paying for his lunch and I started after him. Poppa stopped me: "No, he hungry. It's all right." One year in her off-hours from the Lafayette, Mom went house-to-house taking the census for two dollars a day, but no one who was hungry was ever turned away. As a five-year-old, I remember men sometimes knocking on the back door of our rented house asking for food. Momma could always find enough in the icebox for some kind of sandwich. Poppa was as exuberant and energetic as my mom, Lucille Wright from West Plains, Missouri, was calm.

Of English-French-German stock, she was thoughtful, beautiful, artful and intellectually curious. In playful moods, Poppa referred to her as "the white woman."

From Poppa I inherited a quick temper and mercurial mood changes, which were good for my acting, but oftentimes not for my career. From Mom I inherited patience, empathy, kindness and understanding, which were good for my directing and parenting. They loved their sons, and they never belittled our hopes or doubted our dreams.

After our 21 years together there, I was before them in our living room. I told them I was thinking of going to New York to be an actor. Poppa wanted me to stay. He'd give me half the café. I'd be his partner. "Stay." "Poppa, you didn't want me to get a college education to go on selling chicken fried steaks for the rest of my life, did you?"

He studied me for a moment, put his arm around Mom's waist and trying to hide his emotions (not easy for a Greek) he said, "Yeah, okay. We start it all, so you go. You go be actor."

My parents, my support team.

2

The Cement City

In the mid–'50s, a young actor went to Hollywood to be a star or to New York to be an actor. Off I went to New York to find out what the Goodman Gang was talking about, the Actors Studio, that Method stuff, and Lee and Chuck and Bud. I knew two people in New York, my cousin Gus Andros, now calling himself Dick, and Al Levin, an acquaintance from OU, who lived in some place called the Bronx. I wrote Dick and he said that I could stay with him until I found a place. Dick's brother Plato, a former All-American tackle at OU, also played professional football for the Chicago Cardinals. His other brother Demosthenes (Dee), also All-American, became head football coach at Oregon State. Dick, *né* Gus Jr., had danced with the San Francisco ballet company. He was now teaching ballet in Greenwich Village. An unusual trio of Greeks.

Right before I was to leave Oklahoma City for New York brother Theo tried his best Polonius: "Uh, Gus, Jr. Well … we're not quite sure but we think he's 'indefinite.'"

"I don't know what that means."

"Uh, well, 'on the fence.'"

I didn't know what that meant either and Theo changed the subject.

An OU frat rat advertised that he was looking for someone to share expenses for his drive back home to Connecticut. He owned a 1942 gray Mercury that we hoped would get us there. I was a longish-haired anti-fraternity guy who acted in some school plays and wore overalls and he wore white bucks, was from money and a bit of a snob. We didn't have much in common so most of the three-day drive was in silence which fueled my internal bouts of "What am I doing? Where do I get off thinking I can be an actor? New York City? I don't know big city ways." What a spineless sissy. Poppa had come to America in his teens from a village of 300, no running water, no electricity. He didn't speak English, didn't know one person in New York. So what the hell did I have to shiver about? My God, if my dad could cross the ocean in steerage for weeks in misery and fear, I should be able to sit in a '42 Merc to another part of the United States. I consoled myself: "Hey, I've sold Fuller brushes in Texas, been a sous-chef in Colorado, and acted in Indiana." Okay, not exactly a world traveler, but young, strong, educated and no cavities. Not to worry.

My first sight of Manhattan shrank my bravura. We were driving on the West Side Drive and to my right were these immense stacks of buildings rising higher than oil wells. The city looked as if it were made out of cement and giant Brillo pads. Okay, I can scramble out of the Merc and hitchhike back to Oklahoma. Yeah. Deep breath. All right, a city is filled with people, so if I'd learned enough from my father's "You gotta know how to meet the people," then maybe this unexplored country would meet me halfway.

Because cousin Dick was teaching dance and directing musicals at a summer camp in

Maine, I stayed my first three days in New York with Al Levin and his family on Walton Avenue in the Bronx. Before OU, Al had never seen a cow, and I had never seen a mother and father drink soda pop with an evening meal. For breakfast they ate a toasted donut-shaped thing named "bagel." My first ride on a subway was from the Bronx to Manhattan and when Al said the next stop was ours, I stood up to pull the bell cord.

"Al, I don't see the cord."

"What cord?"

"So the driver'll know to stop at our stop."

The subway stopped on Forty-Second Street all by itself.

Only be an actor if it's the one thing you love most in the world.

My cousin Dick had written that warning to me when I told him I was thinking of going to New York to study acting. I avoided "To be an actor" because I didn't know what all that was. "…the one thing you love most in the world"? I loved my family, my country and blackberry pie. Was it really necessary to include *Acting*?

Dick returned and I left the Bronx for Greenwich Village. His dance studio was on the second floor over the Jericho Tavern on Sixth Avenue near Fourth Street. A large black cloth separated his living quarters from his ballet studio. There was a small bathroom with a shower, a kitchen, and one room just large enough to accommodate two chairs, his bed, and my cot. It was clean and comfortable, and my rent was seven dollars a week. A dollar a day. Dick was not "on the fence" or "indefinite." He told me straight off he was a homo-sexual, but not "flaming," a species he had no tolerance for. ("Gives us a bad name.")

I'd arrived in the cement city with $120 and my first priority was to find a job. Dick got me a tryout with Pam Pam's, a popular Greenwich Village eatery. My Lafayette years made slinging their burgers a snap. They signed me and farmed me out to their Brooklyn Heights Pam Pam's, down from the St. George Hotel, which for some reason advertised a salt-water swimming pool. No hotel in my hometown had *any* kind of swimming pool. My hours were from five in the evening until four in the morning, seven days a week for 50 cents an hour and tips. I'd net about a hundred dollars for a 77-hour week. Here I'd come to New York to be a theater actor, but because of my hours I could see only portions of plays on matinee days.

My first Strasberg sighting was Lee's daughter Susan in a matinee of *The Diary of Anne Frank*. But to get to work in Brooklyn, I had to rush out before the play ended. That night I asked one of my customers who had seen the play, "Listen, so what happened? Did the Germans ever find 'em or what?"

Cousin Dick told me that actors needed a message service whose number you gave as yours. He said all the actors used the Hayes Registry for six dollars a month. Usually there was no message, so embarrassed actors like me left messages for themselves. British accent: "Yes, Clive Barrett here. Mr. Antonio has the number. Tell him I rang. Thank you."

Then I'd call in to Hayes.

"Hi, it's Lou Antonio. Any messages?"

"You have three," and they'd relay *my* three "messages." Pitiful.

Actors have been second-class citizens for centuries. The story goes that in 1960 while *El Cid* was filming in Spain, the Ritz Hotel in Madrid would not allow its star Charlton Heston to register because he was an actor. When I applied for my first telephone, they asked my profession and I told them, "I'm an actor." They wanted a $50 deposit, which I did not have to spare. Dick advised me to call and tell them I was a waiter.

"What is your business?"

"I'm a waiter."

"We can install that in four days."

No deposit required.

One night he let a friend sleep over on my cot, while Dick and I shared his bed. While I was just dozing off, I felt movement from Dick's side of the bed, and then his hand crossed under the sheet and lightly touched my penis. I lightly lifted his hand, steered it back to his side and dropped it. In about five minutes he was snoring and I was wondering, "Now what?"

The next morning he was fixing breakfast. I sat silently at the kitchen table, with not a notion of what to say. "Good morning!" he sang out. Jeez, what was he so cheery about? He slid a plate in front of me with some odd thing on it.

"Uh, what's that?"

"It's called an English muffin. They even have them in Oklahoma. Try it."

Studying my breakfast gave me a reason not to look at him. He sat down with a cup of coffee. "Give me a minute, then I have to run. Last night, well, you can't blame me. You sit around here in your letter jacket with your legs spread open, leaning back flashing your basket like, well, some butch trade. I thought, 'If my cousin's *gay*, this could be fun. So I had to find out and I did and that's that. Finish your muffin. I've got to go to my dentist.'"

Cuz became my guardian. He pretty much watched over me from then on, told me what bars were gay bars, which bars were physically dangerous, "Don't ever get into a fight with a bull dyke." Do not lock eyes with guys on the street or compliment any of his male friends on their looks. Ever.

Slinging burgers in Brooklyn Heights was teaching me important New York stuff.

Customer: "Gimme a soda."

Me: "We don't carry soda,"

Customer: "Whaddya? It's right dere. Pepsi, Coke…"

Me: "Oh, a soda *pop*."

Customer: "A what?"

Johnny, another waiter, helped me out when I needed a translation. He wanted to be a singer-actor and I mentioned him to Dick once or twice. Cuz said, "I'll come in tonight and check him out. Act like you don't know me." He arrived around eight, ordered a burger and left. I got home at four-thirty in the morning and Dick was sitting up waiting for me. Before I could say a word, he pronounced, "Gay as a goose!"

"Oh, Cuz, you think everyone is gay."

The next night at closing, Johnny yawned, stretched and said, "You know, Lou, why take that subway ride back to the Village? I only live two blocks away so why don't you just spend the night at my place?" Secret Agent Andros prevented a possible unpleasant scene. Dick also taught me how to douse a flasher after one popped open his overcoat and pointed his bare erection at me. Cuz tells me his lesson for the day includes the ladies too: "Look at it, point at it, laugh at it."

I was now immersed in subways, sidewalk markets, incessant sirens, yelling, beggars and a bum's "Who's got a buck for booze for a bum?!" The Manhattan streets were not for strolling. Ah, but then chess players in Washington Square, funky outfits on women and men of all ages, lots of smoking, guitars, hats on sidewalks awaiting coin, sidewalk food vendors, people eating standing up, tourists galore. Not a speck of any of it on the streets of Oklahoma City. After observing, learning big city ways, now I had to learn about acting.

The Goodman gang had rhapsodized over Lee Strasberg, but not how to contact him. I knew no one who could help. The Manhattan phone book? He was listed! I spoke to his secretary about joining his classes. She told me the waiting list was long, He had only two classes and a limit of 30 students per. She booked me for a meeting two months down the road. On the appointed day I stood on the Central Park West sidewalk of his apartment building in my clean shirt and freshly ironed black chino pants. What is a Lee Strasberg?

A smiling, dark-haired young woman opened his door and introduced herself as Lee's secretary. She led me into his front room. It was larger than Dick's entire dance studio. Where there weren't windows, there were bookshelves all filled with untidily stored record albums and books, hundreds of each. Seated in a large cushioned armchair sat a small man wearing glasses, open white shirt and gray sports coat. He was soft-spoken, with a sometimes glottal sound that was almost like a snort. Neither friendly nor imperious, he didn't present himself as an icon at all. My slight nervousness subsided as he asked me questions, questions that seemed surprisingly chatty. He asked in a noncommittal monotone: Favorite baseball team? (Boston Red Sox) Favorite player? (Ted Williams) Favorite movie? (*Singin' in the Rain*). After he asked, "Who's your favorite actor?" he seemed to focus on me. For the actor question, I was evasive, I'd never thought about that.

"Depends on what I'm watching, you know, a comedy or something serious. Brando's good, though, I like him."

My only answer that he commented on was when I mentioned Ted Williams and he countered with Willie Mays. "Nobody could move and catch a fly like Willie Mays."

"Yessir. Williams though…Williams had the best swing in baseball: .406 in '41."

Strasberg rose from his chair.

"Uh, Mr. Strasberg … uh, when will I know if—"

He left the room.

In such a short ten minutes and with no probing questions, how could this man possibly have gotten a sense of me?

His secretary entered. "We'll call you, one way or the other." That was my first "Don't call us, we'll call you."

A month later, his secretary called. I was accepted. There would be a spot for me in February of next year (1956) in his Tuesday and Thursday 11 a.m. class at 50th and Broadway.

My "hot diggity" lasted two weeks. I got my draft notice. I was to report for my army physical in Brooklyn on Friday the thirteenth of January. Friday the thirteenth, mind you. The Korean War had ended in 1953, but we had forces in South Korea and the possibility of being sent there faced all young soldiers. I called Strasberg's secretary and told her I'd have to give up my place in class to defend my country.

I spent all the money I'd saved from Pam Pam's on airfare home and Christmas presents for my family. I returned to New York with no money, quit my job in Brooklyn Heights, and was given a going away party by Dick, who counseled me that when they saw "actor" on my sheet, they'd send me first to their psychiatrist. He advised, "You're an actor, chew your fingernails down before you go, act nervous and be vague when they ask you if you're a homosexual."

A fateful Friday at the Army induction center in Brooklyn, New York.

"I'm an actor." Uh-huh. The psychiatrist saw right through my pathetic performance of trembling hands and stuttering. I sneaked a look at his review of my performance: "Various complaints not substantiated by findings." Damn, if only I'd had a Strasberg class.

Standing naked and shivering before the final doctor, I was asked if I had any injuries that might prevent my being fit to defend our country. I unfolded the letter I was carrying from my Oklahoma City orthopedist. The doctor looked up at me suspiciously.

"Throw your arm out of place."

"Sir?"

"Let's see this 'injury.'"

Taking a deep breath, I dislocated my left shoulder. Pulsing with pain, my arm suspended in midair, the doctor leisurely circled me front and back.

"Okay, put it back in and go over there and wait."

"Uh, yessir. Wait for what?"

"Our surgeon."

I slammed the shoulder back in place. Still naked and shivering, I sat on a cold bench for another hour and a half. The surgeon called me over, then looked at my letter and not at me.

"Dislocate your shoulder."

"I already did that for the other doctor, sir."

"I have to see if it is a recurring injury. Dislocate your shoulder."

Again I hoisted my arm and popped it out of place. It hurt worse than before. Boss Surgeon Guy walked slowly around me scribbling on a form. With one last look, he turned to walk away muttering, "You can put it back in."

Wham, bam. As my left arm dangled useless at my side, a buzz-cut sergeant looked at me as if I were a Commie-loving traitor, dropped my clothes on a counter and handed me a form, "Sign this. You're *4-F.*"

On the subway back to Cousin Dick's, I didn't quite realize that I was to be a civilian for the rest of my life. I didn't feel right being unfit to serve my country. Theo had served in World War II in the Army Air Corps and Jim was doing time as an Air Force lieutenant in Alaska. Look, I can't help it, I still choke up when I hear our national anthem. Theo, Jim and I were on this earth with a sweet mother because America had welcomed our father.

All Dick said when I walked back into the Greenwich Village digs was, "What? Now do I have to give you a Welcome Home party?"

I called Strasberg's secretary and she put me back in for February. My Pam Pam bosses said all the waiters' spots were filled, but I could be a short order cook on weekends.

Now all I had to do was be an actor.

3

Some Strasberg,
and Then Some

I was nervous, shy, excited. There was not a familiar face in sight. My first Strasberg class was like any first day at a new school. While the actors waited for Strasberg, there was no horsing around, mostly they were preoccupied with themselves. With a few exceptions they were all young, but older than I, and most certainly beyond me as actors. The Tuesday class was for stuff I'd never seen before: sense memory exercises, like imagining and creating an object handled every day. I saw a lot of feeling the cup and feeling the heat and tasting the coffee. And a lot of pretty girls, several of them former Miss Americas. Strasberg was demanding, encouraging, insightful, never indifferent. He spoke quietly, almost solemnly at times, analyzing the work with precision.

"Don't just indicate it, feel it. Take the time to realize you have it. Don't rush it, search it out, explore it."

A middle-aged actress (about 35) got up to do the Song and Dance exercise. Alone on stage and looking us all straight in the eye, she elongated the vowel in a monotonal "Happy Birthday." Tears popped out, she laughed, she cooed, she lashed out yelling, "HAAAPYYYY BIIIRTHDAAAYYY TOOO YOUUU," stomping her feet hard into the floor! What the hell was that? Happy Birthday my ass. Strasberg explained that the "singing" released and expressed whatever impulses arose in the actor, such as anger, sorrow, laughter. That it also was to promote awareness of self and that the actor was to be curious about what was happening and why.

Oh.

The Thursday class was for scene work, two actors per scene, two scenes per session, or monologues. After the scene, the actors would state what they had "worked on" (tried to accomplish) a sensory task, a personalization (thinking of a real person or a parallel situation in real life), a substitution (creating a real person in their scene partner) and other tools of their trade. All new to me, exciting, challenging, and baffling.

J.D. Salinger's *Catcher in the Rye* was a revered novel amongst us, and for my first time up I adapted some pages from it and played Holden Caulfield. It took place in a urinal and, being more keyed up than nervous, I tossed in a tap dance, a bit of Gene Kelly from *An American in Paris*. It felt good up there on that small stage. I was loose and knew I was "doing the work," but also showing off a bit. Well, that's what actors do, isn't it? Strasberg's critique followed. These are a few of Strasberg's reactions to his first viewing of my acting:

> Good stage aliveness. [But] you took general attitudes about relationships. Work was nicely done, but the problems of the character were surface. You say he's bored, but bored about what? Find the overall

18

problem of Holden, it will change the scene's behavior. Some of the acting is believable, both in yourself and in what you do. When you come on you are there (good). Your acting is in response to words (bad). Your behavior did not coincide with the character. The boy is about to be kicked out of school, he's afraid of sex, too shy to say hello, he has a mental breakdown and ends up in a sanitarium. See the problem first, and then solve it. Wonderful quality on stage, nice to see the aliveness.

That spruced me up and spurred me on. I plunged into the demands of "learning my craft."

The first time Strasberg threw me out of his class was a year later. I had just returned from visiting my family in Oklahoma City. In the Tuesday session I did an exercise of my two-year old niece Connie eating spaghetti. After the exercise, Strasberg asked me what I was doing. I told him and he hit the roof!

"That's not one of my exercises! You think you know more than we do, then get out and teach your own classes!!" I wondered what he was so mad about. The next class I quietly slipped in, sat down, and neither one of us mentioned my expulsion. I reverted to *his* exercises. (But a year later I did start teaching a beginner's class at the Theatre Studio of New York.)

The second time Strasberg tossed me I wasn't even on stage. The scene was *Cat on a Hot Tin Roof*. Ellie Wood was doing Maggie and my first line was off-stage, something demanding like, "What, Maggie?" Strasberg stopped the scene and I came on stage. "Why'd you stop the scene?" I asked.

"You weren't in another room, your voice had no projection. It wasn't real."

I got hot. "I was preparing, I didn't give a damn about being in another room! Raising my voice is not a problem of mine, like right now. If you'd have let us do the scene, then you could have seen what I was working on, why I was doing the scene!"

His glasses magnified the anger in his eyes. "I will not let you challenge my ego with your ego! Get out!"

Poor Ellie didn't know whether to cry or apologize. So she did both. A week later I silently returned to class. At the Actors Studio, Strasberg never challenged me. It might have been because stars and big shots were allowed as his guests and he didn't want *that* kind of scene to be played.

The first Broadway musical I saw was *The Pajama Game*, Bob Fosse's first choreographic triumph. I was high from the dancing, the humor, the songs, the performances. For class I adapted a scene from the novel it was taken from, Richard Bissell's *Seven and a Half Cents*. Fellow student Estelle Parsons and I did the scene complete with *à cappella* songs. Our classmates applauded, which Strasberg hated. "We're here to learn, not to please an audience!" He said it with an intensity that made it a command. In the following weeks, two students did a musical scene with tape recorded music. A month or so later two actors dragged in a piano and an accompanist! Parsons and I had put a little knot in Strasberg's straight line Method. He banned musical scenes.

My cousin Plato Andros had told me before I left home that he'd been on the OU track team with Lonny Chapman, who was now an actor in New York. Plato suggested I should give him a call: "Maybe he could help you with this Barrymore business." I was told by another waiter/would-be actor that Lonny Chapman was teaching an acting class.

Crossing Sheridan Square in Greenwich Village, I recognized Chapman from a movie, *East of Eden*. I stopped him and introduced myself. Taciturn and wary, he nodded and walked away. The Manhattan phone book had got me Strasberg and it got me Chapman.

He wouldn't talk to me, but I mentioned Plato to his wife Erma Dean. My first show biz name dropping paid off. Chapman later told me the only reason he let me in his class was because I was Plato's cousin.

A member of the Actors Studio, Chapman used some Strasberg in his class. Whereas Strasberg's students seemed under self-imposed pressure, introspection and anxiety, Chapman's class was relaxed and loose with lots of camaraderie and after class drinks at Jerry's Bar with intriguing classmates: a bareback rider from her family's circus, a bony, white-haired man dipping into acting at age 65, the gorgeous model Barbara Bain and her slim, funny, intense paramour Martin Landau, a mysterious and beautiful young blond woman who would disappear for several weeks and return with stories of the casinos and beaches of Havana.

We'd "second-act" plays (sneak in after the first intermission) to listen to the words and cadences of Inge and Williams and the new playwrights. Or to study the actors, who in just the 1955–56 season staggered me:

Mary Martin (*Peter Pan*)
Paul Muni and Ed Begley (*Inherit the Wind*)
Ray Walston and Gwen Verdon (*Damn Yankees*)
Ben Gazzara and Tony Franciosa (*A Hatful of Rain*)
Julie Harris, Boris Karloff, Christopher Plummer (*The Lark*)
Ruth Gordon, Bobby Morse, Arthur Hill (*The Matchmaker*)
Lotte Lenya (*The Threepenny Opera*)
Kim Stanley, Elaine Stritch (*Bus Stop*)
Colleen Dewhurst (*Taming of the Shrew*)
Jason Robards (*The Iceman Cometh*)
George C. Scott (*Richard III, Children of Darkness*)

I had never seen anything like it. Could I ever accomplish any of that? Should I go back to Oklahoma City?

Instead of intimidating me it inspired me.

We couldn't get enough of our small world. We clung to one another after class at Jerry's Bar or in small dumpy apartments, bringing our own beer or booze, talking, smoking, drinking, sleeping on floors, exhausted from our energy. From instant attractions and sexual discoveries came hurt and healing, and we "used it" in our work. Eisenhower was president so politics was boring. Our world was actors, directors, writers, Camus, Freud. From the nosebleed balcony in City Center I saw my first ballet, New York City Ballet's *Petrouchka*. I understood cousin Dick's devotion to dance. At the Metropolitan Museum of Art, I could gawk at paintings I'd only seen pictures of in books. The soul in the cold marble of ancient statues made me wring my hands from the intensity of this new visceral experience. The more I discovered what was outside me, the more I discovered what was inside me.

To save money we lent each other books, plays or records. Reading habits from college changed: no more classics or the new novels, it was plays, adaptable short stories, theater actor bios. No more *American in Paris*. It was Bergman, Truffaut, Chabrol, Olivier's' *Hamlet*, Kurosawa and Buñuel. Though my world had opened up, it had become narrower.

We told each other about jobs. Once I was recommended for a World War II prisoner-of-war TV show. It was one of my first auditions. I gave an excited audition; the trouble was, the role was of a Jewish-American soldier and I had to read words I'd never seen before. Thus Chanukka was Oklahomaized as *Chanóoka*, Yom Kippur became Tom Kipper. The reaction was silence. A few blocks from the reading, I saw Martin Landau on the street and ran up to him. "Hey, Marty, aren't you a Jew?"

"Yeah…"

"Well, get over to *Kraft*, they're looking for Jews!"

I was getting antsy. The classes were stimulating, but I wanted to get some sort of acting job too. We all did. I decided to use my one connection. My very first interview with a *motion picture* casting person was with Arnold Hoskwith, head of casting for Warner Brothers in New York. Charles Suggs, a drama teacher at OU, had gone to Yale with Hoskwith, wrote him a letter about me, and thus my interview. I put on the suit and the tie (I had one of each).

He sat at a large shiny desk, his back to the window wearing a dandruff-speckled dark suit. He had a thin, interesting face. Interesting in that his prominent nose seemed to point toward his left ear. We chatted pleasantly about his Yale days with ol' Charlie Suggs and then he got down to the business of me. This is how my first eager interview with a professional casting person went:

Hoskwith: "I don't know, kid, your nose is a little too big, one of your eyes sort of goes in toward your nose, and you've got that bit of a double chin. I don't think you'll make it in this business. Say hello to Charlie."

Unlike the homeless, we had a home. During one period of about two years, I was studying concurrently with three different teachers, Lee Strasberg, Lonny Chapman and Curt Conway, plus a four-hour workshop on Saturday mornings. Conway, this old lefty from the Group Theatre, had been a hot young live television director in New York and was once married to the brilliant actress Kim Stanley. Then came the House Un-American Activities Committee in the '50s, and along with many prominent performers, writers and directors, he was tagged as a Communist. Barred from employment in television and films and with only occasional theater employment, he opened an acting school, the Theatre Studio of New York. A couple of students come to mind, Barbra Streisand and Dustin Hoffman. In lieu of paying for my classes there, I taught a beginning actors class.

From each of these teachers I learned something different and useful. Generally from Strasberg, working on your own instrument, the given circumstance (the situation that precedes the scene), sensory work, emotional recall (creating an emotion through sense memory), relaxation, concentration. From Chapman, using the imagination, the fun and excitement of acting, being bold and fearless. From Conway, the discipline, the no-nonsense part of technique, only using what worked for you. Whereas in preparing a scene for Strasberg or Chapman you could take as much time as you wanted to get it ready, Conway would say, "Do the death scene from *Cyrano* and I want it Friday!" He got you ready to do the job. If one ever came along.

Sure, some of the actors' goal was stardom, but most of us were satisfied if we landed the occasional job for the experience, for classes, for rent. We seemed to thrive on the thrill, yes, *thrill* of creating something within ourselves and transforming it into a character with life and spontaneity, not acting, but *living* onstage. Or, not acting a toothache, but creating the toothache through sensory belief. And, oh, the wonders of the unexpected strengthened our drive. In Strasberg's class I was doing a sensory exercise of the smell of a perfume that

I liked. I was getting it and had it, and smiling, then my pleasure of the aroma turned into sudden fury. After the exercise, Strasberg asked where the anger came from.

"I don't know, Lee, it's a smell that I *like*."

"What is it?"

"Well, it's just from a perfume that an old … that an old *girlfriend used to wear*!" The affair had not ended well. You can bet *that* one went into the file cabinet for later use.

Most actors have an addiction: themselves. The product (the acting) cannot be separated from the person (the actor). The pianist plays on a piano that any other pianist can play on, a painter can give his brushes or tubes of paint to another artist. But if you think my acting stinks, then *I* must stink because my acting is me and no one else can use it except me.

Alfred Hitchcock infamously and popularly mocked actors as cattle. Yeah, well, Hitch, in the theater you don't need a director, playwright, producer, set designer, costumer and all that. Know what you do need? An actor. Or puppets.

4

Dribbles and Drabs

In trying to snare any sort of job, the beginning actor would jump at the chance to be paid a day's pay for being a TV or movie extra. An *extra*, you sneer? You betchum. (Ricky Gervais wrote a series about them.) Once I was paid five dollars for sitting in a quiz show audience to laugh loudly at the jokes when cued. A fellow student in Chapman's class, Joyce Geller, got her name in the theater section of *The New York Times*. We were impressed. At a performance of *Look Back in Anger*, she stood up in the audience and started yelling at the actors and condemning the play. Wow. Then she confided in us that the play's producer, David Merrick, paid her $25 to "make a scene." Merrick got thousands of dollars of free publicity for that 25.

As an extra, the neophyte New York actor was able to learn the technical basics of film techniques, like hitting marks, lenses, sound, matching, watching actors striving to keep a performance fresh take after take, on-set behavior, learning idioms and expressions such as gaffer, best boy, clean entrance, room tone, camera right-camera left and so on. By the time the actor got a role, he or she wasn't intimidated by the mechanics. We also doggedly tried to get cast in Army training films, because they paid $50 a day. Some of the roles required not much more than looking sick with applied syphilis or gonorrhea sores. The makeup department swayed the viewers more than our performances.

Chapman recommended me to Jack Garfein, a 26-year-old director who was casting *The Strange One*, Ben Gazzara's 1956 movie debut, from Calder Willingham's book about a Southern military school. It had been developed at the Actors Studio as a play, and went from there to Off Broadway and then to Broadway. I read well enough for Garfein to be given a screen test for the part that Pat Hingle had played from its inception. Hingle tested and so did another young actor, Steve McQueen. Pat got the part, I got an offer to play a cadet in the movie and competitive glares from McQueen. It was an opportunity to go on location to St. Petersburg, Florida, to learn about filmmaking in the big time, get a salary of $350 a week, something called per diem, and my Screen Actors Guild card, which cost 200. It was a fruitful beginner's education. Acting my few "yessirs" and "no sirs" didn't seem to offer much creative return from the on-set tedium of waiting to act. I yearned for the inside of a stuffy theater or acting class. Being on the inside of moviemaking also was a class. Watching the sprouting Gazzara, George Peppard, Pat Hingle, Paul E. Richards, Arthur Storch and the old guy Larry Gates (42) rehearsing and filming a scene held endless fascination for me.

After the movie, in the fall of 1956, Garfein was directing a play on Broadway by N. Richard Nash, who had written the successful *The Rainmaker* the year before. This one was *The Girls of Summer*, being produced by Cheryl Crawford, with Pat Hingle, George

Me right, as a prisoner in an Army training film (others unidentified).

Peppard and Arthur Storch, all from *The Strange One*, and starring Shelley Winters, also a Studio member. I auditioned and snagged the understudy for Peppard and Storch. They also gave me the job of assistant stage manager for a $5 boost above Equity's minimum of $85 a week. Ninety a week! Hi, ho!

Here I was at the Longacre less than a year out of college working in a Broadway theater! But where was "Wow, I'm on Broadway!"? The stage was dusty, spare and dowdy. Hardly a setting for magic to be made. it was more like I was a student in a master's class, scrutinizing the work of formidable actors.

As a member of Screen Actors Guild and now Actors Equity Association, I was a card-carrying *professional actor*. One of my more important tasks was to professionally fetch coffee and bagels for the cast every morning. After bagel banter, I had the priceless opportunity to study these pros' rehearsal techniques. Though Storch, Peppard, Winters and Hingle were all members of the Actors Studio, each worked "the Method" differently, mainly because of their individual temperaments: Winters, a shouter, would argue with and scold Garfein. Storch ambled slowly into the part. Hingle searched for his character by jumping right into it, trying different approaches every rehearsal. Peppard coolly intellectualized his scenes.

Peppard and Hingle were rehearsing a scene and Garfein jumped up from his seat in the theater and exclaimed, "Wait, I've got an idea!" He hurried onto the stage and whispered to the two actors. They did the scene again.

Garfein: "That's it! Great!"

Darn, I must've missed something, it seemed exactly the same as before. Our scenic designer, Boris Aronson, a 56-year-old Russian who had won seven Tonys, came walking slowly up the aisle past Garfein and me. He muttered a reprimand in his Eastern European accent: "Dat's a good *secret* you got dere, Jack."

As an actor and director, lesson learned.

When a play "tries out," that's exactly what it does, to see what works and what doesn't. From the reality of rising costs today, that decades-old out-of-town custom is pretty much gone. The $17,000,000 *Spider Man* toured, then "previewed" for nine months before opening. My first tryout: New Haven, Connecticut. As assistant stage manager, I went with the property man while he shopped for a few props for the show. When we returned to the theater, six or seven of the New Haven stagehands were angrily exiting it.

Prop man: "Hey, where you guys goin'?"
Crew member: "We don't have to listen to that kind of language!"

I found out "that kind of language" was an expletive-loaded rant that Shelley Winters had inflicted in high volume on their tender ears.

After only mild reviews in New Haven, we were in Philadelphia and it was opening night. I was checking my assistant manager's to-do list when stage manager Irv Buchman put his hand on my shoulder. "Lou, George is really sick and can't go on tonight. You'll have to do it."

Oh, swell. I'd been so busy with my crew duties, I had never rehearsed the part and only scantily had I studied my lines. Forty-five minutes before curtain, I was in Peppard's dressing room. His tee shirt was too tight, his blue jeans too baggy. Script in hand, Arthur Storch came into the room. "You go ahead and do your makeup and I'll cue you, okay?"

Though far from word perfect, I at least had a sense of the lines and Storch told me not to worry about it: "We'll take care of you." In putting on

The **PLAYBILL** *for The Longacre Theatre*

Girls of Summer

Shelley Winters, and almost my Broadway debut.

my makeup and my wardrobe and running my lines, I was too concentrated to be frightened.

"Hey, Lou…" It was Peppard at the door. He was all bundled up and his voice was weak. "Cheryl told me I had to go on. Hal Wallis is in the audience." The play had been pre-sold to the Hollywood producer Hal B. Wallis.

A perfect good news–bad news scenario. The good news was I wasn't going on for Peppard, the bad news was I wasn't going on for Peppard. Mixed feelings? Oh, yeah. But more relief than disappointment.

The Philadelphia critics were "on the fence," as *Variety* and brother Theo would say, not a slam, not a rave, somewhere in the middle. A bit below middle to the New York critics; the play ran 56 performances and was never a movie.

Here's a bit of theater trivia: In *Girls of Summer*, Stephen Sondheim had his Broadway composing debut—an off-stage trumpet solo.

Garfein had another play, *The Sins of Pat Muldoon* with Elaine Stritch and James Barton. He again offered me the jobs of assistant stage manager and understudy. I thought, hell, I didn't leave Oklahoma to be an assistant stage manager and understudy. I've only been here a year. A movie, a play, New York is easy. I wanted to get back to class. I turned it down. *Muldoon* closed after five performances. It was 13 months before I got another acting job. So much for "New York is easy."

As the OU sophomore asked, "I don't get it. This play got bad reviews and isn't going to Broadway. Can't those Broadway guys just read a play and know if it's any good, if it's gonna be a hit or not? What's the deal? Huh?"

5

A West Side Story

Cheryl Crawford knew me from *The Girls of Summer* and asked me to audition for a new musical she was producing, *West Side Story*. Her office was large, unkempt and casual, but with a baby grand piano, Jerome Robbins, Leonard Bernstein and Stephen Sondheim. Miss Crawford, mid-fifties, thin-lipped, short henna hair, a stern but kind face, had produced some 50 productions of opera, comedies, musicals, Shakespeare, Ibsen, O'Casey, Williams and on and on. Robbins was a choreographic giant in ballet and on Broadway. He created dozens of ballets, and prior to 1957 had done *Peter Pan*, *High Button Shoes*, *Call Me Madam* and *Bells Are Ringing*. Bernstein, aside from his classical calling, had composed the music for Robbins' ballet *Fancy Free*, later on Broadway as *On the Town*. He had written the score a few years earlier for the successful Broadway musical *Wonderful Town*. As I stood before them, I was not aware of their artistic fame, they were just introductions.

With my accompanist at the baby grand, I slayed 'em with "A-Wanderin'," my "sensitive ballad." Crawford had tears in her eyes, the guys were nonplussed. Then I sang my "up song," "Sit Down You're Rockin' the Boat," and as I raised my right hand in a midair gesture I saw that it was shaking. It threw me. Being shaky-nervous was a first and I forgot the lyrics, but I continued with: "ta duh ta duh ta duh, sit down you're rockin' the boat." In the second verse I came to the same phrase, same gesture, same shaking hand, and I forget the lyrics again. I dropped my quivering hand and turned to the group, "Well, I'm pretty sure you know the lyrics so why don't I just stop now?"

I got a call back! This time at a Broadway theater. I'd never auditioned from a Broadway stage. It's not a chummy, intimate room with interested faces ten feet away. It is big and bare. Ten rows back, surrounded by a thousand empty seats, are five dimly lighted people, some slumped, some leaning back or flipping pages of a script. My name is announced by a stage manager, theirs are not. My "hello" rang weak and hollow and unanswered. My accompanist, a musical veteran, was in the orchestra pit and started playing. I took a deep breath and then held it. What song was he playing? I stepped down stage to him and whispered, "That's not "A-Wanderin'." He hissed, "Yes, it is!" Again he played, and again I stopped him: "It's not my song!"

From the audience, "Is there a problem?"

"No, not really. I'm just … uh, no."

My music started and I'm pretty sure I sang what he played. I think it was Robbins who then asked me to read a scene, the role of Riff. Thank God no "Sit Down You're Rocking the Boat," just acting. After the reading, he came to the edge of the stage.

"Do you dance?"

Using the cliché all actors use: "I, uh, move well."

"Have you ever studied dance?"

"Oh, yessir."

"Oh? Who with?"

"Dick Andros."

"Who?"

"My cousin."

Robbins sent me off to study with the famed exponent of modern jazz, Anna Sokolow. He was interested! Boy, I threw myself into her warm-ups, exercises and combinations like it was football practice. I was skinned, scabbed, bleeding and loving it. After two weeks, Sokolow said Jerry wanted to see me.

"So, Madame, what do you think, how am I?"

"Lou, as a dancer … you have a high threshold for pain."

No songs, no shaking, I was undaunted by the empty theater. With Band-Aids and bandages I read two scenes for Robbins and the dim faces. I had done the two scenes well and in a few calculated stage crosses managed to move well.

At my new job that night at Julius Monk's Upstairs at the Downstairs, I was serving drinks to a table of four which included a nice young man, suit, tie, neat, and my age. He said to me, "You gave a good audition today." I went over to one of the wiser waiters, all of whom were actors. "See that guy, the young one? He says he saw my *West Side Story* audition today. How do you figure?"

"That's Hal Prince, one of the producers."

Jeez, he looked like a kid.

Robbins kept calling me back, but after five auditions a real dancer was chosen, Mickey Calin. What a group of guys Robbins put together. Tough guy dancers didn't crowd too many dance classes in those days, but he found them. Cousin Dick shrugged, "If you had come to my classes every day, you'd probably be on Broadway."

Cold economics for the acting aspirant: In 1960, Strasberg charged $30 a month for a pair of two-hour classes a week. I earned about that amount in tips per night at Julius Monk's club. A girlfriend at The Gaslight got 60, but she wore black net stockings. An acting teacher today charges 200 to 400 a month for class; can an actor earn that in a night's tips? Depends where he's working, but yes. Dance was about $6 per class, now 15, and the most expensive of all was voice lessons at 40 bucks a session, now 100 to 150. If you wanted your accompanist playing for you at your audition, not only did you have to pay 25 (now 50 to 70), but you had to pay the cab fare!

Nervous auditioner starting his up song: "Beyond the blue hori—"

"Thank you! Next!"

That particular audition cost that actor like 50 bucks a note.

Pat Hingle once likened acting to being a pilot who might be brilliant in a mockup training cockpit, but truly earns his wings flying during turbulence, a bad engine, lives at stake. Where better for actors to earn their chops than actually in front of audiences?

Summer stock. The excitement and hard work in exploring six to eight different characters in a season of stock was a constant and invigorating test and teacher. The cast rehearses one play during the day and performs a different play that night in front of a paying audience. Some not-so-method shortcuts were necessary. All of those lines from different plays roiling in our brains necessitated a reliance on Cliffs Notes pasted on our

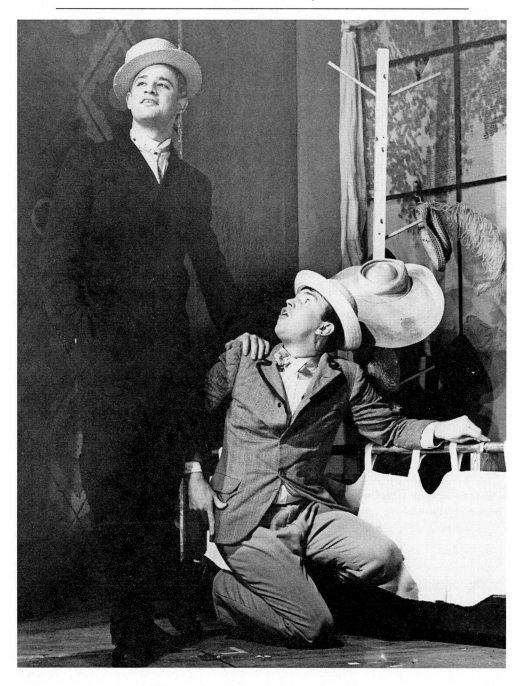

Leaning on George Furth in *The Matchmaker* in 1958.

makeup mirror. "*Hatful of Rain*. Me Polo, fun loving, in love with brother's wife, but a no-no. Loves brother (Johnny), mixed feelings about father. Don't be too drunk for drunk scene. <u>Don't hesitate</u>, *indicate!*" Is Stanislavski *anywhere* in there?

Sometimes summer stock spawned other talents.

Thirteen years later, George Furth wrote *Twigs*, his first of seven plays as a Broadway playwright, most notably two for Stephen Sondheim, *Company* and *Merrily We Roll Along*. He started writing one-acts which were seen and encouraged at the Actors Studio, and then, eureka!, *Twigs* went from scene work at the Studio to the Great White Way. No more summer stock for Furth. Nor for a lot of us, but for a different reason.

There were over 300 Equity summer theaters in the '60s, now there are 39. It's a loss to actors, directors, playwrights, everyone in every aspect of the theater who could profit from failures and successes, from experience. It's a loss to audiences. To all of us.

There were other experiences, some remembered, some forgotten. We didn't call it summer schtup for nothing.

While I was doing Brick in *Cat on a Hot Tin Roof* at Fishkill in 1958, some guys saw a matinee and wanted me to act in an independent film (read very low-budget) called *The Treehouse*, to be shot in Sault Ste. Marie, Canada. Paul Sills was the writer and here's the who's who associated with the film: Irvin Kershner, the director, went on to do movies, including *The Empire Strikes Back*; the producers were Haskell Wexler and his brother Yale. Haskell also was the cinematographer, long before he won Oscars for *Who's Afraid of Virginia Woolf?* and *Bound for Glory*. The cast: Barbara Harris, Michael Landon (hot from *I Was a Teenage Werewolf*), Ed Asner, Barnard Hughes. We doubled up in our small motel rooms, and we all ate family style at one table in a mom and pop diner. Except for Landon; I think he was married to a nurse at the time.

One afternoon on location I was awakened from my nap and pulled outside where the camera was pointed at a cabin wall. Kershner was in a hurry.

"Action. Lou, lean against that wall."

"Why am I—"

"Just lean against the wall. Now look up and smile."

"What am I smiling about, what kind of smile?"

"Just look over here, Lou, and smile. Okay, now look mad."

"Who am I mad at, why—"

"Be mad at anybody and for any damn reason, just look mad! Okay, print. Let's go back inside."

My Method crumbled to the ground. Stanislavski kicked the dirt in my face.

After the tenth day of a 15-day shooting schedule, we were told that the movie was being suspended for a rewrite and that we'd all be called back. We never were.

Hiccups occur in most careers. They are not necessarily career-threatening. Asner, Harris, Hughes, Landon all went on to many memorable performances.

Within two weeks of the Canadian cancellation, I segued into an Off Broadway play. David Ross, a young Off Broadway producer, was getting attention for his fine productions of seldom-produced classics, mostly Chekhov. He hired me to play Eva Gabor's lover in Frank Wedekind's *Lulu*. I jumped into my character with ease and relish. For three days.

"I'm going to have to let you go, Lou," Ross said to me after my third rehearsal.

"I'm fired? How come?"

"You're too young. Eva thinks you make her look old."

Don Fellows replaced me. He was in his mid-thirties, I was in my early twenties. "Too young." Of course when fired, the actor is always too *something*. Or *not enough* something.

6

Selling Soap

Love of Life was a popular half-hour soap opera in 1958. I was hired to play a heavy for a minimum of one episode a week for five weeks at 150 per pop. Some weeks I did *two*! Three hundred bucks for two days work! Glorious wages when you consider that Off Broadway paid $30 a week.

My first day of work, the director Larry Auerbach asked me if I'd ever done a soap before. "No sir."

"Here's the way it works. Rehearse in the morning, tape from noon to 12:30, on the air at one. We don't stop tape unless your pants fall down or you throw up. Got it?"

I hoped I got it. An actor's day on a soap set—pages of words, marks to hit, holding a line until your camera's little red light goes on, doing a close-up alone while your acting partner runs to another set for her next scene.

The Boy Scout Fighting Song goes here.

For instance, an excellent actor, Scott Marlowe, had only done stage and film work when he was cast in a New York soap. Beverlee McKenzie, a veteran daytime drama queen, (and OU grad) took him aside and gave him some advice: "This is a one-hour show, Scott. You'll have a ton of dialogue to learn, which means you will not have an outside life until you find your groove." Essentially it was a warning of stringent work habits, no partying, and the dedication of a monk. Marlowe batted none for three. His acting was without conviction because he could not learn his lines. His character, and his income, were quickly killed off. "Be prepared," sing it, "be prepared."

Jean McBride had been a *Love of Life* leading lady for 12 years. She was in Curt Conway's acting class with me and to us unemployed classmates, her salary was to drool over. Yet she quit the soap opera to get "real parts." She came to class one night near tears. Her long-time agents at the powerhouse William Morris agency didn't know she was a client. "It's like starting over," she cried. A year later she landed her first post–*Love of Life* job, *The Ed Sullivan Show*, which booked a lot of variety acts. Looking beautiful, her "real part" was to walk past the comedian Lou Costello and take a pie in the face. That was it. She married an upstate judge.

Back in Oklahoma, *Love of Life* was on the air during the Lafayette's lunch hour, the busiest time of the day. When I was on the show, Poppa, ignoring his customers, would sit down in front of a TV set he had brought in. With a "Thatsa my boy," customers were invited to watch at no extra charge.

In 1958, after two years in the Air Force, a master's degree in drama from OU and a season of summer stock in Colon, Michigan, brother Jim came to New York to chase an acting career. I was living in a loft on Eighth Avenue and 26th. It was one large room, a

31

hundred feet long, heated, only within a seven-foot radius, by a single potbelly stove. The toilet and shower were some 80 feet away from those seven feet. It was illegal to live there and what with a $50 fine for dumping garbage in a street refuse container, we'd take our garbage to acting class or to a friend's and unload it. We burned coal in the potbelly, but wood was needed to ignite the coal and there wasn't exactly a lot of spare wood lying about the streets of Manhattan. But I found an infinite supply: police barricades, which I'd haul off at four in the morning. In the winter, Jim and I sat around the loft wearing gloves, hats and overcoats reading, improvising *Peanuts* cartoons, or talking about pursuing projects that interested two young Greek boys from Oklahoma.

Oklahoma idea: "Jim, did you hear yet from Harold Blumenthal about *Bound for Glory*?" (Jim's screenplay of the Woody Guthrie tome had been his master's thesis at OU.)

"Yesterday. Said he'd give us a three-month option for $5000."

Greek idea: "Maybe let's go ahead with our *Zorba* idea then. You know—"

"Yeah. A play with music. George C. Scott. Nobody better. Maybe we should try to option that."

I thought a moment. "Wonder how much a *Zorba* option would cost?"

We were silent. "What with last night's tips, I got about two, two-fifty cash. You?"

"Yeah, little more maybe. About three."

We resumed reading.

7

Getting In,
and At the Actors Studio

In the '50s and '60s, the Actors Studio was *the* status level sought by actors young and old. A typical year of 2000 auditioners found only two or three accepted as members. The process was palm-sweating. For the preliminary audition, the actors are led up a narrow darkened stairway and into a shadowed room where their acting in a five-minute scene was evaluated by unlighted members. If you passed the prelim, next came the final audition. Up those non-consoling stairs again, knowing this time those shadowed judges would be Lee Strasberg, Elia Kazan and Cheryl Crawford.

My first audition was *Desire Under the Elms* with the beautiful Barbara Bain. I didn't pass and Barbara was chosen to do her final with another partner. For a year after that, I'd get calls from actors who had passed their preliminary saying the Studio had recommended me to do their final with them. I would.

Alice Drummond, whom I'd never met, called me one February day in 1958 and asked if I would partner her for her final at the Studio. Warmed by my potbelly stove, she and I rehearsed her scene from Tennessee Williams' *27 Wagons Full of Cotton*. In the audition, that slight, frail woman slapped me with the force of a welterweight. My head snapped around, I spun down stage and got a big laugh. It hurt and felt good. That night I got a call from the secretary of the Studio saying I'd been accepted, but not Alice. Later she made it all the way. That audition was my fourth trip up those dark stairs.

For my first scene as a Studio member, I chose Sartre's *Kean*, a play about the legendary nineteenth century Shakespearean actor Edmund Kean. What the hell, I still had my dance belt, I donned tights, spoke well and stood up straight. Not a torn tee shirt or a mumble to be seen or heard. My first two years at the Studio, I don't think I ever chose a contemporary scene. I felt that safe there.

My days and nights at the Actors Studio were an adventure. It gave us a place to take a chance, a place to *practice*. Some of the chances were a thrill: Anne Bancroft doing *My Fair Lady* and singing like a bird, Eli Wallach doing his periodic *Richard III*, George Gaynes, in a far jump from his roles in *Tootsie* and the *Police Academy* movies, sang an aria from *Boris Godunov* while working on an emotional memory. Astonishing. Patrick O'Neal, hilarious in a Dorothy Parker short story. Roscoe Lee Browne, transforming his pear-toned sophistication into a self-proclaimed "nigger" in *Bohickey Creek*. It was devastating. Geraldine Page doing anything.

Eli Rill adapted and staged Edna St. Vincent Millay's *Conversations at Midnight* with Gerald O'Loughlin, Bill Smithers, Don Fellows, and Arthur Storch. Rill also directed the first act of Thomas Wolfe's only play, *In the Mannerhouse*, with Academy Award winners Franchot Tone and Mildred Dunnock playing my parents with me as Wolfe. What lessons I learned from them in trusting full and alive simplicity on stage. Years before *Cats* crawled in London and New York, Lonny Chapman staged T.S. Eliot's *Wasteland*. He adapted a section of Steinbeck's *East of Eden* long before Kazan's film.

Or watching Marilyn Monroe at the Studio, sitting quietly, blue jeans, a sweater, innocent eyes, no makeup, shy. She did a scene from O'Neill's *Anna Christie* with Maureen Stapleton. In Strasberg's private class she did Blanche from *A Streetcar Named Desire*. At that time, 1960, Marilyn Monroe, the most celebrated movie star in the world, was doing scenes and sensory exercises before a class of 30 unknowns.

She once telephoned a fellow classmate, Brooks Morton. In her little girl Marilyn voice: "Hello, Brooks?"

"Yes."

"Lee said I should call you about doing a scene with me in class."

"Well, who is this?"

"This is Marilyn ... from class?"

One of the truly positive things about the Actors Studio (or any class or workshop) is, as Eli Wallach said, and many thereafter, "It's my gym, it's where I work out as an actor."

I hear from time to time, "An actor can't learn to act in a class. You can't give a person talent." The second sentence I agree with. Someone Else does that. I have seen actors not only improve from taking acting classes, but find and release the talent that's been there, untapped or trapped. True, we cannot bestow talent, but, boy, if it's there it can be uncovered, nurtured, disciplined, guided, exercised, stretched and challenged by going to the gym. Yes, there are actors who will degrade a play by showing off their abilities, not the playwright's intentions. Watch me cry, watch my anger, listen to my voice, aren't I great! Watch me, watch *me*! "Watch me" is quicksand to an actor. It's a danger to the art in any artist.

As a person, director or teacher, Strasberg was not infallible or incorruptible. He has been judged harshly by his critics, sometimes rightly so. There are books written by his son John and his daughter Susan; read those if you must. My time with him was well worth his ego, pride and desire for celebrity. His insights and knowledge were gigantic.

Every teacher knows something, but not everything. If not challenged, concepts at least should be questioned—especially those of self-appointed gurus who deem themselves incapable of error, expecting adulation and obeisance, defeating and repelling any artist's independent discoveries.

We've lost our giants—Strasberg, Stella Adler, Sanford Meisner, Harold Clurman, Bobby Lewis, Uta Hagen. We have no one to replace them.

Lonny Chapman was writing a play and he'd give us scenes from it to do in his acting class. One

Lee Strasberg.

of his students, Fran White, a prosperous businesswoman, liked what she saw and scraped together $12,000 and produced the play, *The Buffalo Skinner*, Off Broadway. Jim had a part and my character was Woody, rebelling against strict religious parents. Woody opens the play by addressing the audience, and never leaves the stage. Opening night, waiting behind the curtain, I yawned and stretched and was Woody, rebellious and loose. Oh, and talk about youthful confidence, I'd read a piece by Eric Bentley about how American actors are always leaning on mantels or furniture and sticking their hands in their pockets. So what did I do? I asked the costumer to sew up all my pockets. The curtain opened in the small 199-seat Theatre Marquee, and there I was throwing an opening monologue into the faces of New York's top theater critics: Brooks Atkinson, Walter Kerr, Richard Watts, John McClain, all of them. To Woody, they were unknown faces.

The opening night party was at the loft, a perfect party space. The evening was enlivened by the reviews. Chapman was hailed as an "exciting new playwright," including praise of his past Broadway performances. He joked, "As a playwright, I'm getting better reviews as an actor than I ever got on Broadway as an actor." Then he asked me was I happy with my reviews. If I may...

"Lou Antonio, making his Manhattan bow, is a budding actor to watch." Robert Coleman, *Daily News*

"...a bright new discovery." John McClain, *Journal-American*

"...an attractive, romantic young actor." Brooks Atkinson, *New York Times*

"A fresh and engaging vitality that one would have thought had been copyrighted by Ben Gazzara." Walter Kerr, *Herald Tribune*

The play and the party were a success. I woke up the next morning and Jim was sitting in a chair by the potbelly wearing his overcoat and gloves, reading our review in *The New York Post*. The front-page headline: BROADWAY ACTOR FALLS DOWN ELEVATOR SHAFT. Next to the headline was a picture of Pat Hingle, who was playing Job in *J.B.* He had joined us after his show, participating in the enthusiasm for Chapman, his friend of many years. I had said good night to him only six hours earlier. Jim read the article to me. The elevator in Hingle's apartment building got stuck halfway between the fifth and sixth floors. He had forced the doors open to jump down to the hallway below. His overcoat got caught on the door and swung him under the elevator and down the empty shaft. A hip was broken, he lost part of a finger, there were internal injuries, but he was alive.

My New York stage début, as Woody in *The Buffalo Skinner.*

There was some interest in the new kid in the new play, thus I was being sent up for interviews and possible jobs. I got a call from Alfred DeLiagre, the producer of *J.B.* He was urbane, well-dressed, well-spoken, well-groomed and casual. "James Olson may be leaving the show. Kazan [the director] might be interested in you for the part."

"Okay."

"We'll know by the end of the week."

"Okay." I got up to leave.

"Oh, by the way … Pat was at your party that night, wasn't he?"

"Yessir."

"How much did he have to drink? Was he drunk when he left your place? Suppose that's why he fell?"

"I wouldn't know. I was doing my own drinking, not his."

The bastard was sniffing around for something, possibly an insurance payoff. Not a word of, "Have you talked to Pat's wife? How is he doing?" I left.

Chapman invited his MCA literary agent, the legendary Audrey Wood, to see his play. She did and wanted me to read for a new play by another one of her clients, William Inge. Maynard Morris, an influential actors' agent at MCA, was promoting and guiding a young client named Warren Beatty. Morris and I had met, but he was more enamored with Beatty's potential than by my reviews. An MCA agent later told me that Morris was such a power in the agency that he personally made sure I never got so much as a reading for the Inge play, *A Loss of Roses*. It ran for 25 performances and Beatty was a 1960 Tony nominee for Featured Actor, and won a Theatre World Award for a Most Promising Newcomer.

A few years later, Kazan asked me to do a day's work in his movie *Splendor in the Grass*. I bargained: "I'll do it if you cast my brother Jim. He's from Oklahoma, too, and he's good." Kazan studied me for a moment. He lowered his head, laughing. "Okay, okay," and walked away.

You probably can't recognize either me or Jim. We're covered in oil in a crowded kitchen, and no close-ups. Well, Maynard Morris had an eye all right, Beatty has the leading role in the movie and seems to have done quite well from that. *Very* promising, don't you think?

8

The Fervid Years

The play that brought Edward Albee recognition in America, *The Zoo Story*, was first presented in the U.S. in 1959 at the playwrights unit at the Actors Studio. Jerry, a young man who is consumed by loneliness and its ancillary disturbances, starts a conversation with a mild older man on a Central Park bench. The man ends up killing him. John Stix directed me as Jerry and Shepperd Strudwick as the older man. Albee was quiet, non-intrusive, with a crew cut and attractive Ivy League look. The material was not Ivy League and a rush to work on. This shy and reserved young writer could strip a character clean, reveal unadmitted aspects of our lives, and still make us laugh. Albee's people live in dangerous waters, filled with poisonous unseen things. When we presented it in the playwright's unit, the reaction was strong, heated, divisive, pummeled and praised. Norman Mailer was ready to take on anyone who dissed Albee. However, any negativity that rained down on Albee did not drown his perseverance or voice. A 1960 production of *The Zoo Story* was a success Off Broadway and two years later came *Who's Afraid of Virginia Woolf?* Subsequently Albee has pulled three Pulitzer Prizes for his work. Years later I asked him if he had learned anything from our doing *The Zoo Story* at the Studio. He replied, "The performance of the play you all did at the Studio set me off in the right direction with a sense of what good actors can do!"

On this matter I refer to a 2005 *New York Times* interview with the award-winning playwright Horton Foote:

> As a playwright, Mr. Foote said, he has learned to rely on actors to find the saving grace in even the most shameful behavior.
> "I adore actors," he said. "I always learn something from them. Another reality takes place when you hear the words spoken by someone else. They use their imagination and raise questions you may not have asked. I learned a lot about all the characters after we began rehearsals. An actress like Estelle Parsons, for example, finds meanings that you didn't know were there."
> So since rehearsals began, Mr. Foote has been writing and rewriting every day, changing the play in subtle ways as actors brought a broader view to it. And it is in that broader view that the humanity of the characters takes shape, puts on flesh and bone.

Albee was an active and loyal member at the Studio until it became a producing entity. The story goes that the Actors Studio had first call at producing *Who's Afraid of Virginia Woolf?* Strasberg wouldn't sanction it unless Albee made large cuts. Albee refused, and Strasberg passed on it

Dodging in and out of unsuccessful plays, the unemployed actor is grateful to snag a TV gig wherever they can. In the late '50s and early '60s, jobless theater thespians were disdainful of soap operas or worse, doing a *commercial*. Yaagh. Become a regular on a TV series? Beneath us. Snobs we were. Certainly not so these days. You've no doubt seen movie stars doing series television and/or cable movies, heard them or watched them extolling the virtues of automobiles, telephones, medicines and erectile dysfunction. (Is there a pill to take for a limp career...?)

For one-line parts, supporting parts, leading parts, New York casting people like Alan Shayne, Rose Tobias, Marion Dougherty, Shirley Mitchell and Terry Fay started many a career. They scoured workshops, plays in every imaginable venue, mining actors from the dark caves of anonymity, and sometimes striking pay dirt with the likes of Robert Duvall, Redford and Culp, Dustin Hoffman, Gene Hackman, Faye Dunaway and Peter Falk. Being young, broke and hopeful was what New York was about. Alas, I don't know how those with the burn to learn can afford New York today. But the tenacious will find a way.

All kinds of aspirants drank and danced at my loft. These were mostly dropper-inners, not friends, usually friends of friends: Jack Kerouac, Warren Beatty, Roscoe Lee Browne, Georgia Brown, Gerry Mulligan, Jean Seberg, Rip Torn and so forth. I wasn't close to any of them, except for Browne and Brown. In those times, the young comers were not only talented individuals, we were part of a swarm. Talent attraction. It's not as if we all knew one another, but we knew *of* one another. It seemed a connected community respectful of shared ambitions, envy, competitiveness, dedication, empathetic to the reality of our needs, our failures, our successes large and small.

Sometimes rehearsing a scene was just another way of dating. And a lot cheaper. It was no impersonal "wham bam thank you ma'am" or "thank you sir." After the sex, there was always the work to talk about, plays, movies, actors. We allowed ourselves to bust out, examining who we were without the pressure of parental opinion. Our peccadilloes were side orders, our entrée was the dedication to our art, subsisting on that ever-flickering burn to learn.

The theater was popping with new ideas and forms, scuttling old language and sexual taboos—Jack Gelber's *The Connection* at the Living Theatre with junkies cast and portrayed; Mart Crowley's gay-themed *The Boys in the Band*; Eugene Ionesco's wacky absurdist *Rhinoceros*; Jean Genet unsettling audiences with *The Blacks* and *The Maids*, and with *The Balcony* bringing forth Peter Falk, Roscoe Lee Browne and Cicely Tyson. *A Hatful of Rain* was conceived at the Actors Studio. The drive of a young dynamo named Joe Papp materialized free Shakespeare outdoors! Ellen Stewart's Café La Mama in Greenwich Village is still alive and active. The face of the New York theater establishment was changing expressions.

There were Murray Schisgal, Israel Horowitz, Edward Albee, Arthur Kopit, Jack Gelber and Jack Richardson, touted as the American theater's best prospects since the emergence of Tennessee Williams and Arthur Miller. Lorraine Hansberry became the first black playwright with a hit on Broadway. Nichols and May from Second City and Theodore Flicker's *The Premise* were drawing crowds to improvisational theater with legit actors like George Segal, Gene Hackman and Tom Aldredge winging in from the classics into comedy. As a waiter at the Upstairs at the Downstairs, I laughed at our comedy harpist Tom O'Horgan, who went on to direct Broadway's *Jesus Christ Superstar* and *Hair*, the latter co-written by my Lonny Chapman classmate, Jerry Ragni. At the Actors Studio, Kazan was directing Aeschylus' *The Oresteia*. The Old Vic captured us with Franco Zeffirelli's production of *Romeo and Juliet*. Carmen Capalbo scored with the Brecht-Weill The *Threepenny Opera* that sprang Bea Arthur and Ed Asner from obscurity. Papp had Central Park ringing with Shakespeare. José Quintero raised Robards and Dewhurst to prominence with Eugene O'Neill.

Leonard Bernstein was the composer for two Broadway musicals mounted in one year, *Candide* and *West Side Story*, with a much respected but mostly unknown Stephen Sondheim doing the lyrics. The British were coming, the British were coming! The Angry Young Men sent us Pinter's *The Caretaker*, Osborne's *Look Back in Anger*, Bolt's *A Man for All Seasons*, Arnold Wesker's *Chips with Everything* and Leslie Bricusse and Anthony Newley's *Stop the World I Want to Get Off*.

We were inspired by all that surrounded us, and though most of us were frustrated by not being a part of it, we welcomed it, waiting for our turn.

9

Overseas and Back Again

On Broadway, Frank Corsaro had directed Michael Gazzo's *A Hatful of Rain* and *The Night Circus*, both born and raised at the Actors Studio, and he was putting together a cadre of Actors Studio members for a series of plays to be presented at Gian Carlo Menotti's Festival of Two Worlds in Spoleto, Italy. It was 1959, the festival's second year, and I was fortunate to be chosen by Corsaro, along with Patrick O'Neal, Gene Saks, Arthur Storch, Vivian Nathan, Rosemary Murphy and Sondra Lee. We were to do a new one-act play by Tennessee Williams, *The Night of the Iguana*; a one-act by the Italian poet Nicolo Tucci; Saks was to do a monologue by the Beat poet Gregory Corso; Storch and Lee had a one-act by William Inge, *The Tiny Closet* (long before "closet" had a gay connotation); with a wacky revue by Steven Vinaver with Saks, Lee, me and opera star Patricia Neway, who had sung in Menotti's Pulitzer Prize production of *The Consul* and three other leads in Menotti pieces.

We flew coach to Rome in a propeller aircraft on Alitalia Airlines. Storch had the fear of flying, but he had a formula for fearless flying. After we took off, Storch, sleeping pills in hand, ordered a double Scotch. But this was more akin to steerage than coach; alcohol, magazines and hot food were denied us. Arthur offered Yankee dollars to the temperance-controlling stewardess, but to no avail. The passengers were then treated to one of the finest mad scenes ever enacted aloft or anywhere.

Storch played it effectively, shouting, cowering, shaking, fear in his eyes, distraction in his aspect. It so frightened the passengers and crew that three stewardesses forced fists full of little Scotch bottles into his flailing hands. With a smile on his face, he slept the entire 13-hour flight.

Our salary was a scant $125 a week in lire, therefore, Storch, Saks and I shared the rent of an apartment with a kitchen. We had hot water. Yes, every morning a woman would come in with an armful of little sticks, arrange them under a copper tank and light them. Thirty minutes later, hot water!

Iguana went well. My part, Jake Latta, was small, and I was able to watch Corsaro and those Studio actors creating their roles. We only had about ten days to rehearse the three plays and everyone went swiftly, efficiently and effectively. Williams would air mail us his revisions on lightweight onionskin paper. No faxes or e-mails, only envelopes and stamps kept those new words flying across the ocean.

The Nicolo Tucci play, *Posterity for Sale*, was a different experience. Tucci had written it in English as a plea for respect for writers. But it was tedious and heavy-handed, until we turned it on its ear and played it as low comedy. I played an overblown Texan with a 20 gallon hat, Storch the tormented writer and the five-foot Sondra Lee as his pregnant wife with an oversized belly that looked like a dirigible was due. We had to learn a new type of "wait for the laugh." You see, most of the audience were non–English-speaking Italians, so we'd land a joke, hold, wait for whispered translations into Italian, and *then* the laughs would come. In artistic shame we dreaded Tucci's reaction for turning his high-minded drama into an over-the-top sketch. Opening night he came into our dressing room with tears in his eyes. We looked away guilt-ridden.

"Grazie! Mille grazie!!"

He embraced us all, thanking us for saving his play!

Saks' wife, Bea Arthur, joined us. What an original! At our daily trattoria, a young blonde waitress took a liking to Saks, which was obvious from her lingering looks at him. His wife caught it. In her basso profundo voice, Bea commented for the small room to hear, "She's got a mouth like a chicken's asshole."

I had a sweet affair with an actress from the Piccolo Teatro. She didn't speak English and I was doing my best to learn Italian. We spent hours together talking, I in English, she in Italian. I got a slight summer cold and she took me to a *farmacia*. The pharmacist gave me a capsule the size of my thumb. With broken Italian and gestures I told her I could never swallow it, it was too big. Through quiet laughter, slow Italian and her talents as a mime, she made me understand it did not go in my mouth. It was a suppository.

That summer was a plethora of talent and artists of all genres. If only I had been less shy. I met but, dammit, didn't linger with Jean Cocteau, the conductor Thomas Schippers, the actor John Gielgud, the author Irwin Shaw, dancer-choreographer Herbert Ross (later a movie director) and his wife Nora Kaye, and Glen Tetley, later artistic director of three international dance companies. I snuck into an outdoor rehearsal of Jerome Robbins refining his *Jazz, U.S.A.* ballet. He would start rehearsals for *Gypsy* a month later. I saw my first two operas, the Corsaro-directed *Angelo del Fueco* and Luchino Visconti's production of *Duc d'Alba*. In the country of Puccini, Verdi, Vivaldi and Rossini, I fell asleep in each.

My mind and senses were open and heightened every day by other venues of which I knew so little. At the Uffizi Gallery I wrung my hands and broke into a sweat standing before the statues, staring and touching. There were artists doing set design, firing glassware, Schippers conducting Verdi's *Requiem* in the village square. I walked through narrow streets in a nighttime candlelight procession of Spoleto citizens to Menotti's apartment in an homage of thanks and reverence to their maestro. Cream rises to the top and I was swimming in it. Seldom would I be in the nexus of such elevated art and committed artists.

Returning to New York at the end of that summer, I was cast in a daunting role in Leo Tolstoy's *The Power of Darkness*. My *Buffalo Skinner* reviews five months earlier were for naught, I had to audition twice. It was an Off Broadway production under the direction of Wynn Handman, a highly regarded acting teacher who later founded the American Place Theatre. His wife Barbara had adapted the story about nineteenth century Russian peasants with murder, adultery and infanticide in their lives. Lots of fun stuff to work on. Mary Alice Bayh and Nancy Pollock were cast in the play.

A student of Handman's, the popular comic Jan Murray, was personally bankrolling the entire production. During one rehearsal I got a telephone call that pulled me down from my Spoleto high. My girlfriend informed me that she was having an affair with a close friend of mine and was breaking up with me. I was shattered. I didn't know friends did that to each other. Head down, I slumped back into rehearsal for my next scene, sobbing

Mary Alice Bayh, me, and a bit giddy Nancy Pollock from Tolstoy vodka shooters.

Tolstoy dialogue for a good 15 minutes. Handman and the cast thought I must be doing some Method crap and probably rolled their eyes at my bleeding heart slaughtering of the Method. Of course I "used it" in my character of Nikita; he gets a young peasant girl pregnant and is forced to kill his baby. Like I said, lotsa good stuff to work on.

We opened on October 12. The critics who had reviewed me with such clear-eyed praise in *The Buffalo Skinner* had apparently donned sunglasses for *Darkness*. Mixed reviews assailed us. Vincent Gardenia was playing the gardener to whom I cry in despair after killing the baby. Since we were obviously not a hit, Vincent left our show to take a play on Broadway. His understudy Peter Falk and I had a quick afternoon rehearsal before Falk's first performance.

"Uh, Peter … which eye is your good one, which one do you want me to look at?"

"Dis one."

That night after killing my baby, I do my "Olivier yell," emerge from the basement and fling myself onto the thick layer of real dirt that covered the stage. As the gardener, Falk started his page-long speech with an *Irish accent*, switched to a Puerto Rican accent, then an Italian accent. I was laughing so hard I had to bury my face in the god-awful dirt. He did it with his even-then Columbo pacing so that one page seemed to drag on for two days.

Darkness closed after a four-week run and my pantry was bare. Nothing saved from Italy, and though Off Broadway minimum had increased to $40 a week, before taxes, I didn't exactly have a nest egg. Producers, directors, hey, it's me, don't you remember, "a budding actor to watch"? Uh-huh, but apparently not to hire.

Television to the rescue.

Walter Matthau was set to do a series in Florida called *Tallahassee 700*, a half-hour cop show. Matthau was a gambler and apparently not too good at it. The story goes that he owed his bookies such a bundle that he was afraid to leave his apartment, which is the only way he could get to Tallahassee. For Matthau to be able to leave town alive, his entire salary had to go to the bad guys in advance. He was to live solely on his per diem. Matthau had a tough life when he was a boy in New York City, destitute, sleeping in doorways under newspapers for warmth when his mom had a caller.

Driving to location one day in Tallahassee, I asked him, "Walter, why do you gamble?" He laughed and said, "Dunno, I'm paying this psychiatrist guy a lot of money to find out."

He'd bet on anything. As we pulled up to a dock for the day's shooting, he saw a seagull on one of the pilings. "Bet you ten he stays on that post until we get out of the car," said Matthau. I declined. And he would have lost. His enthusiasm for acting was contagious. When we got back to our hotel after a hot Florida day's work, he asked if I'd mind doing one of our scenes again for his wife Carol. As an actress, formerly married to William Saroyan, she didn't seem to find it odd watching her husband doing a scene in their hotel room from a second-rate TV episode. She applauded. Walter poured us a drink with a toast: "To thespians everywhere. But mostly in Tallahassee."

My first encounter with a Hollywood director was a few months later on a series shot in New York called *Naked City*. Robert Duvall and I were guesting as bad guys with Sylvia Sidney playing Duvall's dippy aunt. At the Gold Medal studios in the Bronx, my character was supposed to fire his machine-gun into the floor and then run. We rehearsed, I fired, I fled. David Lowell Rich, the Hollywood director, said he wanted me to fire the gun, wait four beats, and then run. Well, with my character in a crisis situation, I hadn't figured to pause four beats after firing a machine-gun. Rich wanted it so in my head I tried about five different adjustments: fearless, no, nonchalant, maniacally, no, no, and so on. I went to Rich, "Sir, I really need some help from you. I can't find a reason for staying when I know that he'd get the hell out of here. Can you give me some kind of reason for staying?" Rich looked at me square in the eye for a full *two* beats, turned on his heel and walked away without a word. Big Hollywood Help he was. I think I used some cheap-ass trick like my gun jamming, trying to fix it, and then running. Seems to me that at least one part of the director's job is to help an actor in trouble. Perhaps I ask too much, the actor has to find his solution to the problem. For instance, on Broadway I've auditioned in a love scene, emoting, "You're sexy, you're pure, I want you to be the mother of my children," to a balding male stage manager reeking of a damp cigar and body odor. It's part of the territory. In *Close Encounters of the Third Kind* (1977) Melinda Dillon and Richard Dreyfuss had to convince us a spaceship and aliens were real. After "action," the actor has to trust his old pal and companion Imagination.

David Janssen on *The Fugitive* was always off-camera for your coverage. For his close-up he'd say to the guest actor, "Thanks, but I'd really rather have the script supervisor read your lines. So take a break. I won't be any better if you do it. It'll be the same one way or the other."

With David Janssen (front) in my first *Fugitive* episode.

With grueling 13- to 15-hour days, some actors take to a series and some don't. In four continuous seasons I acted in one *Fugitive* per season with Janssen and in with one *Defenders* per season with E.G. Marshall. A chart of the two of them over four seasons:

First season: gung-ho and never a nip.

Second season: gung-ho and a six o'clock toddy.

Third season: gung, and drinks at lunch.

Fourth season: ho, E.G. laughing and roaring at a 6:30 a.m. makeup call, a Bloody Bull in his hand.

I watched in wonder as he strode before the jury, the camera on the jurors' backs, giving his closing arguments word-perfect. What an actor. But on the next take I saw how he did it. He was reading his dialogue off script pages taped on each juror's chest.

After a *Fugitive* day, Janssen and I were having a drink across the street at the Formosa Inn. I was teasing him about the wondrous women who'd visit him on the set from time to time. "You met Ellie, right?" he asked, referring to his wife. He caught my reaction to his question. Once he had asked me over to his house for an after-work drink and she had related to me as if I were one of those non-entity *actors*, yaagh.

"Right. Another season or two, I'm going to divorce her."

"Got it. But what I don't get is, why wait?"

"I want to stay with the show until I've got two million dollars."

"Two. Okay, why *two* million?"

He took a drink. "Because she'll get a million from the divorce, and then I'll have *my* million."

10

Garson Kanin

January 2, 1960, just under a year from my debut reviews, I was in New York rehearsing the small part of a Latin American insurrectionist for a *United States Steel Hour*, a network show that was broadcast live, with George Grizzard and Mark Richman starring. During the dinner break before air, my agent called and told me to rush down to the Plymouth Theatre and read for a play.

"What's the play, what's the part?" I asked.

"I don't know. Just get down there!"

In the wings, I scanned the part called the Shady One. I was antsy, I had to get back to CBS in time for the show. I was called to the stage and introduced by the stage manager to the director Garson Kanin, a friendly man, who smiled and said, "I understand you've got very little time so rather than tell you about the play, just read the scene and take as a clue the name of the character, the Shady One. All right?"

All nerves and energy, I did the scene and ran off the stage. Grizzard and Richman were finishing their meal and Grizzard was having a Scotch on the rocks! He was going on the air live in 30 minutes?! I was dumbfounded. Seeing him throw back his drink reminded me that one of my jobs as assistant stage manager on *The Girls of Summer* was to make sure there were shots of vodka hidden in three separate spots upstage. During the performance, Shelley Winters, with her back to the audience and a quick snap of her head, would drain the vodkas. Never did ask her if that was Actors Studio or Hollywood training.

Live TV could put many an actor in the grip of fear. Millions of people were watching you and there was no take two, or getting a line thrown to you from a stage manager. In that *U.S. Steel Hour* I stood there running my three lines over and over in my head waiting for my cue. Not a morsel of the Method in my head. Red light on, my cue! I'm told my lines were expressed more or less coherently.

Mr. Kanin cast me in that Broadway play, Felicien Marceau's *The Good Soup*, scheduled to open in March 1960 at the Plymouth. All that attention I snared Off Broadway for those leading roles the season before? Fuhgeddaboudit. Not just the Shady One, but two more, Le Casse and Third Patron. Notice that only one has an actual name. Humbling, but the play had a cast that any young actor would be honored to act with, watch work, or just hang with. As an experienced novice I leapt at the offer. Here were some of the venerable veterans of the cast: Ruth Gordon (Kanin's wife), Zero Mostel, Sam Levene, Mildred Natwick, Ernest Truex and the gorgeous Diane Cilento. These actors had traveled many roads in theater and film and I anticipated what my spying on them might yield.

La Bonne Soupe had been running in Paris for two years. Kanin had seen it many times and to duplicate the staging for his version he had taken dozens of photographs during the Paris performances. In our rehearsals, he didn't allow the actors to leave the stage area. Even if you weren't in the scene, you damn well sat on a folding chair up against the back wall. No smoking, no talking. A perfect seat to study the lapses and accomplishments in a Broadway-bound play. I had kept notes in Strasberg's private classes and I wasn't about to let this experience go unrecorded either. Here's excerpts of the first day's log of my first Broadway play.

The Good Soup Log, January 4, 1960

The New Amsterdam Theatre is now a dinghy old theater used for rehearsals, the elevator service is as slovenly as the drunks one encounters every morning as a course of natural 42nd Street life. Garson Kanin makes a short speech about how he wants none of this mumbling, inner business, it'll just waste time, so everyone speak up. No sit-down read-through of the play either. On your feet and let's beat it out.

Top: Ruth Gordon, Sam Levine, Ernest Truex. Bottom: Diane Cilento, Mildred Natwick, Jules Munshin.

The old pros have eagerness and enthusiasm, younger ones quiet, reading, sizing each other up for possible relationships. Kanin to Mildred Natwick: "Do this, darling, it's funny. I don't know why, but it always got a roar. I don't know why." I note, "Yeah, but it was in French when it got the roar." He finishes blocking the entire show at 5:45! Day has mostly been about "getting it on its feet" and copying the French production from the pictures. So, this is Broadway.

Kanin is a charming man, with a facility for giving direction succinctly, clearly and in a non-accusatory tone. "This is not," he says, "*not* a French farce. It's naturalistic, real. Brecht influences it, it's epic, but in style it is naturalistic." He says that George Abbott once told him that the most important thing for a director is "to keep the play as a whole in his head" and therefore run-throughs are important, that there is more benefit from a run-through than from stopping, because the unconscious starts to work and the unconscious is where all creative art begins.

Mostel is a marvel to study. His pantomime of fly-fishing is like a ballet, smooth, exact and flowing. While I was at OU, the House of Un-American Activities Committee subpoenaed him. He told them it was against his religion to name names, was blacklisted and essentially was barred by networks and movie studios from doing television and films. There was no blacklist in the theater and between an occasional nightclub job and as a

Me, Morgen Stern and Diane Cilento in *The Good Soup*.

respected artist, selling his paintings, he and his family scraped by. He was a fascinating man and actor. One lunch hour we went next door to Grants, a thriving hot dog joint. He buys me a frank (15 cents) and a cherry smash (five cents). In our conversation there was no litany of his misfortune, he seemed to be always in a state of discovery. I asked him what he thought of the play. He shrugged and mugged, "My damn wife made me take this play. I hate the part."

Here I am in my early twenties watching the zest and energy of Sam Levene, age 55, Ruth Gordon, age 64, and Ernest Truex, age 71, who seems to bounce when he walks. (At our first preview I marveled as I watched him putting on old-age makeup.) Ms. Gordon conserves her energy by not rehearsing at a performance level, but when she does let go she belies her years and is a whirlwind. Role models? You bet. She gave this advice to the young Dorothy Whitney, who was playing a couple of small parts: "Don't try to get laughs out of your lines. You're playing a small part and nobody will remember what they laughed at. You're in your twenties, be vital and look as good as you can."

Kanin softly draws out actors, says he knows more about the play now by watching us, learning from us. One day as he and I were standing there taking a wiz in the urinal, he says what every actor dreads to hear, "You know the best time you did this part, Lou? When you read for it." Ouch.

Zero, who would be 45 in February, got hit by a bus on January 13 on his way home from rehearsal. He would be fine in a few months, but he was out of the play. The comedic actor Jules Munshin replaced him. Too bad. Zero's an artist, Jules a charmless comic.

We opened in Philadelphia at the Forrest Theatre. Ten minutes into the first act on opening night, Pat Harrington Sr., a former vaudevillian playing a wordless waiter, hears the reaction of the crowd on our dressing room loudspeaker and crows, "We're kicking the shit out of 'em, we've got a hit!" The show gets raves from the *Philadelphia Inquirer*, calling it a "wise and witty comedy … brilliantly staged, with a dream cast." But Kanin is quick to warn us about the hokeyness and broadness that have crept into a few performances. "You're going for the laugh, not the moment."

Some actors handle out-of-town pressure better than others. The less experienced seemingly suffer more from hold me, hug me, love me. When the huff and puff is over, seldom are there soft murmurs of affection or two a.m. life stories. It goes more like roll apart, stare, silence, then:

Actor: "The audience just doesn't get what I'm doing in the second act. Is the playwright *aware* of that? Where should I throw this?"

Actress: "I think my monologue was off tonight. Do you have any ideas, has anybody said anything? The wastebasket. Tie a knot in it first."

Most of the flings die on the train back to the Cement City where actors, fearing the New York critics, now seek solace from family, friends, lovers and Manhattan habits. As Suzanne Pleshette once said, "Location doesn't count."

In Washington, D.C., we opened during a snowstorm at the National Theatre. In understudy lore, "Go out there and come back a star!" Carrie Nye has to go on for a flu-felled Cilento. Nye had never run the play, yet she performed admirably.

"Nye does a dandy job," as critic Tom Donnelly wrote. Cilento returned and stardom eluded Nye. She married Dick Cavett and had a respectable career.

The reviews: one positive, two negative. We traveled to New York without eager expectation, just hope.

On February 29 we settled into the Plymouth Theatre in New York. Levene said, "I was here 20 years ago and had Ruth's dressing room on the first floor, now I'm a floor higher. Another 20 years and I'll be on the roof."

Levene was a member of the Group Theatre during the Depression and I appreciated his advising me to put $50 a week into something I never heard of, mutual funds.

"But, Sam, I only make a hundred twenty-five a week and clear maybe 90."

"So make it 20."

I wish I had listened to him. Another lesson in Levene economics: "You know what I'd do if I were your age? Buy a little hot dog stand or fruit stand on the side, just to pay the rent."

Walking to the Plymouth opening night I see Kanin getting out of his limousine a half block from the theater. It's chilly, but he sees me and waits for me. I relate to him what Truex had said about being at the Plymouth, "Here I am on 45th Street in my forty-fifth Broadway opening night."

We walk the half-block to the theater arm in arm. He says, "Why should we worry, we know how the show goes, we've done it 40 times. The audience doesn't. They're worried that they might be bored, that they won't like it. Let them worry."

The reviews came as a shock.

Times: "A commonplace, repetitious story ... dull."
Herald-Tribune: "Both the fun and the substance run thin."
News: "Frequently funny, but now and again my attention wandered."
University of Oklahoma sophomore: "I don't get it. Can't those Broadway guys just read a play and know if it's any good, if it's gonna be a hit or not? What's the deal? Huh?"

We close in three weeks. After our final curtain, Ms. Gordon, still in makeup and costume, sits in a chair center stage. The actors were told she wanted to say goodbye to each of us individually. I wait in line until it is my turn. With a warm grip and a crooked smile she says, "Tonight was your best performance. Thank you for all of them." She probably said the same line to each actor, but if so I did not care, I wanted to thank her and her husband for my first game in the Big Leagues.

In various venues I'd done about 30 to 40 plays, but none could compare with being on stage with this production's rehearsals, problems and the solving of them, decades of treasures offered by the older actors, out-of-town tryouts. From the creative lift from those actors and Kanin I'd never felt so deeply and confidently that I was an actor.

11

From Burt Lancaster
to Summer Stock

Strasberg was always sneaking producers and directors or stars into the Actors Studio, which pissed the actors off. We wanted no part of showcasing. But Strasberg was somewhat star-struck and wanted to be admired by the big guys. That's how director John Franken-heimer saw me doing the poet Scipio in a scene from Camus' *Caligula*. Burt Lancaster was to star in *The Young Savages*, which his company was producing and Frankenheimer was directing. Sydney Pollack, his assistant, may have put his job in jeopardy when he swayed them to audition me for one of the gang leaders. For Pollack this movie was an important step toward immersing himself in film. He wanted to be a motion picture director. I snagged the part and Pollack became a masterful director.

Hollywood. Hollow-wood, Hollyweird. The Land of Fruits and Nuts. Such were the sneers given the film capital of the world by some of New York's Fundamentalist Thespians. My fundamentals had an escape clause. So far that year I had short runs of one Broadway play, one Off Broadway play, parts on three half-hour TV dramas and earned $2370, gross. Unlike Romney, Trump and the Big Guys today, hefty taxes were deducted from my meager bounty. Knowing how Poppa had barely squeaked through the Depression, I had pledged never to carry the "starving artist" label. I was winging westward ho toward 500 dollars a week for four weeks!

As the plane climbed quickly and steeply into the sky, the force pushed me to the back of my seat. I turned to my Actors Studio mate, Vivian Nathan, also in the movie. "What the hell was that!?" I'd never been on a jet before.

She patted my arm, "Don't worry, Lou, you'll get used to it."

Whoosh! My Chapman classmate Ruhl Samples was speeding us along the middle of what a sign called the 101 Freeway in Los Angeles. Again I was pressed back into my seat. Out of an instinct to live, I shouted, "Ruhl, slow down, man!" He laughed. "I'm only doing 65. We're okay."

"You're crazy. In the middle of all this traffic? Really, Ruhl, you gotta be going too fast!"

"Not in Hollywood."

I was having ice cream in some hip Hollywood Blvd. ice cream parlor with a New York actor friend in Hollywood shooting a movie. He was in good spirits, a job can do that, but then he spoke quietly and with emphasis. "Listen, don't mention to anyone out here that I'm gay."

Spoon mid-air: "I don't get it, why not?"

"It could cost me work. If it was between me and a straight guy, they'd hire the straight guy."

If America knew a leading man was a homosexual, he could never be a star. The cover? An arranged marriage and *photoplay* magazine "dates." That was Hollywood in 1960. In 1960, homosexuality was illegal in Great Britain. A man could actually go to jail for such a "crime."

In 2002, I was directing a television episode and a young woman was on set observing me. "Shadowing" me was the term. She was hoping to direct one of the episodes. Not unusual. At the end of the first day's shooting, she came to me and put her arm around my waist. "Lou, I wonder if you'd do me a favor."

"What is it?"

She walked me to a quiet area. "Would you mind being my boyfriend when I come on set?"

"I don't get it."

"I'm gay. If the producers find out, I'm afraid they won't hire me. Happened to a friend of mine. Please. Think about it."

For the rest of the episode, I had a girlfriend. That was America, 2002! In 2016 she's having a solid career as a television director. What with a few well-known actors, NFL guys and Congressmen "outing" themselves, maybe those days are over. But as Yogi Berra said, "It's over when it's over."

My first day on *The Young Savages*, I reported to the Columbia Studios makeup department, curious to learn how their magic would make me pretty. They spent two hours jamming a rubber tube up my left nostril, slathering putty on my nose and gluing fish tissue across my left eye to simulate a scar. Plus a baby Quasimodo hump on my back. Every morning for two weeks they did that, and in those first ten days I worked one day.

It wasn't wasted time: Being on set is 101 in moviemaking. The crew and extras showed professional competence, but little enthusiasm.

The Fourth of July was approaching and Frankenheimer asked me what I had planned for the four-day holiday. "Dunno. Maybe fly back to New York and see my girlfriend."

"Why don't you stay? Come over to the house for barbecue and roasted corn on the cob."

"I dunno…"

"See the extras over there, the girls?"

"Yeah."

"Pick one. Or two. They're yours, that's what they're here for."

More hillbilly than Hollywood, I flew back to my girlfriend.

My important scene was to be shot on the

I feel pretty, oh, so pretty.

last two days of my four-week guarantee. It was around a pool table with Burt Lancaster. Right before the scene, Frankenheimer called me into his trailer and nervously acted my entire part, line readings, indicated emotion, facial expressions. I felt like I'd just been given a halftime "Win it for the Gipper" pep talk. Good thing Frankenheimer's a director; as an actor, he was scarily hammy. Lancaster and I were introduced, and we rehearsed our moves. Immediately Lancaster started directing me: "Kid, hold the cue this way when you point it at me." Was I supposed to take his direction? I turned to Frankenheimer. He immediately turned to the script supervisor and wouldn't look at me. Lancaster was never imperious—quite gentle, in fact. I studied his performance. It was odd; even though appearing natural, he seemed to be over-acting. And definitely overseeing the scene. I finished my two days around the pool table, and ended up appreciating not so much the acting of Lancaster as the style of Lancaster. Pollack arranged for me to see my dailies. I'd never seen myself in dailies. I sat there alone, moments were happening that I hadn't worked on, hadn't expected. Good stuff. All in all there was a sense of colorful reality that I thought was right for the scars, hump on my back, bump on my nose. I was excited. I liked me.

Right after I finished *The Young Savages*, I read for Frank Pierson (who later wrote *Cool Hand Luke* and *Dog Day Afternoon*). He was producing a half-hour Western series called *Have Gun, Will Travel* starring Richard Boone, an Actors Studio member I learned later. When we shook hands, he had a portable radio next to his ear listening to a John Kennedy campaign speech. The role was interesting, a villain. Cowboy boots, cowboy hat, six-shooter. Sheeit, I was loving it. And another 500 acting acorns for New York. My first scene was a dolly shot along the Western street. I had about two pages of dialogue. The assistant director called, "Andy, we're ready!" This Andy was sitting about 50 yards away from us in a chair marked DIRECTOR. With his back to us! He waved "okay" and went back to reading a script. Don't know if it was ours or not. No rehearsal, we did the scene and, damn, I dropped two important lines. The assistant director yelled, "Cut. Okay, we're over here." Andy kept reading. The crew moved quickly and I moved quickly to the a.d. "Uh, I'm sorry, but I dropped some of my lines."

"It's okay, don't worry about it."

"But they're plot lines. They tell what the whole story is about. Shouldn't we do it again?"

"Kid, it's okay, don't worry about it."

Well, we did it again, but because of forgotten plot lines? No. The camera operator had caught a crew member's reflection in a window. The only time Andy, to whom I was never introduced, got out of his chair was when I did my own stunt, which was getting shot, hurling myself backwards and falling forward on my face dead.

The a.d. asked me, "You want a wire?"

"A wire? No, I'm fine." I didn't know what a "wire" was. (I learned later that it would have been hooked to a harness and I'd have been yanked backwards.)

Dick Boone shot me with a sawed-off shotgun, I threw myself back five feet, hit the wall and fell face down dead onto the hard wood porch. The director, full name Andrew McLaglen, came up to me and congratulated me: "Great stunt, good going. Okay, we're at the saloon!" It's the only words he ever spoke to me. What kind of place was this Hollywood? Stars directing you, "Kid, it's okay, don't worry about it," the director not bothering to watch the scenes? I hurried back to New York and the sanctity of summer stock and $67 a week.

At Lonny Chapman's summer theater, I did two premieres. One of the plays was written by Chapman and the other by Studs Terkel, a Chicago radio personality and author. One night we were all having a beer and one of the actors said he liked cool jazz. Terkel shot back, "Cool. I don't like cool. It means detached, uninvolved. I want to be involved!" He stayed involved until his death at age 96. Quite a man.

Not Gleason, me, wearing a mattress stomach in *Amazing Grace*.

His play was called *Amazing Grace* and the leading part of Jack was written for Zero Mostel, who was unavailable. Chapman started rehearsing the play, doing the lead and directing it. After rehearsing for two days, he told me it was too much, he couldn't direct and act in it. He asked me if I'd step into the part. I was probably a hundred pounds too thin and 20 years too young so I said yes. We cut a hole in one of those thin mattresses, I put my head through it and voilà, I was Jack.

Curt Conway was also in the play and it was great to be on stage with one of my acting teachers and directed by another one. I'd like to hear what Al Pacino has to say about acting with Lee Strasberg in *The Godfather*.

During *Amazing Grace* I got two letters from Los Angeles on the same day. One was a two-pager from John Frankenheimer and the other was from Burt Lancaster's producing partner, Harold Hecht. Frankenheimer's opened with, "First let me say you are a very talented actor…" Then the rest of the letter informed me that my part was being re-filmed with another actor. Hecht's letter was also a thoughtful one: "[Y]our tie did not match in the scene. The first day of shooting you wore one tie, and on the second day a different tie. The makeup looked phony…. [D]ue to the schedule and time etc. …"

Though thoughtful, the tie tale was hollow. He had a first class crew and wardrobe matching is Film 101. Plus he did not know I had seen my two days of dailies. In essence I was fired. An actor has to be sensitive and vulnerable as an artist, and yet thick-skinned and tough enough to survive as one. An ever-present possibility of rejection follows actors like Joe Btfsplk's dark cloud in the *Li'l Abner* cartoon strips.

The audition—will I get the part or not?

You get the part: Will I make it through the Equity five-day clause?

You make it to day six: Will they fire me before we open?

You open out of town: Will the critics like me?

Show's in trouble: Will they think it's my fault?

Broadway opening: Will the critics like me?

The play closes, and it starts all over again. Hi diddly dee…

After that summer I did a scene at the Studio and as Shelley Winters was critiquing my work, she skidded into a 180 on how Burt Lancaster had thought I was "too interesting" and replaced me with a conventional looking actor, no putty, no hump. Accurate or not, it wasn't the first time that a star pulled rank in the interests of self-protection. Right, Ms. Gabor? (Nor the last, as you'll see.)

I would have to dig my trench a little deeper, but brother Jim put the right perspective on the Hollywood episode. "Why would anyone want to make his movie debut with a hose up his nose, scars on his face, and a humpback?"

12

38 At-Bats, Three Strikeouts

Just when you think you've made the Big Show...

The year 1960 was a busy one for me: a Broadway play, my first trip to Los Angeles for a movie and television show, six TV shots in New York City, a day's work on Kazan's *Splendor in the Grass*, four plays in summer stock. Feeling like a real actor, I auditioned in Otto Preminger's office for *Critic's Choice*, a play he was producing and directing, starring Henry Fonda and written by novelist-playwright Ira Levin. I was hired. The play was set for a December opening in New York at the Ethel Barrymore Theatre. In early negotiations they wanted me to sign a run-of-the-play contract, but before rehearsals began, management dropped that contract request. As I wrote Jim, "I'm glad they changed that run-of-the-play thing, don't think I'd want to be bogged down in this play for a whole year. So it's okay with me." I saw the upside of life in those days.

Our loft was scheduled to be torn down by the International Ladies Garment Workers Union to make way for a huge complex of apartment houses. I like quiet, I like solitude and a tree here or there ain't a burden. Not a lot to ask for, unless you're living in New York City. In an expiring 1950-something Chevy I was driving up to New City to see a friend when I impulsively decided to turn off the Palisades Parkway at the Route 9W exit. A realtor's office was not ten yards off the exit.

"Sort of looking for a place to rent," said I.

"One is opening up, but it's probably too small for you."

"How small?"

"Two small bedrooms upstairs and a kitchen, shower and living room downstairs."

"Uh-huh. What else about it?"

"Probably too isolated for you. Nearest neighbor is a quarter mile away."

"Uh-huh."

Taking in my faded Levis and tee shirt: "And the rent, the rent might be too high for you."

"How much exactly is it?"

"Well, it's a hundred dollars a month."

"Let's take a look."

The tenant was there and we were introduced. He had a European accent and asked what I did. "I'm an actor."

"Are you in a play now?"

"Actually, I'll start rehearsing a new play in the fall. Henry Fonda has the lead."

He smiled. "Ah, tell Hank hello."

"You know Mr. Fonda?"

A painting of my castle above the Hudson. Mom was the artist.

"Yah. We were both with the Princeton Players. I was the set designer. Tell Hank that Yuri says hello."

"Hank?"

It was in a wooded area on a hill overlooking the Hudson River. My nearest neighbor, the never noisy Jewish Convalescent Home, was a quarter of a mile away. I lived there for the next seven years.

Though it was only a 40-minute commute into the Actors Studio, my agent Peter Witt screamed in his Teutonic accent that I was being idiotic. What if I had an emergency reading and had to be there right away? Well, they'd just have to wait, I told him. Swearing loudly in German, he hung up the phone.

In the summer I'd walk up the driveway to my mailbox on 9W. Coming back through the blooming dogwood, I'd pick wild raspberries for breakfast. I leveled part of the steep hill below the house and stabled a bony horse on loan from Burgess Meredith. I rode through tall trees and foliage on the abandoned Erie Lackawanna railroad tracks adjoining my property, the Hudson River below, not a slab of cement in sight. Those were good years, creatively and personally.

Meredith lived nearby, and one night he, Franchot Tone and I had a long night of drinking and theater-acting-movie "discussions." I wasn't interested in winning the arguments, only in learning from theirs. Those two had done everything and to hear them hold forth on their experiences was mind-blowing. They described the theater and movies of the '30s and '40s, the Group Theatre, plays, audiences, directors, salaries, actors, producers. A first-hand cram course in decades of theater and motion picture lore that you could never get from classrooms or books. We even argued about how to take curtain calls. Finally we called a recess at about three a.m. and agreed to resume six hours later when the sun was up and we were sober.

Oh, here's just one piece of advice from Tone that had nothing to do with the arts, but, well, maybe being in the arts, "At your age, Lou, get all you can. But be choosy, be careful."

I returned the next morning. Tone was sleeping in and Meredith was scuffling around the kitchen in a bathrobe pouring what looked like dark brown twine into a bowl. "What's that?"

He put some in a smaller bowl, opened a large cage sitting on the kitchen counter and shoved it under his monkey's face. I didn't remember a monkey!

"It's something I just heard about, organic wheat pasta. Supposed to be good for you. So I guess it's good for a monkey."

I would never equal their achievements, but could I even hope for into-the-night arguments with the young talents of the day?

Back to *Critic's Choice*. A quick plot summary: A drama critic (Henry Fonda) is married and has a son. His wife (Gena Rowlands) writes a play. Dion, a young Greek director (me), is hired, the wife and the director have an affair and the critic-husband's dilemma is that he has to review her play.

Bogus concept: Another critic from his paper could have reviewed it. But this is a comedy and certainly comedy needs conflict. Which there was on…

October 15, 1960, *Critic's Choice* log, edited

Steinway hall, third floor, first day of rehearsal of *Critic's Choice*, director Otto Preminger, playwright Ira Levin, cast: Henry Fonda, Mildred Natwick, Virginia Gilmore, Gena Rowlands, Seth Edwards, me. No speech by Otto, no "What we want to do with this play is…" Play doesn't seem as funny hearing it as it was reading it. Otto says I'm too charming, be grosser, pretentious, not a nice guy, tactless, obnoxious. (Preminger on Preminger?) Think of those World War II movies with Nazi officers and you'll remember Preminger. His shaved head and German accent scuttled the image of a light comedy director, whereas Ira Levin, in dress and manner, was the very image of a successful writer of plays and novels—cigarette, reserved, sleeveless argyle sweaters and a distracted air. A pretty pro group it appears, but we'll see, won't we?

Preminger and I did not much like one another. The second day of rehearsal, his first note to me was, "Don't try to be so charming, Lou. Wait until you do Mr. Fonda's part in summer stock, then you can be charming." All I was looking for in that rehearsal was the creative and physical energy of the character. Charm? How do you even work on that?

Fonda was a technical master. The second day, he came in with the blueprints of the set, which had not as yet been built. He informed Levin that he might need two lines added in one particular speech because a stage cross would probably take longer than Levin imagined. And the scene hadn't even been blocked yet. His mechanics were so exact that when we played in front of an audience, Fonda would silently belch in every performance on the exact same lines of my dialogue.

Actor's Technique Department: Every year H. Adrian Rehner brought his Chicago senior acting class to see Broadway plays and after curtain always arranged a Q&A with one of the actors and his students. Fonda graciously met with the students on the stage of the Booth Theater after his matinee of *Two for the Seesaw*.

Critic's Choice. On left, clockwise from bottom: Seth Edwards (back turned), me, Virginia Gilmore, Henry Fonda, Gena Rowlands, Mildred Natwick. Otto Preminger (far right) is already glaring. Others are unidentified.

Budding ingénue: "Mr. Fonda, when there's a part where you have to cry, what do you do?"

Fonda: "I don't take the part." Technique.

On the bare Barrymore stage, scripts in hands, we started getting the play on its feet. Preminger regarded rehearsals as performances, thus to be immediately criticized, cut and mended by him. He had no regard for an actor's way of working. As a preparation for my first entrance, I did a quick dance and a twirl (spiking the enthusiasm of the character) and then entered the taped area of the room for my scene. Preminger explained as if to a four-year-old that my "pranks" were very amusing but did I know there would be scenery in front of me and the audience wouldn't see me? One morning he said, "I hope you get as many laughs as I got describing you at a dinner party last night."

Gena Rowlands, playing Fonda's wife, was treated badly by Preminger. She and I labeled our Bald-Headed Bad Guy "Butt Head." One rehearsal he interrupted Gena in mid-scene, yelling at her, "I don't believe you! I've told you for two weeks how I want it and you won't do it and the way you are doing it now is *wrong*! I don't believe you, nobody talks that way, you talk unlike anyone else in the play, your talk is planned, people don't talk that way." Then he acted it for her. Rowlands never blinked, listened quietly until he ran down. Leaving the scene, she muttered to me, "I'm going to take up pottery-making, professionally."

Preminger not only acted Rowlands' part, he did all our parts, even Mildred Natwick's, the ultimate actress. Only Fonda was spared. We were never given the opportunity to create, only copy. Here's a sample:

Preminger (to me): "What was that, you changed it again!"

Me: "I chose something different to work on and, yeah, sometimes that'll change it."

Preminger: "Change it?! I don't care if we run five times or 50 times, you will do it the same way!"

Natwick got off an accurate observation: "He *might* be an excellent director, but he lacks one little quality, making you believe that *someday* you'll be able to do the part."

A week later, he fired Gena Rowlands. She seemed relieved. She had lost seven pounds and had a young son who was certainly more important than putting up with Butt Head. Her understudy, Georgann Johnson, started rehearsing after lunch though no official word of Rowlands' departure was given to the actors. Subsequently Rowlands has been nominated for two Academy Awards and has won three Emmys, talking like people talk.

During our tryout in Wilmington, Delaware, Preminger yelled at me and I yelled back at him. He yelled back at me, "I am the only one permitted to yell here!"

"Not when it's me you're yelling at!"

He smiled, lowering his voice to conversational. "You know, we're not holding you here, you are free to leave. We don't want to hold you if you don't like the part." A cheap shot, literally. If I quit, they don't have to pay me two weeks salary.

Part of the Wilmington review: "[Lou Antonio] is quite funny until his role turns into a caricature."

On to Philadelphia.

Panic was making Herr Otto flounder more. During an evening's performance in Philadelphia, between the second and third acts, he gave new blocking and dialogue changes for the upcoming act three! No way could he and Levin tell if the new stuff worked because all they saw were actors trying to remember, "What do I say here?," "Where do I go now?" Even Fonda.

The next day, our playwright got his head handed to him. Preminger declared that the affair between Dion (me) and Angie (wife) would be cut out of the play: "It makes her unsympathetic." For the first time we hear Levin raise his voice, and he is furious. "You can't do that! It's the spine of the play! And the Dramatists Guild has a rule, there can be no changes without the playwright's permission!"

"Fine, Ira, fine. Then I just close the play here in Philadelphia."

So much for the Dramatists Guild and Ira's fury. No affair.

We left the City of Brotherly Love and headed to our last tryout city, Boston.

The night before opening, I threw up bad Boston food all night and my voice sounded as if it were shredded rags. Opening night the audience seemed to like the play. Preminger came into my dressing room. I won't write in his Teutonic accent; it'd be too reminiscent of his Nazi in *Stalag 17*, and of him.

"I've decided to replace you with another actor in the part."

I stopped, white sock in hand.

"Was a difficult decision but I had to make it. You get all the laughs, your timing is good, character good, energy good, but you can't play comedy! Even if you get good reviews tomorrow. You're a very talented actor, you are, but you can't give it what it needs. All the readings are right, but—"

"Who's the actor?"

The red starts rising from the back of his neck and climbs up to his forehead. "What difference does that make? It's none of your business!"

"'None of my business?' You are doing me out of a season's work, I want to know who's doing it."

"Murray Hamilton."

"How long do you want me to stay around?"

"I don't know, but you won't open in New York. I wanted to tell you myself. You will be given your notice tomorrow."

"Then you don't want me at rehearsal tomorrow?"

"No."

Boston reviews:

Play: "...very pleasant sophisticated comedy of Manhattan mores."

Play: "...little substance but much fun ... slight and more than slightly fraudulent."

Preminger: "[He] served this soufflé on the Shubert stage last night, it proved flat as a French pancake."

Preminger: "[He] directed with results that seem to vary."

Me: "...menacing and quite far-out as the youthful director."

Me: "[He] shines in the part of the young director, the youngest dirty old man I know."

Several of the cast offered their opinion and Dolores Dorn-Heft offered a Valium. They believed that Fonda was wearing the Black Hat, that the affair was cut because it emasculated his character, that I was fired because of my testosterone. My last performance was without any regard to previous Preminger direction. It was free and fun. I had no doubts or insecurities about my talent or my portrayal, but I would miss Dion. Fonda had Fonda to protect. Understandably so. He would last years longer than the play and indeed gave us the pleasure of his performances the rest of his days.

After my matinee, I ran into Murray Hamilton on his way to the theater. An excellent actor, maybe ten years older than I was. He and Preminger had worked together before in several movies; *Anatomy of a Murder* was a good one. Considering the circumstance, it was not a painful meet. He was gracious and I wished him luck. Later I heard that Preminger had Hamilton's hair cut short, put him in a baggy sweater and had him play it a bit gay. Fonda was safe and Hamilton got a season's work.

It's a given: The day an actor lands a job, the actor is fully aware that it will come to an end. That unemployment bone is always being chewed on, or choked on. I had arrived from Oklahoma City in August 1955. In five years I'd done five plays, three movies, 13 television shows, 25 plays in summer stock, and been dumped from two plays and one movie. Sounds plentiful, but every year I had to sling burgers or serve drinks to make a living.

The odds of living above poverty level for an actor are chancier than hitting double zero on a roulette wheel. In 1983, Colleen Dewhurst and I were keynote speakers at a Southwest Theatre Conference in Oklahoma City. She had just left *You Can't Take It with You* on Broadway to take another job. In blue jeans and chambray shirt, she cautioned the actors in the audience, "Most of your days will be spent unemployed and if you can't live with that, then get out of it. Not too long ago I left a part on Broadway in which I was on the stage six minutes. *Six minutes.* And I hope they'll have me back." She had been in the theater 40 years, played some of the great parts, O'Neill, Shakespeare, leading roles on Broadway, received two Tonys and four Emmys. Her words were a hatpin poised over their balloons of imagined careers of success and respect.

I'd maybe been in New York a year when an admired and talented actor at OU, Jim Maguire, called me at two in the morning and told me to get over to his apartment house quick because a woman next door had just died and the apartment would be up for rent. I rushed over. The woman's dead body was still in the apartment. I was fifth in line. A year or so later, Jim, dressed in a tuxedo with his address book next to him, killed himself with an overdose of barbiturates. I prayed there was no line outside his door. Joanna March, a deliciously whimsical actress whom I had met when I was a sous-chef in Colorado, killed herself a few months after Jim died. They were in their twenties. They had studied with respected teachers, Jim with Uta Hagen, Joanna with Mira Ristova. Both were interesting, talented, dedicated actors, but the jobs never came to them. I have known more than a few young actors with scars on their wrists who have survived and went on to occasional employment, which is about all any actor can realistically hope for. Though their crystal ball may become cloudy, the dream, flickering, still lives. For some it was too great a dream to live without. For Marilyn Monroe, the dreams may have been too great to live with.

Actors Equity
Association Statistics for 2013–2014 season
Membership (includes, chorus, and stage managers): 42,676.
Average number of working weeks a year: 16.
Members working per week: 5931.
Annual average earnings per working member: $7,463.
16 percent are stage managers.
Members earning 75,000 or more: 1260.

SAG/AFTRA (would not offer equivalent AEA statistics)
160,000 actors total membership
4,000 work in a year
Day performer makes: $859
Weekly performer makes: $2979

Department of Labor
Actors: 59,210 actors total surveyed.
Median pay was $19.82 an hour
They don't break it down annually because it is a freelance occupation.

Though a bumpy ride, in 1960 I grossed $6,000, more than I'd ever made. The Infernal Revenue Service decided to audit me. I went into the city with my receipts and met with the man in the suit behind the desk. Not as well-dressed as Otto Preminger, but similar in attitude.

"Mr. Antonio, with all these *alleged deductions*, how do you have enough money left to live on?"

"Well, sir, when I'm not working, I get $50 a week unemployment insurance."

"Oh, I see, I sit here eight hours a day, five days a week, *working*, and you get $50 a week for *not* working!"

I was ordered to pay the United States government $167 for not working.

13

From Streisand
to Paxinou to Olivier

In the summer of 1961 I sang "Pass That Peace Pipe" and was cast in an Off Broadway revue called *Another Evening with Harry Stoones*. Already cast was a stringy young woman named Barbra Streisand, who was getting some buzz after a late-night Mike Wallace television interview. We knew each other from Curt Conway's acting classes. She was mostly quiet, and mostly talented, but during her rise the media hardly ever mentioned she also had a tight, sexy body. She didn't seem to notice it either.

For a comedy revue it had some oddball casting, from the ferocious dramatic Diana Sands to Dom DeLuise, fresh and funny from the Off Broadway hit musical *Little Mary Sunshine*. Dom and I were downstage rehearsing a comedy sketch and we noticed the director Glenn Jordan looking upstage, not at us. Dom and I dwindled to a stop and looked over our shoulders. That little Streisand gal was doing some outlandish comical bit, and she wasn't even in the sketch! Remember Satchel Paige's advice, "Never look back 'cause someone might be gainin' on you"? That doesn't apply in show business, an actor should *always* look back. I'd seen Barbra in the role of the French maid in *The Boy Friend* at Fishkill, where she exasperated the director Curt Conway with her onstage misbehavior. She also drove the more experienced actors to distraction with her over-the-top "Watch me" tricks. And "watch" the audience did.

During a lunch break one afternoon, I was in my Fishkill dressing room going over my lines for the next week's play when I heard the sensitive sounds of Streisand singing a Harold Arlen song, "A Sleepin' Bee," from *House of Flowers*. Intrigued, I stood off-stage and watched and listened. She was downstage center facing the darkened empty theater singing *à cappella*, strongly involved in the story of the song. Good phrasing, good voice, honest, a little indulgent, but so what? Alone on stage, an empty theater, a work light shadowing the actor in half-light … always a turn-on for actors and their dreams.

We had been rehearsing *Stoones* for about two weeks when I got a call to replace an actor in a Broadway show, *The Garden of Sweets*, starring the Greek theater's national icon Katina Paxinou. It was in rehearsal and who wouldn't want to work with Paxinou? She had done everything from Socrates to getting an Oscar for the 1943 movie *For Whom the Bell Tolls*. Back in July of 1961, I had read for *The Garden of Sweets* twice and had one long discussion with the director Milton Katselas on philosophy so he could see if I could "think." I don't know if I flunked philosophy or acting.

'Twas all forgotten until that Broadway call. The *Sweets* company paid *Stoones* $500 for the immediate release of my contract and it was done. It would mean leaving the revue

***Another Evening with Harry Stoones*:** **Bottom, left to right: Kenny Adams, Sheila Copeland, Diana Sands, Dom Deluise. Standing, left to right: Virgil Curry, Susan Belink, Barbra Streisand, me.**

and all that singing and sketch-ing with terrific people. Everyone wished me luck. I said goodbye.

The Garden of Sweets was about a dysfunctional Greek family that owned a candy store. Stavros, my character, had left the family to be a writer, fails and returns to recriminations and reconciliations. The cast had been in rehearsal for almost three weeks. They made no effort to welcome or help me. My presence seemed an imposition. When costumer Patricia Zipprodt asked me how I saw my character dressed, I had to answer, "Hell, I don't know."

Katina's insisted that acting is "rhythma" (rhythm) and every actor must have it. "I don't learn lines," she says. "I know the rhythma, the rhythma tells me what to say." And, "When I see someone who says he is Method actor, I pack my suitcase and run. If I cannot concentrate enough to believe that my daughter in the play has died, I cannot think of a lost lover and carry that on the stage for my daughter. That's nonsense. Motivation, bah! Genius needs no method."

At one point in the second act, she shed copious tears in every performance at the same moment. Eager to learn her "belief" technique, I asked her how she did it. "Iss eassy. I tell you. I look up at de lights, and *I don't blink!*"

After four desperate days of rehearsal, we opened in Philadelphia at America's oldest legitimate theatre, the Walnut. We got through it without incident, or much audience response. As I removed my shoes and socks after the performance, I noticed my toes were bleeding.

The play was ill-fated, but at least I got to share a playbill with Greek theater icon Katina Paxinou.

On stage I hide my tension in my feet. An audience will notice clenched hands, but they can't see through shoes. An infection came from the black dye in the nylon socks. Oh, pain. To this day I only wear white cotton socks.

Flash forward: White socks. Elizabeth Taylor and I went to a toney party at Halston's one night in 1983 when I was directing her on Broadway in *Private Lives*. The famous couturier's penthouse had an impressive view of St. Patrick's Cathedral and Rockefeller Plaza, along with all the Beautiful People. I loved being introduced by Taylor as "my director." Her director had on his tuxedo and white socks. Drinking champagne and staring at famous faces, I heard Elizabeth's whisper,

"Lou, about those socks…"

"It's all I wear, Elizabeth. Sorry."

"Well, all right, I guess it's who you are."

The next day she gave me a present, a pair of white cotton socks with the tops dyed black. They went beautifully with the tuxedo.

In the *Sweets* previews, I knew my words and moments but not the character. A precurtain note from director Katselas: "Less balls."

Okay, sensitive writer, okay, I'll try wearing glasses to have "less balls." It definitely changed the performance. Ben Frye and Irving Squire, the producers, came storming back after the curtain rang down. "What are you doing?! That's why we fired the other actor, we don't want a homo up there!"

I dumped the specs.

I suppose there have been worse reviews for a play in Philadelphia, but it's difficult to imagine they could surpass the ones for *The Garden of Sweets*. Just a sampling from two Philadelphia papers.

> "[N]ot a long play, but it is a tortuous and cloudy one."—Henry Murdock, *The Philadelphia Inquirer*
>
> "[M]urky and tedious ... very much is made of very little."—Jerry Gaghan, *Philadelphia Daily News*

For some unfathomable reason it was decided that the play would open in New York at the ANTA Theatre. In New York, Katselas called rehearsals as if he had the magic bullet in his director's bag. He re-staged an exit of mine almost like a Martha Graham dance piece. It was out of character and made no sense, just fancy. Pressure was weighing on both of us, his Broadway directing debut, my first leading role on Broadway. After six or seven frustrating and fruitless attempts to fulfill his vision, I turned to him in exasperation.

"Milton, listen to me. I have more experience as an actor than you do as a director. I'm a better actor than you are a director. We are wasting a lot of time on a sour idea. I won't do it. And that's that." It was obvious that even a brilliant exit would not pull the play out of "murky and tedious."

Omen upon omen, opening night was October 31, Halloween, and to boot, Khrushchev had scheduled his atom bomb test for that date.

The autumn night air was clear and crisp as I walked to the theater. An hour early, I wanted to see my name for the first time on a Broadway marquee and inhale my success. Like Clinton I never inhaled. The marquee was blank, only a dull gray paint adorned it. Ah, but on the sidewalk a sandwich board was propped up with an 8x10 glossy of Paxinou on one side and a glossy of me on the other side. Class. Opening night, closing night? The same night. Half the seats were empty. Unfortunately, several were occupied by critics.

> "[The] only show I ever saw in which the principal actors had so little to do that they could afford to stop everything and listen to the mood music."—Walter Kerr, *Herald-Tribune*
>
> "There hasn't been a gloomier Greek family on the stage since *The House of Atreus...*"—Richard Watts, *New York Post*

Khrushchev's bomb worked, ours was a dud.

Yep, a one-nighter with Paxinou. And, oh, Streisand added a one-nighter to her résumé. *Another Evening with Harry Stoones* closed after a single performance.

Though *Sweets* went silently, the news that Sir Laurence Olivier would be in town taping Graham Greene's *The Power and the Glory* set the talent pool buzzing. Every actor in town was after a part. And the actors who signed on! George C. Scott, Julie Harris, Roddy McDowall, Patty Duke, Keenan Wynn and both the Mildreds, Dunnock and Natwick. I was given a ten-line part except, damn, I didn't have any scenes with Olivier. I whined and somehow my agent traded the tenner for an eight-line part. Yes, two lines less, but I'd have three scenes with Olivier! I excitedly told my friend Ina Balin about the job. "Oh, be sure and tell Larry hello," she said. Larry? Wow.

Oh, that all the spoiled and overpaid actors of today could have observed "Larry."

Playing a Mexican priest, he put in brown contact lenses every day of rehearsal. He was always prepared, polite, attentive, never calling attention to himself.

The show was taped in Brooklyn. On set getting my Mexican makeup put on, I overheard the crew talking about how yesterday's first day of taping ended at three in the morning. Olivier had slept in a dressing room and was up for today's seven a.m. call. In a scene that was essentially an Olivier monologue, I had been placed next to Roddy McDowall. After a rehearsal, the producer David Susskind whispered something to Marc Daniels, the director. Daniels looked over at me: "Paul, you be next to Roddy, and Lou take Paul's place to the right of Larry."

I guess I looked puzzled and Daniels, a sensitive, nice, man came over to me. "Lou, Susskind thinks you look too much like Roddy, wants to separate you."

I peeked at Roddy, at his Mexican makeup, at his large putty nose with a wart on the end, and a hair in the wart! Had Arnold Hoskwith been right about my nose?

In my scene (get that, *my* scene!), Olivier was having trouble finding the key to his monologue. I was standing right next to him, watching and listening to this extraordinary actor. He worked effortlessly and honestly, but the hook for the speech eluded him. After about six or seven takes he finally nailed it. He watched the replay on a monitor. You could see the pleasure on his face. He nodded to Daniels. We moved to another set and started rehearsing the next scene.

Voice over loudspeaker: "Uh, Larry, we're going to have to go back and do that last one again. Focus problem."

No tantrum, no accusations, no threats. His head drooped, his body sagged, we returned to redo the scene. He tried and tried it several more times, but failed to recreate what he had captured so beautifully before.

Olivier (quietly): "Marc, perhaps we should just move on." A performance at the mercy of the machines again.

At two a.m. he was on horseback and I was leading his horse by the halter. The 17 hours of work had exhausted him and one damn thing or another kept going wrong. He had to mount, dismount and remount the horse about six times. In the middle of another take, he stopped and held up his hand. He had never stopped a scene. It got very quiet; was he going to explode?

"Marc, if I could just have a few minutes."

A particle of the fake dirt had gotten under one of his contact lenses, which I was told can be excruciating. In pain he went to rinse his eye. We finished the scene at three a.m. He had another seven a.m. call, and slept once again on a cot in his dressing room. And again no tantrum, no accusations, no calling his agents.

In his autobiography *Laurence Olivier: Confessions of an Actor*, he wrote, "A couple of days after the last Saturday of *Becket* we started shooting *The Power and the Glory*. The going was fantastically tough."

I had thought that I had only one idol in my life, Ted Williams. Not Brando, not Strasberg, not Truman. The next day, Olivier and I were outside the sound stage in a hallway, just the two of us. He saw me and started walking toward me, as if to start a conversation. He got closer and closer and when he was about two feet away I broke into a sweat and blurted out, "Ina Balin said to say hello!" He stopped, startled, gave me a slight smile, a nod and left me standing alone in the quiet hallway. Damn me. Olivier had become an idol.

14

Two Misses and a Hit

The Big Rejection. No, not Death. Getting fired.

In only one of my Broadway plays did the original cast remain intact. Rejection can be an uppercut to an actor's confidence, and a low blow to his income.

The following is more the story of one veteran actor than it is of a younger one who envisions a career into Medicare. The Old Pro is Rex Williams, an experienced theater actor who was somewhere past 50 at the time he and I were in *The Good Soup* in 1960. Now it's March of 1962.

It started on a Monday at 9:45 a.m. Playwright Henry Denker awakened me with a phone call. He wanted me to read for his play *Venus at Large*. He explained that the show was doing its first preview that night in Philadelphia and Mr. Schenker, the producer, and Mr. Denker ("Good morning, Schenker and Denker") were going to fire an actor and wanted me in Philadelphia to read for the director after the performance. I hurried from the Philadelphia train station to the back row of the Walnut Theatre. On stage was a bearded Rex Williams playing Mandelbaum, a character sort of based on Paddy Chayevsky. I was reading for Williams' role and, well, at least I had the beard for it. That summer I had grown one for the title role in Michel de Ghelderode's *Barabbas* at Woodstock, New York. Brother Jim and Isaiah Sheffer were producing with an eye towards Off Broadway.

It was going to take more than an actor with a beard to save *Venus at Large*. The play was unclear, unorganized, unfunny, un-comedy. David Wayne didn't know his lines, Bill Prince had no energy. The only appealing character up there was Joyce Jameson's vivacious rendering of a sweet, vulnerable blond.

I went to Schenker's suite at the Warwick Hotel at midnight. I told Schenker and Denker that Williams will be fine, it's only the first preview. Denker said, no, the whole play depends on that character. Huh? Albeit he never stops talking (he is a playwright after all), Mandelbaum is only on stage 15 minutes. Rod Amateau, a successful sitcom director, arrived 12:30-ish. Neat, shaved head, short. Man talk, then I read for them and left. Five minutes later, they phoned me downstairs: "Come on up, you got it." It wasn't so much a thrill as it was nailing a part, and a *paying job*. I told them I'd go back to New York, get my stuff, come back, rehearse and go on in three days at the Saturday matinee. That night they got me a room in the Warwick, at their expense. On the way to the lobby, the elevator stopped, and in walks Rex Williams. His beard noticed my beard. He kept peeking at the script I was trying to hide under my arm. "Lou, are you going to be my understudy?"

"I, uh, am here to maybe, you know … uh, teach a…."

He realized that I was replacing him and said a line I'll never forget: "Why don't we go for some Jell-O and talk about it?"

The *Barabbas* beard at Woodstock got me to Greece.

Rex explained that the previous year *Venus* had opened as a tryout at the Westport summer theater with the original Mandelbaum being fired and replaced with Jack Bitner, a well-regarded actor. Bitner was then fired and replaced by Rex, the third actor in the role. I assured him I did not find his performance fire-able, they should just close the play. He smiled and we wished each other good luck.

I signed for a guaranteed two weeks salary at 350 a week. During the day I started memorizing the part, watching the show in the evening to learn my blocking. I asked the stage manager if his assistant could cue me and help me set my blocking after the performances.

"No, that hasn't been arranged," said he.

Rona Jaffe, whom I was dating, came up to help me with my lines. A boring job, but not a boring woman. She was a best-selling novelist and smart as a whip, and certainly smart enough to know that I would be basting a turkey.

On that dark stage I rehearsed all by myself. As an image of the character I indeed picked Paddy Chayevsky. Once when Curt Conway was busy on a job, Chayevsky took over his acting class. With a dour delivery he pummeled our youthful innocence with "Show business is a bag of crap and only through luck will one or two you possibly make a living in it." As our heads hung, Chayevsky continued tolling the death knell for our future.

That's the image I used for Mandelbaum. That Friday, before Williams' last performance, we had a light supper. "Thank goodness I've got a little antique store, so I won't starve," he said.

"Rex, I go on tomorrow afternoon with not one rehearsal. Their attitude seems to be 'It's your problem, fella, not ours.'"

"I think everyone but the producers see it as short-term employment," he said.

Saturday matinee and it's my turn in the barrel. Right before curtain with the actors sitting poker-faced on the set's sofa and chairs, I was introduced to them. "This is Lou Antonio, he'll be playing Mandelbaum." The cast didn't seem that interested in the news or me. No one said "hello" or extended a hand. For my maiden voyage that afternoon, I blew a few, and fluffed a few, but managed to get through it and grab a few laughs. Essentially it was a rehearsal in front of an audience, and my first with actors. More flop sweat than fun. Amateau offered not a word to me. That evening for performance 2, the laughs improved because I found a meager level of relaxation. Rex went back to New York.

My agent had called the day before and told me that because of the play, he had to turn down a lead for me on a *Naked City*. Ah, phooey, a one-hour *Naked City* would have been a lot better-written than this play. At the Sunday rehearsal, Amateau, brimming with insight, addressed the cast with Schenker and Denker nearby.

"Theatre is not a democracy, no more intellectual discussions, what I need is a comedy!" Oh, boy, write *that* down in the Theater Wisdom book. Here's another: "Threads is what it needs, until the whole stage should be like one big ... *cobweb*." I dubbed him Rod Amateur.

At rehearsal that afternoon, Amateur called me over. By now I knew that look. "Lou, let's go into a tight two." A *tight two*? Now there's a *theater* term. Add that to "Action," which he always said in rehearsals. He went on, "We'll have to let you go, Lou, but I wanted to tell you myself, not have the stage manager do it. I'm not that kind of guy." (Why do directors always feel manly when they "do it themselves"?)

"Nothing to do with your talent (of course) or with your acting (of course), I just think you are more a dramatic actor, a heavyweight. Yeah, Lou, you are a heavyweight." The curse of shaved-head directors and "But you can't play comedy!" danced in my hair-laden head.

Rex Williams called me, told me *he* got a call, he'd be going back into the play tomorrow and offered his sympathies. "Lou, over 30 years in the theater and on this one I'm feeling like a yo-yo!" We both laughed at the silliness of it.

My $700 check did not bounce and that's about all I got out of the wasted week.

Wait, one last fillip. Rex played a few previews in New York and then he was fired *again* and replaced by the aforementioned Jack Bitner, the second actor who had been fired from the role. Four actors, two of them fired and rehired had played the part. The play ran four performances

At the conclusion of each season, a season being from September through June of the following year, *The New York Times* would list a box score of the Broadway plays and how long each ran. For the 1961–'62 season I was associated with four plays, which had a total run of 11 performances. I didn't even get my 20 weeks to qualify for unemployment insurance. Brother Jim said I was the most hired and least employed actor in New York.

After seven consecutive seasons of stock, I filled the summer of '62 by going into the Off Broadway *Brecht on Brecht* at the Lucille Lortel Theatre. It was a grab bag of Bertolt Brecht works picked over and assembled by George Tabori and directed by Gene Frankel. A hit, it attracted respected theater names into its cast; the likes of George Voskovec, Dane Clark, Eli Wallach, Annie Jackson, Viveca Lindfors, Michael Wager, Kevin McCarthy and Barbara Baxley would come and go. One night who showed up on stage with us but Kurt Weill's widow Lotte Lenya. I was on stage with history! No frills or artifice, her seriousness spiked with sly humor and charm. Ms. Lenya was enthralling in the subtexts she brought to her scenes and songs. You felt she had lived it and was confiding with the people out front. A better classroom would be hard to find. Today stars going in and out of plays is a heavy-hitting stratagem for theater economics. All to the good if it keeps the theatre pulse pumping.

For seven days I was doing double duty with an episode of *The Defenders* during the day and *Brecht* in the evening. Though tired from the 12 hours of my day job, it was hardly something for an actor to bitch about. Chris Sarandon, a terrific actor, told me that once he was doing two Movies of the Week at the same time, one in Vancouver, on the west end of Canada, and the other in Toronto, on the east end. Each of the two companies wanted him enough to arrange their schedules to accommodate him. Chris would finish his day in Vancouver on say, Monday, fly to Toronto that night, shoot in Toronto until called back to Vancouver to shoot on Thursday. On one such trans–Canada flight he was near exhaustion, bemoaning his eviscerating work schedule, unsure as to what city he was waking up in, what part he was acting that day. Then he took a breath, took a moment and asked himself, "What the hell am I griping about? I've got two jobs! When will this ever happen again?"

In my dressing room, as I slipped out of my street clothes and into my Brecht wardrobe, the evening's aura would envelope me and my energy would surge. All trivial thoughts and concerns were excluded. Through a scene, a song or a monologue, I responded to Brecht, myself and the audience. I've seen actors with migraine headaches, a painful swollen ankle or reeling from the flu, and as they set foot upon the stage the symptoms vanish and they deliver strong, affecting performances. The work takes hold and takes over. An extraordinary act of mercy from the Gods of Us. What was it John Lennon said?: "It's all in the mind, y'know." But Mary Baker Eddy said it first.

15

Elia Kazan

Kazan was doing his project of Aeschylus' *The Oresteia* at the Actors Studio and I was Apollo. I still had my *Barabbas* beard because of the possible Off Broadway production. Kazan had us do our mythology homework from Robert Graves' *The White Goddess* and Frazer's *The Golden Bough*. Our initial tasks were sensory and animal exercises, particularly for the Furies. His ideas and demands were viscerally stimulating. He knew how to give us freedom, take from it and then discipline it. Never once raising his voice. Nothing got by him. In one rehearsal, all I had to do was pose as Apollo and observe the interplay between two actors. I was listening, but not paying attention. Kazan walked by me and casually admonished me with, "Come on, Lou, you're being lazy. Get to him." All of us were in the hands of a mild but firm master.

One day after rehearsal, I had to tell him that it looked as if *Barabbas* was a go, and that I'd have to leave the Greeks to be a Jew nailed to a cross. He whispered to his assistant Barbara Loden, she nodded, then he said, "I'm doing a picture in Greece, Lou." To Barbara: "He'd be good for Abdul, wouldn't he?" She nodded again. "I'll get you a script," he said. I didn't hoot and holler. Kazan had a reputation for telling lots of actors that they would be in his next project, only they weren't.

The script, *The Anatolian Smile*, was a knockout. The part, Abdul, was a *Turk*! It was about Kazan's family sending their son to America in 1900, away from the genocide of the Greeks and Armenians by the Turks. The screenplay takes us through the obstacles and travails the young Greek endures to fulfill the family's dreams and his. During the filming it was retitled *America, America*.

The *Barabbas* investor disappeared. I called Kazan from the pay phone at the Studio and told him I liked the script. His reaction to my reaction was, "You know, Lou, we don't have any money to do this. The part doesn't pay much."

I'd heard that about Kazan. Well-known actors would work for way less than their usual salary because they knew they'd be better than they'd ever been. Besides, what salary did I have to compare it with? I would get to go to Poppa's homeland for three months, even if it was to play a Turk. You have to know that the animosity between the Greeks and Turks is ingrained in me; the Turks killed my father's father in the genocide of the late 1890s. I had my work cut out for me, lose that DNA, do not judge my Muslim Abdul, but understand him, his function in the story.

Kazan had me come to his office several times to improvise with the young man playing the lead, Stathis Giallelis, who had never acted professionally. An intense and handsome young man with a pronounced Greek accent, he had precisely what the script described: "Eyes like dark olives." The office was Kazan, simple and comfortable, books and scripts piled here and there, awards or celebrity-laden pictures absent. Improvisations were set up to establish a relationship between our characters, but I think more importantly between Giallelis and me.

No studio thought the movie would make a nickel so Kazan had to scrape and hustle to get a million dollars to make it. (That year on *Cleopatra*, Elizabeth Taylor was the first actor to be paid one million dollars for a picture, and probably a per diem that could pay for our entire crew.) My per diem was $15, and out of that princely sum I had to pay for food and my Athens hotel room.

Before I arrived in Greece, Kazan ran into trouble filming in Turkey. The company's hotel rooms were bugged; the cab drivers and several crew members were government spies. Charlie Maguire, the producer, told me that to have a meeting, he and Kazan had to walk in the middle of the streets away from hidden recording devices. Another example, in that era of the story, dock workers ("mules") were paid pennies a day, but when the Turkish film liaison saw them dressed as they would've been, shabbily and dirty, he ordered Kazan to put clean clothes and new shoes on them or he wouldn't be allowed to film the scene. So steady were the harassments that Kazan decided to pull out of Turkey and go to Greece. That put even more money pressures on an already skeletal budget. When Kazan left for Greece, the Turks held the film he'd already shot, wouldn't allow a foot of it to leave the country. Days of filming never to be seen? A few weeks later, without apologies or explanation, the film was shipped to Greece undamaged.

Kazan works with actors a hundred different ways. On a Sunday afternoon, the two of us sat on his balcony in Athens going over a scene. Abdul was colorful and full of life and Kazan was encouraging me to go over the top. Then he'd bring me down. Then, horror upon horrors, he'd give me a *line reading*. I thought to myself, "God, I only hope I can do it that good." At one point during the filming, Abdul was supposed to be drunk on a mountainside, drinking from a pottery jar. I recalled those Kazan tricks, e.g., getting Andy Griffith drunk for a scene in *A Face in the Crowd*, having Frank Silvera drink real brandy take after take in *Viva Zapata!* I smelled the jar. No smell. I tasted it. Water. Relieved, I started doing my actor's stuff, a sense memory of drunkenness. Now this is how smart Kazan is: He whispered to a crewmember, *just loud enough for me to hear*, "Look at Lou, he's really drunk." Which gave me confidence and belief in what I was trying to create.

Greece was deep within me, in a sometime psychic way. A hot Sunday morning when I woke up from a dream. I called my girlfriend who had just started rehearsals four days ago in a Broadway play. A bit of "howz it going," then I said, "Had a dream last night about you on stage rehearsing. The director stops the play and says to you, 'We're gonna have to let you go.' He fired you."

She laughed and we exchanged Athens-Manhattan gossip. Three days later, she called. "They fired me. I'm out of the play."

While Poppa was in America, his mother had been killed in a field in Ano Diminio, where he was raised. Her cause of death was not revealed. There was not enough money for Poppa to go to Greece or for a grave headstone. In Athens, I purchased one to be delivered to her cemetery. Poppa's cousin Angelo came from the village to Athens to accompany me there. I spoke the barest of Greek and he spoke no English. He was small, thin, maybe 40, with a solemn, weathered, inexpressive face. We got on a dusty, jangly bus to Ano Diminio. The trip was hot, dry and loud, but when we got off at our stop I was treated to

Elena Karam and Elia Kazan in *America America*.

a beautiful view of the Bay of Corinth, blue, clear, uncluttered by boats or swimmers. I turned to Angelo and said, "ὀμορφη": beautiful. He nodded.

Poppa had started his days with serene beauty. We walked up a narrow dirt road among identical small whitewashed stone houses. Not a car, not a person in sight, the only sound the occasional braying of a donkey. I began walking faster, then inexplicably running full out. Breathing hard, I stopped in front of a small whitewashed, two-room stone house. I stood there shaking, sobbing. Why?! My cousin came up behind me and said quietly in Greek, "Αφτο το σπιτι τοθ πατερα σασ." That's your father's house.

Acting can be dangerous. In *America America*, the turning point in the young Greek boy's life is when he decides to stop being cheated by Abdul and knifes him to death. He becomes a man. We were up in the mountains and the scene was staged so that Giallelis and I would wrestle, then run to the edge of a 600-foot cliff. He would catch me, knife me and I'd die and fall over the cliff. The Italian-Greek crew had built a platform about three feet down the cliff for me to roll onto. It was marked by a single weed at the edge of the precipice. Low-budget, low-tech, a skinny little weed.

Giallelis and I did a couple of takes, no good. We did another, fight, I stumble to the weed, he jumps on top of me and as he tries to throw me over the cliff I look down. Whoa! No platform! I yelled at him to stop, but the little bastard kept trying to pitch me off the cliff. I looked down those 600 feet to the rocks below, heaved him off me, stood up and threw him to the ground! Kazan came over.

"I'll be the only one who cuts a scene, Lou! Got it?"

"Look down there, from where the weed is."

He walked to the edge and looked down to the rocks where I could have been lying.

"Oh. Well, someone must have moved it."

Paul Mann, blacklisted in the '50s, was a well-known acting teacher in New York, but not familiar with film. Kazan had hired him to play Linda Marsh's father, a prosperous, rather overbearing rug merchant. Marsh was a member of the Studio, a beautiful woman who later played Ophelia to Richard Burton's *Hamlet* on Broadway, and in 1979 became a highly successful writer and producer on the sitcom *The Facts of Life*.

Right: **A Greek playing a Greek (Stathis Giallis, front) and me, a Greek playing a Turk.** *Below:* **Kazan setting a shot on *America America*.**

One day Kazan called me aside. "Lou, I want you to find the right time to say to Paul that if anything happens to me, I want him to take over the direction."

"Oh, Gadg, come on, I can't do that."

"No, really. Make him believe it, find the right time."

I was never chatty or friendly with Paul in the first place, but I found the "right time" and relayed the message as convincingly as I could. He listened, didn't say anything. The next day, the wardrobe woman complained that on the way to his dressing, Mann was tossing his costumes to the ground. He started giving orders to the underlings, treating them like lackeys. Paul Mann's character became even more of a puffed-up toad on film and miserable to anyone on set who had to deal with him.

Here's one that Kazan didn't have anything to do with. Well, maybe. There's a scene where Giallelis is walking on a mountain path believing he has finally shed himself of Abdul. I enter the scene on my donkey for a hundred-foot dolly shot and at the end of the dolly track sat the sound mixer. It was an overcast day and on take three I entered the shot just as my donkey expelled a loud burst of intestinal gas. When the scene ended, I shouted to the sound mixer, "Leroy, how was it for sound?" He looked up at the cloudy sky and said, "I don't know, Lou, I got a lot of thunder at the beginning." Oh, Lord, a soundman who couldn't tell the difference between thunder and a donkey fart!

Because of Kazan, I was given a Best Supporting Actor award from the All American Press Association, whoever they were. Good company though. Other recipients that year were Albert Finney for *Tom Jones*, Patricia Neal for *Hud*, Leslie Caron for *The L Shaped Room*. A Brit, a Yank, a dancer, a Greek.

From a Naked City
to Andorra

My first leading role in a network series was on *Naked City* in 1963. I'd done featured parts on three episodes of the gritty cop show, but "Color Schemes Like Never Before," written by Alvin Sargent, was my biggie. My character, Charlie, was a sensitive laborer whose brother was a low-rung gangster. They loved each other, with a relationship similar to that of Marlon Brando and Rod Steiger in *On the Waterfront*. Carol Rossen played a waitress who reads poetry and tries to elevate Charlie above his street level thinking with poetry and books. And I got to kiss her. I was directed by another Hollywood TV director, Ralph Senensky, thankfully the flip side of my previous one.

On the first day of shooting, Charlie is saved from being run down by the bad guy's car by the series star Paul Burke. We rehearsed our scene lying on a March-chilly Greenwich Village street. Paul had one line taped onto the palm of his left hand. One line. Right before the take, he asked me, "Why am I saving your life? Do I know you?" He hadn't read the episode. It gets that way for some series actors and we guests have to work diligently not to let it infect our performances. Burke was truthful and natural and such a solid actor, the audience would never suspect he didn't know what the hell he was talking about.

The writer Alvin Sargent did something that I appreciated even more as the years went by. He wrote a letter from Los Angeles congratulating and thanking me for my portrayal. A most uncommon courtesy. He went on to win two Academy Awards and wrote many successful movies, including *Spider-Man 2* and *3*, *Paper Moon* and *Ordinary People*.

I learned something useful from that television appearance. The morning after the broadcast, I went to my Grand Union market in Nyack for some groceries. Three or four people stopped me and raved about my performance, a first for me. Waking up the next morning, I stretched and thought, gee, maybe I should go back to the Grand Union and get some milk. I was ready with a humble and grateful "oh, thank you" but not one shopper approached me. They had a whole new evening of television faces in their heads. Grocery stores are for shopping.

Ralph Senensky was good with actors. We developed a shorthand. After a take, he'd look at me and I'd nod that it was a good one or shake my head slightly and we'd do another one. That October he requested me for a guest shot on a new psychological series in Hollywood called *The Breaking Point*, with Ralph Meeker and Mariette Hartley already set as guest stars.

Senensky had a theater background and on a weekend he rehearsed Hartley and me in all of our scenes together. Meeker and I played brothers. Meeker had toured as Stanley in a national company of *A Streetcar Named Desire* and starred on Broadway in *Picnic*. He was prepared, quiet, easy to act with. It was great going out to Hollywood to work with New York stage actors to see how they did it. Television, that is.

What did I learn from Meeker? One morning after he stepped out of the makeup trailer, I asked him for any film acting advice. "Makeup's not going to help this mug of mine, or my acting." He wiped all of his makeup off with his bare hands.

During a lunch break, I hopped over to the Goldwyn Studios to audition for producer Quinn Martin. He was quiet, unassuming—and thoughtful enough to have a roast beef sandwich waiting for me. He had just gone into production on a new series, *The Fugitive*, which I was there to read for. The episode's title was "See Hollywood and Die," not, I hoped, a forecast of my future. He read a couple of scenes with me, hired me, we finished our sandwiches and I went back to *The Breaking Point*. Thanks to Senensky, and therefore to Martin, I later became a summertime commuter to Los Angeles for television guest shots. Martin encouraged his casting director Jon Conwell, at added expense, to fly in unknown New York actors for guest roles. Just some of his TV series were *The Untouchables*, *The Fugitive*, *Barnaby Jones*, *12 O'Clock High*, *The Streets of San Francisco*, *Cannon* and *The FBI*. Well, he subsidized many an actor's theater career, and therefore, the theater.

The star of *The Fugitive*, David Janssen, couldn't have been more fun or professional. Brenda Vaccaro, a pal from New York, was also cast in this episode, which helped make it a hoot and a good shoot. I liked these Hollywood jobs, good parts, nice people. My bad-guy buddy in the episode, Chris Robinson, was the actor who had replaced me in *The Young Savages*, but I didn't find that out until years later.

From the two television shows in Hollywood, I returned to my little red house with some change in my pockets, looking for a strong part in a good play. George Tabori had translated and adapted Max Frisch's *Andorra* for producer Cheryl Crawford. To direct she hired Michael Langham, artistic director of the Canadian Stratford Shakespeare Festival. Because I had worked for Tabori in *Brecht on Brecht* and with Ms. Crawford in *Girls of Summer*, I was offered the role of a rapist sergeant. It wasn't a large part, but nuanced and important.

At about that time, Franco Zeffirelli was set to direct *The Lady of the Camellias* with Susan Strasberg and John Stride, a young Brit whom Olivier had pulled into the original company of England's National Theatre. I got a call to read for it. It was not your usual audition. My friend Marty Fried was stage manager and told me the script wasn't ready, therefore, I'd be reading from *The Importance of Being Earnest*. A tie seemed in order. Zeffirelli sat at the head of a long table on the Winter Garden stage. I read. I finished. He studied me. "So, you tell a joke now."

I am terrible at remembering jokes and told him so. Fried whispered in my ear. "Come on, Lou, you know a damn joke! It means he's interested." I looked over at Zeffirelli. Aha.

"I remember one, Mr. Zeffirelli, but it's an Italian joke, is that okay?" Fried winced.

"Ahma' no like Italian jokes."

"I'm sorry, sir, but I'm nervous and it's the only one I can think of. It's short."

Sighing, "Go ahead."

"Do you know the difference between American Hell and Italian Hell?"

Zeffirelli stared at me, not about to help. I struggled on:

"In the American Hell, they boil you in oil and nail you to the cross. In the Italian Hell, well, they don't really boil the oil, they don't really use nails."

Fried needed a cigarette. Zeffirelli looked at his wristwatch. Oscar Wilde and an Italian joke? I'm a Greek from Oklahoma. Oy.

Maybe the tie did it, they offered me the part, but negotiations had already begun for *Andorra*. My agent Peter Witt said I'd have to lose the Zeffirelli play.

The first rehearsal for *Andorra* seemed to be set arbitrarily on a peculiar date, the last day of the year.

Excerpts: *Andorra* log, December 31, 1962

Biltmore Theatre, 261 West 47th Street, 10 a.m. It's New Year's Eve day and the play is *Andorra* by Max Frisch, director is Michael Langham, producer is Cheryl Crawford (bless her). Most of the cast hasn't signed contracts, in fact, this is the first time I have ever arrived for that momentous first day of rehearsal without a contract. Is that legal? The cast is sitting in folding chairs on the bare stage, Cheryl Crawford and George Tabori are seated in the audience. Langham speaks to the actors from the first row. He's slim with a sculpted face and full head of dark hair, not energetic as much as wired, his English-accented words rush out in a stream. The theater is unheated and most of us are still in our coats and scarves.

No introductions. Langham: "The play is a fable, an analogy, like the Bible is. Like the Flood, no one really believes it. Heightened reality. We'll work slowly, first reading we'll dispense with as they're usually depressing. Theme of play is prejudice, shown by anti–Semitism, but if we just show that it's anti–Semitism and the deeper point of prejudice is missed, then we've failed. The town should be *any* town, think of the Middle West, only more south, think of Mexico. We have to have a community feeling in the group. The men are too sophisticated to give in to the heat, respectability is of prime importance to them."

The rolling British accent of Hugh Griffith, prominent nose and slightly popping eyes, clashes with the boyish button-nosed face and German accent of Horst Buchholz. Griffith gestures toward Buchholz: "And what do we do about our ... differences in speech?"

"They should be exactly the same," Langham says, "or it would be senseless." He addresses the cast: "Somewhere between the accents of Griffith and Buchholz." (Twixt British and German ... jeez, how do we do that, go for Swiss?) "The playing must be realistic, although the style of production won't be. We should get the audience's sympathy for these people and hold it until it's too late for them."

We haven't read the play through and it's the first day and our director is giving attitudes, colors and line readings. It's as if we have to perform his direction today to prove to him we can do it. More like he's doing a job than trying to infuse a theatre piece with life. Instantly bits of gloom float among the actors.

Six of us were to share one dressing room (is that legal?). Hugh Griffith got two, one for him and one for his bar. The litmus test of how much alcohol he'd consumed was in the color of his lips: the more booze, the redder the lips. Some nights it looked as if he were wearing lipstick.

The actor playing the rich bigot asked if perhaps Langham could let the play sit with us a while, allowing us to come up with some ideas of our own. Two days later, he was fired. Whoa, fourth day, one actor fired. Thayer David replaced him and got exactly the same line readings from Langham that were forced upon the other actor.

I got directions like "breathe faster," and "you should get your pants cut tight to show your male member." (What other gender member would I have?) He never complimented or encouraged, and we were all so busy trying to fathom his line readings that we could only explore the text at home, never with a fellow actor.

He was cold and rude to the actors. In front of the cast he belittled our ingénue Barbara

Mattes with, "It's pronounced caTTle, with a T, not caDDle. If it were to be pronounced with a D, it would be spelled with a D!"

He wanted Thayer David to fart on Irene Dailey's entrance. David declined. Langham gave Cliff James, playing a town official, a do-it-all-in-one-breath-direction: "Legato here, pianissimo there, crescendo on this line." etc. James looked Langham coldly in the eye for four beats, and then did the speech point by point exactly as conducted by the Maestro. Langham was silent. By trying to belittle James, Langham was diminished.

January 30, previews began. In one of them, I did have a smidge of fun. During our fight scene, Horst miscalculated and hit me square in the face with a hard two-fisted swing. I rose from the floor as my bullies held Horst's arms. I acted like Lou, not the character, and *Lou* closed in on him angrily. Horst was scared shitless. Lou swung, Horst yelped, and my fist whizzed by his face *as rehearsed.* He almost cried with relief, I had a sore jaw for three days.

Here's a short sampling of Langham's directorial encouragements during the ten previews:

> "Irene, where's that fire you used to have? Like when you first read for the part?"
>
> "Lou, you weren't likable enough." (Jeez, call Otto.)
>
> "Where?"
>
> "Why, uh, all through it."
>
> To Thayer: "You are using your 'fat voice.' Don't." (Which didn't amuse Thayer, who was fat.)

February 9 was the date of our opening. Here's an opening night direction: "Lou, do you suppose that just before the curtain goes up, you could sort of play with your member? Let it show a bit more."

I called upon our ingénue Barbara for help. (We'd hooked up in *The Good Soup*.) Barbara wrapped her arms around me to good effect. The curtain wasn't the only thing that rose.

Note on the backstage bulletin board from Ms. Crawford prior to the performance: "No party tonight, but one for the hundredth performance." No one remotely believed there'd ever be a party.

Once I was at the Strasbergs' and Paula, Lee's wife, said to me, "The trouble with young actors, like you and Rip Torn, is that you aren't selecting your parts carefully, building a career."

Horst Buchholz and Hugh Griffith, gracing the playbill for another short-lived effort, *Andorra*.

"That's ridiculous," Lee snorted. "There are so few plays and parts today that an actor has to take what's out there."

Since there was a newspaper strike, no reviews were published in the daily papers, but some were in a rag called *FirstNite*:

"...Langham has permitted a chaotic range of acting styles...."—*The Village Voice*

"...high minded, generally well acted, crisply and imaginatively directed ... doesn't seem to go anywhere."—*Daily News*

"...grows in power and finally achieves a chilling pity and terror..."—*New York Times*

"[O]ne of the best casts of the season ... but almost bloodless treatment of a vastly important subject."—*Daily Mirror*

Who do you trust? Or do you trust any critic? Would any of the above have sent you to the theater? Particularly at today's ticket prices.

The Lady of the Camellias had been delayed and Zeffirelli wanted me immediately. What with some scathing radio reviews and no line at the box office, we all sensed the demise of *Andorra*, just not when. I went to Cheryl Crawford and asked her advice, what to do about my taking a part in *Camellias*.

"Lou, as a producer of this play I can't tell you to go ahead and take another play." A beat. "But as Cheryl Crawford, I'd say I don't think there's any danger of our running more than another week."

She was right, nine performances. No party, no poster. Now, from Andorra to France with an Italian as my tour guide.

17

Franco Zeffirelli

The newspaper strike continued. Not only did the public not know *Andorra* had closed, they never knew it had opened. I started rehearsals on *The Lady of the Camellias* while doing the death rattle of *Andorra* at night.

Camille rehearsals took place in the Winter Garden, where we were scheduled to open on March 20. One of the larger theaters, 1555 seats, it usually housed musicals, thus it could accommodate Zeffirelli's two turntables and a scrim. Scenically Zeffirelli's productions are more operatic than intimate. The 7th Avenue immodest marquee might be a clue:

FRANCO ZEFFIRELLI'S PRODUCTION OF
THE LADY OF THE CAMELLIAS

The production had class written all over it. Marcel Escoffier and Pierre Cardin did the ladies' gowns, *Barabbas'* Anthea Gianakouras was the costume coordinator, Ned Rorem, who'd done six operas, choral works, ballets and other music for the theater, was to compose the music, and the men were to wear corsets beneath their tuxes. The actors were Susan Strasberg (Camille), John Stride (who wowed us Method folk in *Romeo and Juliet*, as Armand), Frank Silvera, John Hillerman (later of *Magnum P.I.*), George Gaynes, Chris Jones (briefly), Carol Rossen (briefly) and Rex O'Malley, playing the small part of a society snob. In the 1937 film with Greta Garbo, he had played Gaston, Armand's friend and side-kick, my part. O'Malley warned the men about the corsets; he still had a bad back from wearing one in the movie.

To show you what an actor has to adjust to in directors, I offer excerpts from

The Lady of the Camellias log

Lincoln's birthday, a Tuesday, 1963. Winter Garden Theatre. First day of rehearsal for *The Lady of the Camellias*. Today is Franco Zeffirelli's birthday (will he emancipate me from flops?). Stars Susan Strasberg, John Stride, Frank Silvera, Coral Browne [the latter did not appear in the show]. To give us feel of times, men will wear corsets, lady's gowns to be made in Paris, designed by Pierre Cardin (coos from the ladies). Ghost writer, Terrence McNally here, Norman Twain and Harris Masterson, the producers. A "fun" first day, but ah, what is to follow?

Zeffirelli was so … so … *Italian*. He greeted everyone with hugs and kisses. As unyielding and stiff as Langham was, Zeffirelli was warm, fun, and huggy. They did have one thing in common: Zeffirelli too acted out all the parts, but in contrast to the Brit's chilled enactments, Z's were with enthusiastic overstatement. Plus he did wait until the *second* day of rehearsal. Most of his directions are unspecific ("Maybe eez fonny to make a face dere…"). Truly enjoying an actor's suggestions, he was not insistent on your hewing to his.

We kept getting rewrites, not from the original British adaptor Giles Cooper, but from

A table reading for *The Lady of the Camellias*.

this sweet, cuddly young Texas boy, Terrence McNally. However, we suspected McNally's private life is not so cuddly, as revealed in his rewrites. Gaston now had to describe Camille as having "a black widow spider between her legs, waiting for a man to enter the web to sting and kill." Oh, Terrence, does yo' momma know?

We had a barometer of Zeffirelli's confidence in the play, the degree of twitching in his right eye. The first grumblings of the cast were heard as we rehearsed with the turntables: "I feel subservient to the set, like I'm ruining the look of the set by being on it." And of course one actor walked into the scrim and tore a hole in it.

Susan's offstage boyfriend Chris Jones and Zeffirelli got into it. New directions to Jones by Zeffirelli caused a tense exchange capped by Zeffirelli's "You are going to have a lot of trouble before we open."

"Maybe you better fire me now."

"All right, you are fired."

"Fuck you."

Jones was bad-boy typecasting. Strikingly attractive, rebellious, but insecure as an actor. The producer Norman Twain brought him up on charges with Actors Equity for insubordination and bringing weapons into the Winter Garden (a gun one day, a knife the next). Jones and Strasberg married in 1965. Four years later, he had a major role in David Lean's *Ryan's Daughter* and was paid half a million dollars. Thrown out and hangin' in.

The days were getting garishly goofy. Zeffirelli yelled at Susan Strasberg, "You will do what I say!" (Preminger with an Italian accent.) He wants her to play it as a little girl, a doll. Susan wants more of the courtesan. She yells back and exits with, "I'm sorry, I'm going to be sick." She went offstage and threw up.

The day before the first preview, March 18, our director was now wearing dark glasses to hide the runaway twitch in his eye. The fun had turned into chaos. Right before curtain, he said, "It can only be disaster, but it will get better."

So now we were another uptight Broadway production with the preview pressure-pot boiling. We all could hear the rolling thunder of approaching unemployment. The scant weeks of creative satisfaction must be immense to compensate for the probable months of unemployment. However, the day before opening, two preview reviews posted by producer Norman Twain tilted us toward slim expectancy:

A rave with good words for all: "Lou Antonio as Armand's gay friend, Gaston, has a pleasant light trick."—*Boston Herald* (no newspaper strike in Boston)

Gay? Light trick? Huh?

"A most rewarding drama."—*Philadelphia Enquirer* (no strike in the City of Brotherly Love)

Stride and Strasberg, *The Lady of the Camellias*.

Susan, nervous and pacing and in tears, threw up this morning. I realized when Zeffirelli was giving me new blocking the day of our opening night that I have never played the same dialogue twice in a row before an audience! As we gathered on stage, Zeffirelli's opening night pre-curtain pep talk to his cast was, "We're not ready to open, but it will be an event, not perfect like we would like it, but it is 70 percent perfect. You must keep in mind pace, voice and rhythm." He never pointed out which 30 percent sucked.

But the show played well enough, solid, no big goofs. Well, one. The down right turntable was to rotate in with a restaurant table and two chairs, one for Stride, one for me. The turntable wheeled us on stage. Stride sat himself at the table, but there was no chair for me. *They forgot my chair*! What to do? My legs hidden by the table-cloth, I strike a sitting pose by squatting. As I played the scene with strained and shaking legs, my butt suspended in mid-air, Stride muttered to me, "What are you doing, taking a shit?" This from an actor from the National Theatre in London?

Kazan came backstage with Lee Strasberg. He smiled and asked me, "What was all that jumping around you were doing up there?"

"It's what Zeffirelli wanted me to do."

"Oh…"

The opening night tradition of waiting and sweating out reviews didn't happen. No papers. No tradition.

On Sunday, March 24, four days after the opening, the producers ran an ad in the *New York Post* (which had gone back to work):

"Stylish and beautiful…. Zeffirelli remains a genius on the artistic level."—*Journal-American*

"There is more elegance, opulence, imagination and drama in the staging than any other Broadway play this season. Franco Zeffirelli has done it again."—*World-Telegram*

"Staged with magic … irresistible … acted by young performers with charm, earnestness and skill … astonishingly moving…. Miss Strasberg radiantly and delicately beautifully acts with sensitive and unerring emotional power."—*New York Post*

Scorched by radio critics and in print by prominent critics including Howard Taubman, Walter Kerr, Judith Crist, and by *Variety*, our *Lady* closed after 12 performances, besting *Andorra* by three. I opened and closed in two plays during one newspaper strike. I had to conclude that Zeffirelli has no idea how to tell a story. He folded at the *most* crucial time, before an audience. I wondered if there shouldn't be two directors on a show, one who does the primary work and another with an objective eye collaborating during the last two weeks, saying, "This isn't clear, you don't need that, cut it, use more gels in the upstage lights," etc. Selection of this director should be as careful as picking the first one. As a visualist, Zeffirelli's strength was his weakness. His scenic ideas always took precedence over the story, the organic life of the play. The director should serve the play, not his reputation.

18

Keeping Busy Until Dewhurst

In my house above the Hudson, I was restless. Something inside me was kicking around. On an old Underwood typewriter, I wrote a short piece (20 pages) with mainly lyrics and dance description. I was writing *Valentine*, about two innocents trapped in a small Southern town who decide to go to New York City and break the stagnation of their lives. A guy I knew, Charles Greenwell, said he'd like to give a try to writing the music for it. He was serving in the army in Fort Benning, Georgia, and aside from "Taps," basic training didn't offer him much musical stimulation.

I mailed him the lyrics and he would mail me freshly minted music. It was a short piece, eight songs, seven dances, and no dialogue scene longer than a page. The story was told mostly through the choreography and songs.

Formerly a Greek church, the space at the Actors Studio is wide, deep and open. Perfect for dance. I was fortunate to grab a stellar cast from the Studio membership, but due to their upcoming commitments I had only 12 days to get the dances, songs and scenes pulled together for the Studio's Tuesday session. Kelly Brown, the choreographer and lead male, was a former ballet dancer and had danced in ballet companies and a bunch of MGM Hollywood movies, *Seven Brides for Seven Brothers* for one. Lesley Anne Warren, a dancer-actress, was getting recognition from having played the lead in a *Cinderella* TV special and the ingénue lead in Disney's *The Happiest Millionaire*. Madeleine Sherwood, a Broadway veteran, sang and acted the oppressive and smothering mother. In a trio of male seducers, Ron Rifkin, later a Tony Award winner for *Cabaret*, sang and danced the Sensitive One. Tom Avera, an ex-saloon singer, did a spot-on Suave One. Lane Bradbury (the original Dainty June in *Gypsy*) played the young girl. Julie Newmar, all six gorgeous feet of her, had danced on Broadway and in MGM movies. All that talent, and it was free!

Gene Casey, our piano accompanist, rehearsed the actors as the songs arrived from Georgia. Kelly choreographed in rented dance studios between his acting scenes and song rehearsals. It was marvelous madness: "No, Kelly, it should be more like a horse lifting its legs in high grass" (heavy sigh from Kelly the choreographer, as opposed to Kelly the actor). "Okay, Lou, come back in an hour. Let's see, Julie, let's try this..." At Gene's piano, it's was, "Ron, when you come to 'I tend toward homosexuality,' try it so that we get a sense the guy has worn this mask before." Then back to the Studio to mop the floors that the actors would dance and roll on.

After 12 days, we faced the Method audience of the Actors Studio and Lee Strasberg. I was in the balcony working a rented follow-spot. A musical? At the Studio? Visions of my *Pajama Game* and Strasberg danced in my head.

The actors did better than ever, superb in all the acting, singing and dancing. After the 40-minute presentation I turned off my follow-spot and went before the group to talk about what we had tried to accomplish. There was heavy applause. I was stunned. I flashed on Strasberg's "We're here to learn, not to please an audience!" But he was complimentary and encouraging. The next day, Cheryl Crawford called me: "I understand you did an interesting piece at the Studio," she said in her terse monotone. "Can you do it again? I'd like to see it."

"No, ma'am, half the cast has left for jobs."

"Then send me the script."

"Okay, but know, Miss Crawford, that the dances and the songs tell the story as much as the dialogue. Might be hard to really see what we did."

She read it, called a week later and thanked me, saying that she would have to *see* a piece like *Valentine*. The head of Warner Brothers, John Calley, heard about it and wanted me to send the script and a tape of the songs to a Broadway talent manager-producer, Hilliard Elkins. Calley received Elkins' evaluation: "No one is interested in going to see a bunch of young people in New York." *Valentine* was never performed again. I miss it.

Peter Witt, my agent, was still on my case about living in Grandview. "Dey vant to see you today, but dere you are in trees. So *tomorrow* go see Albee and Alan Schneider about his new play." It was for Edward Albee's adaptation of Carson McCullers' novella *The Ballad of the Sad Café*. I didn't have to read for it, perhaps because of my having done Albee's *Zoo Story* at the Actors Studio. I did have to meet the director Alan Schneider. Colleen Dewhurst was set to play the lead, and she's a big woman, so just in case I stuffed some newspaper in my shoes to make me an even six feet tall. (Garson Kanin once asked my height and when I said 5'11", he advised me, "Always say six feet.") Albee had final casting approval and the meeting was pleasant and short.

Miss Amelia, Dewhurst's character, runs a general store in a small Southern town during the 1930s. Into her solitary existence steps a hunchbacked dwarf who claims to be her cousin Lymon. Miss Amelia is fascinated by the stranger and the two strike up an unusual relationship. Lymon soon convinces Miss Amelia to transform her shop into a café. Things seem to be going fine until Marvin Macy, the man Miss Amelia once married and then spurned, is released from prison and drops in for a visit.

September 20, 1963

Another first rehearsal. *The Ballad of the Sad Café*

One p.m. Martin Beck Theatre. I recognize Colleen Dewhurst, Roscoe Lee Browne, Bill Prince and Michael Dunn. Alan Schneider, the director, wearing a baseball cap, Albee in beige Levis and white shirt, producers Lewis Allen and Ben Edwards dressed for their roles and are properly suited. We are all on the bare stage in folding chairs around a long wooden table. Most of us have never met before and with a theater of empty seats before us there is not exactly a feeling of coziness among us. The perennial bright work light is downstage left. Schneider says, "Most of my work is done. Getting this good cast, I just have to stage it. This play is about loneliness and love, but mostly loneliness. People trying to connect. Everyone, easy on the Southern accents, Roscoe, no accent."

Albee stands and addresses us in an informal tone. "The first day of rehearsal is depressing to me. You're good actors, Alan's a good director, Ben [Edwards] has built a nice set. So if the play's lousy, it's my fault. And that's why the first day of rehearsal is depressing. To me." He then gave small changes and cuts. The play is divided into three acts. He told us when he started writing *Ballad* he envisioned it at 70 pages or so, but it kept coming and kept coming until it ended with 185 pages and it's those 185 he is hacking away at.

We're to have the set in two weeks. No out-of-town tryout. (That's three in a row.) Schneider asks us to pause where pauses in Albee's script are shown by dots. "Those dots mean that the play has a rhythm, so play the pauses indicated." A forestage is to be built over first row. The beginning of another acting adventure.

The Ballad of the Sad Café.

Schneider encourages courage, which is good to hear what with Michael Langham's *Andorra* drills still lingering in my ears. Unlike Kazan, most directors get nervous if they watch actors probing the inner and exterior ranges of their characters rather than performing. The pattern prevails, Betty Henritze replaces an actor on our fourth day. For the actors, the rehearsal times should be the best of times—creating, experimenting, failing, searching for something new, something old, something borrowed. Schneider simply listens and watches us. The extras and townspeople are getting the most attention from our director; he takes an inordinate amount of time to block the crowd scenes. That's where the critics notice "direction."

Colleen and I mostly sit around.

"Do you feel like we're extras in a TV show?" she asks me.

"Yeah. I was hoping those days were gone."

"How does Walter Kerr like you?"

"He did, but now he doesn't."

"Me neither."

I am pissed that Schneider has never rehearsed our scenes. We rely on her husband George C. Scott for his suppertime suggestions to Colleen: "Only get sensitive where it counts."

Sometimes Schneider is cruel to the actors, mocking them or criticizing rather than helping them. Usually Dewhurst will set her jaws and clench her fists when he does that. A few weeks into rehearsals, she unclenches and lets fly at Alan in front of all of us. So intense is she, the dust stops in midair: "Mr. Browne is one of the most exciting actors in the theater," she says, "and he is dull in this part. There is no feeling of a company because of little cubbyhole notes, no freedom for the actors, itsy-poo directions of 'move one inch into your light.' We are in trouble, actors are hung up!" She continues for a good six or seven minutes. The cast listens quietly with nodding agreement and appreciation. She is spot-on. Schneider doesn't defend himself or argue with her. He makes a few self-deprecating remarks: "I'm doing the best I can, but I'm only a stupid guy."

Schneider begins giving *me* notes to give to Dewhurst! Never been in that position before. He and Dewhurst have absolutely nothing to do with each other, that is, she refuses to let him have anything to do with her.

Me atop Colleen Dewhurst.

Michael Dunn's character was supposed to idolize Marvin Macy and it wasn't happening. Schneider comes to me for help: "Do you have any ideas, Lou?" I suggest that he might ask Michael to substitute a real-life hero for Marvin. "Like I'd choose Ted Williams." Schneider said, "That's one thing I don't know how to do, work with actors."

In Hollywood a few years later, he was directing screen tests for a movie he hoped to get hired for. I was visiting on set and overheard him say to the producer, "I don't know anything about camera, the one thing I am good at is working with actors."

A Hirschfeld! (copyright Al Hirschfeld Foundation).

The Sunday before opening, *The New York Times* ran a Hirschfeld of *Ballad* with Dewhurst, Dunn and me! I'd never been in one of his famous Broadway caricatures and I was surprised and delighted. It's fun and sort of prestigious for an actor to be the subject of Al Hirschfeld's dancing pen and to search for his "NINA"s hidden in the portraits. It also somehow made me acutely aware that my role was of importance to the production. That had never been a consideration before; my primary goal always is in finding my character and experiencing his life on stage. Any *show biz* elements were simply distractions. (Excepting, of course, post-opening interviews and thus gratefully and with pride, striding the streets of New York as a "working actor"…)

October 30, opening night. I am nervous. Totally cool four years ago in my New York debut, but since then nervousness knocks and has risen with each succeeding play. It is not a loss of confidence, it's just that through training and experience I am demanding more from myself, more character complexities, more nuance. The one note that brother Jim reiterates is, "In your curtain calls, *smile!*" I'm usually thinking of something I could have done better in the performance or something I'll go for next time.

There's a letter scene, essentially a monologue, in which Marvin opens his heart for the first time about his feelings for Miss Amelia. Marvin cannot read or write so his brother is writing it down in a letter to be sent to Miss Amelia. Opening night I jump five lines, but then go back and get them. It doesn't throw me, I'm full, real full. Two bursts of applause during the letter. Encouraging to hear, though long ago I learned that opening night applause is not always a true barometer of quality. Dewhurst and Dunn are hot and grab the audience fully.

We get five out of six excellent to enthusiastic reviews! The dissenter. "*Ballad of the Sad Café* keeps us at arm's length. In spite of vivid things in it, it ends as speculative grotesquerie." Yep, Walter Kerr.

However:

"...beautiful, exciting, touching and absolutely enthralling ... a notable addition to the literature of our contemporary stage."—John Chapman, *Daily News*

"...Antonio has a vivid scene in which he dictates a letter brimming with love and hate."—Norman Taubman, *New York Times*

"...an engrossing evening, a salutary success. Lou Antonio is particularly effective ... properly sinister and attractive..."—John McClain, *Journal American*

"...an astonishing and individual play, fashioned into a drama of matchless integrity. Antonio is consistently fine and brilliant in scenes such as the marriage proposal and in dictating his angry letter..."— Norman Nadel, *World-Telegram*

It's a new feeling for me, returning to a theater for the second performance anticipating that I might well be playing and digging into the same part for months. Not so fast, buddy. You can't just trade reviews for success like you can frequent flyer miles. Well, Neil Simon could.

After we opened, Dewhurst and I continued doing our actors' work. In every performance we'd mine for gold. Then, bingo, one night there it was! That nightly search kept us alive on stage. With Dewhurst, a scene never lost its life.

Dewhurst had one fatal flaw on stage. Well, not *fatal*. She would break up, and had a smile too wide to hide. There's a scene in which Macy proposes to her. We sit on the stage

Me, preparing to propose to Colleen Dewhurst.

apron and I take a jewelry box out of my pocket and open it to show her the ring. From the stage to the end of the apron is about ten feet. One matinee it seemed like a bus trip to Iowa. I opened the box, the ring popped out, rolled down the apron and dropped into the front row of the audience. Oh, swell! The scene could not continue without that ring! I crossed down stage and said to this frightened man in the first row, "Gimme da' ring." He was the proverbial deer in the headlights. "Gimme da' ring, please," I repeated. Timidly the guy picked it up and handed it to me. I turned around and my leading lady was flat on her back laughing. I sat down next to her, she sat up, still laughing. I said my line, she laughed. I said *her* line. That cracked her up even more. I said my next line and offered her the ring again. Oh, man, that stirred up a whoop. Colleen Dewhurst, extolled as one of our greatest tragedians, stood up, spasmed with laughter and walked off stage right shaking her head helplessly, waving goodbye to me as she disappeared into the wings. The audience applauded her for a solid minute.

My father came to New York to see me in the play. He had arrived at Ellis Island 45 years earlier and had not been to New York since. It was the only time he saw me on Broadway. Dewhurst told me that after the show, Poppa, along with my brothers Jim and Theo, came to her dressing room to congratulate her on her performance. Also in the room was two-time Academy Award winner Shelley Winters. Shelley to Poppa: "Your son is very good in the play, Mr. Antonio."

"Yah. What *you* do?"

"Well, I'm an actor, too."

Poppa (patting her arm): "Well, you stick with it, you make it."

Shelley graciously accepted the encouragement.

President Kennedy was killed on Friday, November 22, and that night Broadway went

STARS
OF
THE FUTURE   Talented males the pros

think will make it on Broadway . . .

EDWARD ALBEE
Playwright

It is my suspicion that Lou Antonio will never be a "star." He has too many things going against him—his personality, his acting ability, for two. By this I mean that he is too nice a person and far too good an actor to be content to settle for the easy prize. What he will become is merely an extension of what he is now. His craft and art have grown the five years I have known his work. He was in my first play, *The Zoo Story*, and he is now in my most recent, *The Ballad of the Sad Cafe*. The more I think about it, I puzzle that he has not been in them all.

Do not misunderstand me. Lou Antonio will achieve stardom, but he will never be a "star." He will not desert to California or sink into television. Rather, you will more likely find him off-Broadway—or wherever the plays are. Nor do I think we will ever find him behaving like a "star." No true star does. Lou Antonio is merely a fine actor getting better all the time.

DAVID BLACK
Producer

In the Fall of 1961 Sir Michael Redgrave, Margaret Webster and I had almost despaired of finding a Pasquale for *The Aspern Papers* when Clifford David walked onto the stage. It took less than one speech before Sir Michael nodded to me that this was our man. Later, during rehearsals, I watched him grow in the role as he constantly applied new ideas to his interpretation. This quality of dedication is the thing which I look for in a future star. It is this constant dissatisfaction with his own performance and the willingness to search out and accept criticism, which, when added to his natural talent, assures Clifford David success. Since *The Aspern Papers* he has demonstrated his versatility by singing and acting in *The Boys From Syracuse* and playing in two movies. I am convinced, however, that his future lies on the legitimate stage. I also predict that he has the good looks and charm to be a future matinee idol.

Albee got it half right. And, gratefully, his talents helped me sink into television. Sorry, Edward, but thank you.

dark. We played the matinee the next day and when Miss Amelia pointed her shotgun at Marvin Macy, well, it took Colleen and me momentarily out of the play and sent a chill through us. The audience gasped. Everyone in the theater was suspended in the image of the assassination. As in a silent dream, the room was soundless.

After Kennedy's murder, attendance fell sharply. After 123 performances, *The Ballad of the Sad Café* closed on February 15, 1964.

Theo came to visit me at the little red house. We stood on my hill in the February cold looking out at the Hudson River. Theo worried about me. "So, Lou, when will you get another job?"

"Maybe some summer stock, maybe some TV in California. I dunno, probably June or July."

He shook his head, "Let's go back inside, it's getting too cold," he said.

19

Faustus, Julie and Josh

That summer I did a TV guest spot in Los Angeles. One night I was talking with Leo Penn, an Actors Studio actor and director, at the Rain Check, a dark, smoky and somewhat gloomy hangout where the younger aspiring actors gathered to brag and bitch. We got out of there and as I waved good night to Leo I was suddenly on my back on the sidewalk looking up at an angry young man. I got up, he ran. I ran after him and grabbed him by the front of his shirt.

"What the hell was that!?"

As he teared up: "You New York actors think you are such hot shit, comin' out here, taking our jobs."

"You're pissed at me for *working*?!"

"I just had the lead in a movie with Jimmy Caan, *Red Line 7000*, Howard Hawks directed me, and I can't even get a fucking guest shot on *TV*. You come out here, this hot New York actor..."

Frustration and anger seethe beneath many an 8 × 10 glossy.

Actors East and West have a tendency to see things differently. Playing a small part in *Cool Hand Luke*, Dennis Hopper would crowd and push to get on camera. He couldn't be chastised for it, that's the way actors are brought up in Hollywood, agents and managers doing the pushing to get their young ones to "get your face on camera."

I got a call to go the Beverly Hills Hotel to read for a play that Josh Logan was directing, *Ready When You Are, C.B.!*, Julie Harris to star. Josh Logan. His history of Broadway was long and respected and he had been Oscar-nominated for *Sayonara* and *Picnic*. Logan was a big, friendly man, polite and encouraging. I read well enough that he and I flew back to New York to see if Julie Harris and I had "chemistry." That word again.

On a bare Broadway stage, Josh put us in his test tube for about a half-hour, shook well, and our elements fused. I flew back to Los Angeles to finish up my guest shots.

A few days later, a call came from Word Baker, a respected director who had won Obie Awards for *The Crucible*, *The Pinter Plays* and *The Fantasticks*, the longest running musical in theater history. Baker was calling me on the endorsement of Mildred Dunnock. Would I like to play Faustus in Marlowe's *The Tragical Historie of Doctor Faustus*? It was to open at the prestigious Off Broadway Phoenix Theatre for an eight-week run. Perfect. I could do a classic Off Broadway and then segue into a comedy on Broadway. I'd done Hotspur, Mercutio, Kean, Cousin Dick's ballet classes and I still had my dance belt, so tights? Okay, let's do it. I told my Hollywood agent I was taggin' up and headin' home. He protested, "Lou, I get calls for you all the time." Oh, the disgust. "Plays. What is that going to get you, a big six, seven hundred a week?"

"Uh, no. More like 200."

Faustus is a formidable part. My preparation was a bit different from my approach to a contemporary play, but not that much. Era, character, psychology, physicality, goals, intentions, all that stuff. I went into training to be vocally strong, facile, pliant, nuanced and confident. To avoid contemporary physical mannerisms and gestures, I intended to keep an eye on myself.

The opening speech to the audience, though written to be spoken by the chorus, Word Baker gave to Faustus. In that introduction I wanted our New York audience to feel I was at ease with the language. The Faustus I wanted would require a conflation of diction, style and my method. I wanted my Faustus to be free of a moaning dispirited intellectual by pulling from the drug culture credo of the day: Tune In, Turn On, Drop Out. I wanted to propel this brilliant young man into an anticipatory rush of voyages and pleasures that would infuse him with energy, joy and bursts of "My four and 20 years I'll spend in pleasure and in dalliance." The Devil was my dealer.

Sometimes spontaneity can produce pain. When the Devil is coming to collect Faustus' soul, Faustus looks for a place to hide. He implores, "Earth, open." I'd played center in high

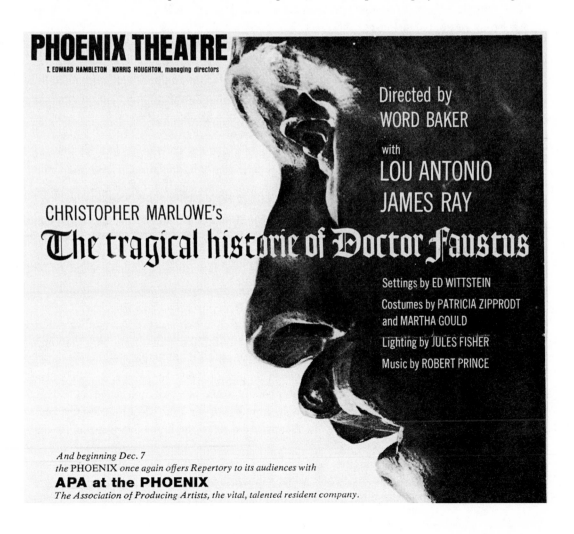

school football and one part of practice was to fling your body horizontally into the air, arms out, and land on your stomach. Right after "Earth open," I flashed back to that teenage image, leaped flat out, arms wide, and hit that wooden stage floor with a whack. In double misery (mine and Faustus'), I said the next line, "'Twill not hide me." My jaw, my chest, my neck ached from the crash. Impulse to expression, gratifying. Spontaneity, ouch.

I should have heeded the wisdom passed on to me when I was 19 working in Colorado one summer. I had rented a horse fresh off winter range. I swung into the saddle, the horse bucked, balked and ran full out up a mountain and down the mountain. I bounced and weaved and finally reined him in. The old cowboy I rented him from nonchalantly told me it was no big deal. "Getting throwed ain't nothin, it's *landin'* that hurts."

The applause during previews was strong. Preview audiences are pure, no critic has sweetened or poisoned the well yet. Opening night, we were confident. Mephistopheles (a terrific James Ray) and I shared a tiny dressing room. (Not exactly a Method idea.) Right before curtain, Robert Prince, who composed the incidental music, came in. He leaned in close to me and said what an actor must never hear before opening night curtain: "Just remember, Lou, the whole thing depends on *you*."

It seemed to go well, high energy, laughs when they were due, quiet when due. We got a strong response during curtain calls. The party afterward was at Baker's apartment. I took a slug of Scotch and said to Lonny Chapman, "They are going to kill us, and me in particular."

Josh Logan called early the next morning: "Lou, don't read the reviews." I hadn't, but thanks for the big clue, Josh! Another clue: The cast was uniformly sweet to me the next night, tiptoeing around me, looking at me as if I were a wounded dog and they wanted to take the thorn out of my paw. Let me dig out some of those thorns:

"Splendid production.... Lou Antonio plays it audibly and gracefully but I thought with a bit too much gymnastics, especially when he takes a dive across the stage..."—John McClain, *Journal American*

"His characterization remains too boyish to the bitter end ... too much spirit of Till Eulenspiegel and not enough of the savage quest for experience."—Norman Taubman, *New York Times*

"Antonio, in a rather brief career, has been growing in favor as one of the better young players, but I doubt if many playgoers regarded him as having the range and power that he displays here. In a limited run of eight weeks, his performance will last well beyond that."—*Rockland County News*

"Colorful, but sprawling.... Lou Antonio, as Faustus, turned in a solid performance in the difficult part."—*Daily News*

"A man's reach should exceed his grasp." Yeah, thanks, Bobby Browning, but when you go out on a limb, there is liable to be someone with a chainsaw howling. What I wanted to accomplish I got, but the critics saw the role differently. Still, we must climb onto that limb, even though it has been used for many a lynching.

While I was in *Faustus*, rehearsals began for *Ready When You Are, C.B.!* After what was required from Faustus, I thought that a comedy would be a walk in the park. Get your laughs, take a bow. Finally, a play that would support me for a full season, or two! A one-set comedy with a cast of five with Julie Harris and directed by Josh Logan? Boffo. A winner!

Marlon Brando had disappeared from *The Egyptian*, a 1954 toga movie, and hid out in playwright Susan Slade's apartment. What happened between them is what the play was based on. It was funny, lightweight, and good parts for everyone. Julie, as she admitted, was almost 20 years too old for her role, but when she came on stage wearing snug blue jeans on her trim cute body, she was 20 years younger and passed easily for 22. I certainly believed it, eight times a week.

c.b. log, October 12, 1964

The New Amsterdam Roof Theater. I am too bone-tired to be here in this good ol' dusty, ratty haunt at ten a.m. This place is as filthy as ever, and the elevator service is as slovenly as the morning drunks on 42nd Street. This possible heartache of the future is a comedy called *Ready When You Are, C.B.!,* from the joke of the same name. Our producer is David Black, a young man with balding pate, long sideburns and longer cigar. Susan Slade, the author, is thin, attractive short black hair, and nervous. Joshua Lockwood Logan, director and theatre legend, is over-coated and genial. The actors, Julie Harris, Estelle Parsons, Arlene Golonka, Betty Walker and me. We are the cast for now, but given the history of my previous plays...

A talk from Logan: "Leave it free, but let's get it on its feet, we'll set things only loosely, I see it as a rough sketch, I'll give you freedom—except for the ones who don't want freedom."

The Devil is coming to collect a debt, the soul of Faustus.

In her first four lines, Logan gives Parsons three line readings. He starts setting business immediately, interrupts every minute to direct and say, "I'm not giving you a line reading, just want to get the meaning clear." He directs with his head in the script, not once looking up at the actors, asks Susan Slade questions all the time, like what kind of cheese is in the icebox? Swiss. He follows Slade's parentheses explicitly. Keeps repeating that he wants to do the play as she wrote it, because after all, that is what interested him. Tries to establish immediate attraction between Harris and me. Mrs. Logan is watching part of the rehearsal. "My sort of good luck charm," Logan explains. Let's hope so.

At the end of the second day of rehearsal, he says, "Well, we've finished blocking half of it."

"You mean the other two acts are that *short*!" asks I.

"Lou, this is a two-act play."

"Oh ... yeah..." Unfortunately, because of *Faustus* I hadn't read *C.B.* since I auditioned in July.

Julie Harris, what a load of talent in that petite person. *Not* petite: her lunch. She brings two gigantic sandwiches, plums, apples, banana and thermos. Is gluttony a fuel for talent?

Parsons is hilarious, she goes full-out when she's manic, conversational when she's depressive. Golonka is cuddly and funny.

Julie Harris on the playbill for *Ready When You Are, C.B.*.

Logan acts out a moment for Julie. He will try anything as an actor, but lets his actors try very little. He says his technique is to "throw a play on its feet in some shape, like mud on a fence, so I get the idea of the thing, then to dig under and find the emotion, but then try not to show it." Some days he's brilliant and I can see where *Mister Roberts*, *South Pacific*, *Fanny* et al. came from.

He is now starting to tell me how much more charming, attractive and good-looking I am when I don't press or come on strong: "You don't need to. You are a strong personality."

I get sent off to Mr. Kenneth, Jacqueline Kennedy's hair stylist, who says to me, "There's no reason you should look like a mouse." I spend two and a half hours getting my hair reconditioned and dyed from my Faustus blonde back to its natural color, and then Mr. K comes in with his tools and starts cutting and pinning and shaping while I'm hoping to hear, "Jackie, darling, over here!"

We opened in Philadelphia on November 12. As *Variety* (and Theo) would say, two on the fence.

> The evening is sluggish except for occasional comedy punctuation…—Ernest Schier, *Philadelphia Bulletin*

Harris' performance wasn't mentioned at all. The play is dismissed, as are the actors. Logan re-directs the next day in reaction to the reviews.

After our second performance, Logan asks me to take a walk with him. On the dark, cold, quiet streets of Philadelphia, he drops a bomb: "Julie wants to quit."

"What!"

I'm not getting fired, but the star wants to quit. This is a new one for me. What happens now?

Julie Harris watches Josh Logan directing, or perhaps dancing?

Logan rings me at four a.m. Manning Gurian, Julie's husband, told him that her outburst was Julie's pattern and he reassured Logan she would stay with the show, as she always has.

A day or so later, Logan cut a line of Golonka's and she said, "Josh, that's my only character thing." It finally happened, Josh Logan blew his mustache. Voice quaking, he seemed on the verge of tears. "Do what I tell you and stop treating me like a child. I've been in this business a long time. I'm a gentle man, a nice man, I'm tired. I've been working all day and all night on this play. I'm not concerned about your little personal exasperations, the only important thing is that we have a hit. We've got to have a hit!"

After the performance that night, Slade, Golonka and I repair to a bar. Slade is angry. "Estelle is not the girl I wrote any more. Lou, your costumes are bad and—"

"Yeah, I still think I should be in old blue jeans."

"Right. and so are Estelle's and Julie's. Josh wants a happy ending, for you and Julie to get together. I would have been happy to open with the play and performances we gave Tuesday night. But the play is getting worse. Josh says I have beginning playwright's disease, blaming the director and actors. I don't know what's happening on that stage any more."

It's two in the morning and I'm studying my script and I hear some guys having a loud, good ol' drunken time in the hotel hallway. A door opens: "You motherfucking cock-suckers, shut up! Go to goddamn bed and let us sleep!" Oh, me, oh, my, was that our little Julie?

Next morning at rehearsal, Estelle bursts into my dressing room raving about this new singer who's fantastic, Bob Dylan. I give her a "Yeah, yeah" and go to Julie's dressing room.

"Julie, did I hear you swearing at some sailors last night?"

In her reverential voice: "Oh, weren't they just terrible. And me with a son who needs his sleep. Oh…"

The next day I'm walking to rehearsal and see Julie waiting for a traffic light to change. I come up behind her with a dirty-old-man whisper in her ear: "Hey, little girl, how about a bit o' huff and puff before lunch?"

Without a look: "Fuck off!"

I break up, she turns and punches my arm with convincing fuck-off strength.

We escape the City of Brotherly Critics to the Brooks Atkinson Theatre in New York. Our costumer, Theoni Aldredge, seems to be making as many costume changes as we've been getting line changes. Logan is trying to get me to look like a "leading man." Before a preview one night, he said, "Cut and peroxide the hair on your chest and upper arms." Whereupon he rushes out of my dressing room and clambers back with a large pair of scissors and starts cutting the hair on my chest, explaining all the while that Bill Holden had shaved his chest for *Picnic*. Well, you don't disagree with a frenzied director holding a pair of sharp scissors over your heart.

Before my next rehearsal, Logan mentions my resentment at his cutting my chest hair. "It was only to make you appear more attractive. Irwin Shaw, a man, a real man, said you looked like a second-rate prizefighter." Logan gives me handsome notes.

> Keep your chin up, it gives you a better profile.
>
> Don't look down, we see where your hair is thin.
>
> Stand up straight.

Didn't he know what I looked like when he cast me? Why don't they just get Rock Hudson or Robert Wagner, for God's sake? Brando wasn't *pretty*. Well, okay, he was beautiful. Logan isn't even happy with my shirts. My shirts, my hair, my posture, my *chest* hair, dare I ask about my acting?

Poor man was probably being pounded by the panic of producer David Black, who was not smelling the intoxicating aroma of "Hit" in the prophetic gossip of Shubert Alley. Or Downey's, or Sardi's.

My second Hirschfeld, and alas, my last (copyright Al Hirschfeld Foundation).

Julie Harris, and me with Mr. Kenneth's bouffant.

Opening night was Pearl Harbor Day, 1964. No great goofs or anything to make theater lore. Parsons was late on an entrance and I ad libbed, Julie dropped a few lines, I was better than ever (I think).

The show was okay, but the audience was listless and there were no "Bravas" for Julie. Didn't sound like a hit to these callused ears.

The opening night party was at 21. The first review in was Howard Taubman's in the *New York Times*. "Julie Harris is an enchantress," it began. "The new comedy distills charm, laughter and a touching sense of truth…. Harris makes Annie a creature you quickly lose your heart to."

A good review in the *Times*, and a rave for Broadway's sweetheart! I ordered a 12-year-old Johnny Walker Black and sat back in the booth in relief. Finally, after 11 plays in New York, a full season's employment!

The other reviews came in:

"Lou Antonio is an attractive man though I can't see him as a Hollywood type so devastating to women that he'd be worth $500,000. Nevertheless, he's adept at comedy, and undeniably charming."—Norman Nadel, *World-Telegraph*

"Lou Antonio is expert and believable as the errant movie star."—Richard Watts, Jr., *Post*

"[C]ertainly not the worst play I ever saw, but just possibly the least interesting…"—Walter Kerr, *Herald Tribune*

"I don't get it. Can't those Broadway guys just read a play and know if it's good, if it's gonna be a hit or not? What's the deal? Huh?"-—Lou Antonio (sophomore, University of Oklahoma)

I switched to the bar Scotch. Julie didn't have the power, Taubman didn't have the power. We closed in ten weeks.

20

Not-So-Lovely Hula Hands

That summer I flew to Los Angeles to bank some of those West Coast acorns. Bless his heart, Quinn Martin gave me a couple of guest shots, a World War II series called *12 O'Clock High* and another *Fugitive* episode. While I was doing the *Fugitive*, my West Coast agent Paul Kohner set up a reading for director George Roy Hill, who was prepping *Hawaii*, from the James Michener book. I was up for the part of a missionary from New England. My makeup man on *The Fugitive*, Emile LaVigne, said to fit the period, it might help my audition if my hair were longer. He put a fall on me and I read for Mr. Hill, a most pleasant man. I kept thinking, "Oh dammit, he's gonna spot this stupid fake hair and think 'Another desperate actor.'"

LaVigne, however, was one of the best. I was called back for a second meeting with Hill. While I was sitting in the hallway looking at the script, a small, bespectacled, dark-haired man surreptitiously began giving me the eye. Circling me, studying me. I thought, jeez, can't a fella prepare for an audition without being cruised? "Oh, excuse me," the apparition said. "I'm Walter Mirisch, the producer of this picture, and I just wanted to make sure you didn't look too Italian. 'Antonio,' you know." He nodded and left.

Kohner called to tell me they wanted me. The part and the salary were lame so I didn't care if I did the movie or not, but the Hollywood agents said do it so the Hollywood "community" would know about me. I did some math and figured I could live almost a year on the salary, small as it was. Damn. Five months on Oahu followed, five long months.

A batch of New York actors were hired for the movie: Michael Constantine, Gene Hackman, John Cullum, George Rose. Then there were those non–New Yorkers Julie Andrews, Max von Sydow, Richard Harris.

Andrews and von Sydow were both unaffected, nice people. She cracked us up on the beach one day. We were all lying about in our swimsuits and she started singing a tune from *My Fair Lady*, but with a slight difference in lyrics, or rather lack of lyrics. In her pure contralto she sweetly sang, "I could have ____ all night, I could have ____ all night, and still have begged for more. I could have spread my ____ and done a thousand things, I've never done before." I'm not bleeping words here. Miss Julie simply left the operative words out. Sing it her way, but not in front of your mom.

In makeup one morning, I was talking to someone about a comedy I was writing. Von Sydow spoke up: "Lou, I play comedy. Everyone thinks all I do is Bergman, but I play comedy." Actors never know whence a job might spring. Too often it's a Virgin Spring.

The New York contingent was treated shabbily. Dorothea Jeakins had designed the costumes so authentically that in the Hawaiian sun we were being parboiled in our heavy, scratchy, woolen wardrobe. No chairs, no dressing rooms, we were itchy and sweaty and

Me being comforted by Julie Andrews and Max von Sydow in *Hawaii*.

miserable. A new production manager, George Justin, was hired out of New York. We had worked together in New York and I went to him. "George, you know they're breaking SAG rules here. We're supposed to have chairs. Sitting on the sand in this wardrobe is torture."

"Now come on, Lou," said Justin. "If I give you guys chairs, then I'm gonna hafta give every one of the 200 Hawaiian extras a chair or they'll think we're doing the *haole* thing."

We got no chairs.

Hill had cast two Polynesian non-actors in major roles. He was wonderful with them, patient and coaxing believable performances from them, sometimes to the tune of 22 takes. Meanwhile, during those takes I'd watch the consummate Max von Sydow struggle to keep his performance alive. He was going downhill and Hill didn't seem to notice. A director gets no huzzahs if Max von Sydow is good, but if two amateurs get good reviews, then the director is brilliant!

The Hawaiian cast and extras were treated very well by the company, and particularly by Hill. Which paid off for him. The movie got so far behind schedule that Hill was secretly fired, and Arthur Hiller was sneaked onto the island to replace him. Whoops, the word leaked out. A note was slipped under Hiller's hotel door threatening his life. Something along the lines of "Direct and die."

Mirisch sent him home and rehired Hill. No director was going to risk being murdered to direct a *movie*. One might *commit* murder to direct a movie, but...

At that time on Oahu, you could easily have hired someone to do it for you. One morning a 6'3" local extra came to work looking wiped out. He said he had to take care of a yacht last night and it kept him up late. "What do you mean, 'take care of a yacht'?"

"You know. I had to blow it up."

Another morning he again looked like bad road. "Been yachting?" I joked.

"Nah, just some Chinese guy wouldn't pay up, only had to throw a couple of bricks through his windows. Lou, if you ever want anybody to disappear? $200."

We could not leave the island and I was battling boredom with Mai Tais. John Cullum's wife, Emily Frankel, came up with an idea to snap me out of my mild despair. I had told her and John about two teenage girls in Grandview who used to come to me for advice on subjects they couldn't talk about with their parents. "Write a play about it," she ordered.

I'd write some and after lifting a few, well, quite a few, Richard Harris and I would act the scenes at night in my hotel room. He was fun to be with. But there was this one night.

The Watts riots had just torn up Los Angeles. John Cullum and I and a few others were having drinks in the garden of Harris' house. Our host was telling us what idiots we Americans were about "the blacks."

"You have to do it like they do in Holland. They bring in a black, let him live with his customs for a week or so and then slowly start getting him accustomed to the Dutch way. Then there's no problem."

I had to take that to task. "That's just dumb and makes no sense at all. It's not like we bring over one black a week, we already have over ten million living here now. They are Americans! And you're saying—"

Island fever? He swung on me and we pounded on each other until the others separated us. But our revels that night had not ended.

Cullum, one of the most talented, thoughtful, and kindest of men, spoke with a mild Tennessee accent when not acting. The yacht-exploding extra was there that night. Cullum was toasted and leaning on a car. Because of Cullum's Southern accent, the big guy's haole-hatred must have doubled. He started walking toward Cullum, whose back was to us. I sensed what he was up to: "Don't touch him." The big guy turned to me: "Okay, brudder, then *you*."

He raised his hands in that karate stance thing you see in movies.

Don't ask me where it came from, but I stepped up to the big guy and said, "Take a step and you'll have a bullet in your belly."

He dropped his hands and backed away. He must have thought I had a gun with me, not unheard of in his circle.

I think Harris was afraid I'd sic a lawyer on him, and the next day he made nice and invited me for lunch, but no drinks. Smiling, he told me confidentially that the movie was so far behind schedule that they would have to dump big sections of the script to catch up.

The boredom of waiting days to act a little bit, sitting in hot sand, the disregard we experienced from management was maddening. We wanted to get the movie over with and get out. I showed George Justin how my character could be dropped out of the rest of the picture! No deal. Michael Constantine was the first to finish up. "I've served my time, I'm outta here," he said. We all liked Constantine, and as jealous as we all were, I threw him a small New Yorkers party in my hotel room, which had a balcony facing those striking Hawaiian sunsets. In the orange glow of the sinking sun we were drinking, telling war stories, wishing we could be on the plane back to New York with Constantine. The telephone rang, it was for Constantine. He listened and slammed down the receiver. "Shit! There was a scratch on the film, I have to stay another week. Shit!" He poured himself more vodka, looked out at the ocean and shouted, "Not another goddamn beautiful *sunset!!*"

As Harris anticipated, the producers were throwing out giant chunks of the script, including the rest of my part. My character's later years were to have a Mark Twain look. Twain got dumped too. A bit of movie trivia: In the movie *Argo*, the makeup man John Chambers, played by John Goodman, was in real life the John Chambers who did this makeup with Dan Striepeke.

So I was out of Hawaii, the state and the movie. Free, free at last! I called Harris to wish him well. He *was* well, his salary for the picture was $300,000, and to get his "script approval" he bargained for *another* $300,000. So that's what he was smiling about!

I returned to Los Angeles for a quick handful of acorns: Quinn Martin's *12 O'Clock High*. The director was William Graham, offbeat and talented, a 40-year-old motorcyclist pixie. The star of the series, an earnest Robert Lansing, and I finished a scene. Graham didn't say *cut*. Lansing and I improvised dialogue. Still no *cut*. Finally there was just nothing left to add, so we stopped and looked out at Graham. He was sitting 20 feet away in his director's chair engrossed in a yachting magazine. The assistant director hurried up to him,

"Billy!"

Talking into his magazine: "What?"

"The scene!"

Into his magazine: "Oh, *action*."

"No, Billy, the scene's *over*."

Never looking up: "Then *cut*."

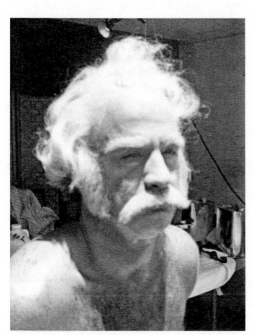

My best Mark Twain look; wish I had that hair now.

21

Cool Hand Luke

In 1965, I was finishing an episode of *The Virginian* at Universal when I got an offer to do an episode on a new television series in New York, *For the People*, starring William Shatner and Lonny Chapman. My established price in Los Angeles was 2,500 to 3,000 dollars. *For the People* offered 1,000. My summers were for my theater savings account so I declined. They came back with 1,500. I again said no. Back with a last offer of 1,750. Exasperated, I asked who was directing the episode. "Stuart Rosenberg."

"I'll do it," I said. I'd seen his work and thought he was an inventive director. The part had some good things to go for, a skanky, scroungy heroin addict. I finished my cowboy in California and went to my New York dope addict.

Right before my first scene, I noticed my hands were too clean for my junkie guy. I kneeled down and dragged my hands on the filthy sound stage floor, getting them as grimy as I could. Out of the corner of my eye I saw Rosenberg watching me. He gave me one note before a emotional scene I had in the witness chair. "Go for the fences." I must've gotten a lot of wood on it.

That episode was the thirteenth and final one, was concluded the day filmed television died in New York. Only *The Nurses* survived. In that Harlem studio, the farewell episodes of *The Defenders* and *For the People* were being shot. The stages were a carnival: crew, secretaries, actors, drinking goodbye to New York television employment. A story darted through the stages about E.G. Marshall, the star of *The Defenders*. At a long table, his cast and crew were eating and drinking and Marshall got up to propose a toast to their producer Herbert Brodkin. He laid a picture of Brodkin on the table. "Here's to our beloved Brodkin," he said, whereupon he unzipped his pants and proceeded to pee all over the picture.

The next year, a short-lived new series cranked up in New York, *Hawk*, starring Burt Reynolds. I did a guest shot on it and took to him immediately. Though he was still suffering divorce pangs from Judy Carne, he was easy to be with and Hollywood-savvy. He was slim and trim, but I reminded him when he was, as he put it, "a lardo." We had auditioned a few minutes apart for the same role in *Look We've Come Through* for Broadway. He got it. Hollywood was paying off for him. A few days into shooting, he was smiling broadly: He had just bought a used Cadillac for his father. He was happy and proud that he was financially able to do that.

No car, but Reynolds gave me his personal Hollywood cosmetic advice:

- A better smile? Cap your teeth.
- Need hair? Plant some or buy a hairpiece.

- Cheekbone emphasis? Have your molars removed.
- "Whatever you need to get done," he said, "get it done."

Later, when I worked with him on his *Dan August* series in Los Angeles, he came to work on my first day with his right wrist in a cast. I asked the producer Tony Spinner if Reynolds had broken it doing a stunt (he liked doing his own).

"A stunt? Nah. Doing this 'dramatic' scene, he slammed his fist down on a table. Broke his wrist *acting*."

Reynolds was a good guy. When he owned the Jupiter Theatre in Florida, he treated his guest actors with respect and warmth and provided luxurious living accommodations. Years later, when he closed the theatre, he gave Florida U, his alma mater, all of the lights, equipment, props, costumes, everything and anything that a drama school could use.

After *Hawk*, I went out to Los Angeles to do another *The Fugitive*. My modus operandi was to cash in my first class plane ticket and drive out. That way I got to stop by Oklahoma City, visit my folks, eat a chicken fry at the Lafayette and relax in the strengthening peace of their love.

The ticket refunds paid for my room and board in L.A. and I didn't have to rent a car. Rosenberg called me in to meet the producer for a movie called *Cool Hand Luke*, from a novel by Donn Pearce, an ex-convict. Sorta like *Ballad of the Sad Café*, just a meet, no audition. I was cast as Koko, who survives in the camp by sucking up to whatever prisoner held the most power among the convicts.

In Stockton, California, doubling for Florida, the sagging barracks and prison camp had been built to Cary Odell's set design. Spanish moss hung from the trees. Donn Pearce showed us how to use a shovel, how to talk without moving our lips, all the habits and tricks prisoners used to get by.

After a day's work, we'd go back to our Greentree Inn Motel to dance with each other, drink and play lots of poker. The bullshit flew fast and friendly. We developed an *esprit de corps* in no time. The poker games were not for big stakes, but Dennis Hopper and Warren Finnerty did lose their entire paychecks. Not too difficult with the low wages we were being paid. I was winning on luck and losing on stupidity.

One night a new actor arrived and dropped by the game. You've gotta picture

That guy who played Luke (Paul Newman) and me.

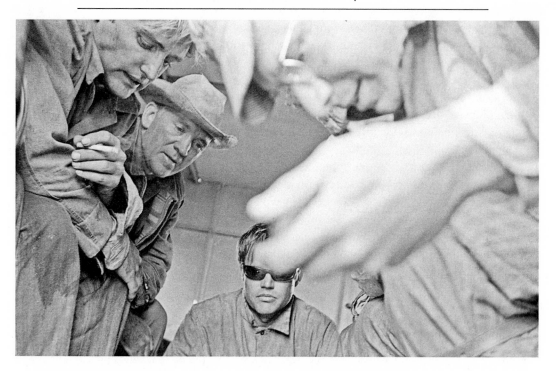

Between takes, Dennis Hopper, John McLiam, Joe Don Baker and Wayne Rogers in *Cool Hand Luke*.

Strother Martin, holding his cards with nicotine-stained fingers, ashes on his shirt, saliva on his lips.

New Actor: "Hi, Strother, whatcha been doin'?"

Strother, deadpan into his cards: "Ummmm … playgrounds, mostly."

New Actor backed out of the room to moral safety.

We all put our cards down and fell down laughing.

The poker games, the drinking, yes, the dancing, Rosenberg encouraged all of this because it made us a unit with nuances of our off-screen relationships. And how could we not respond to Paul Newman as our hero? A fine actor, a fine man, easy to be with over a drink, a stand-up guy, and terrific to act with. The motel converted a linen closet into a sauna for him, and his morning ritual included a sauna, 200 slant-board sit-ups, face dipped in ice water. We were all envious of his six-pack stomach, before that phrase was in the national vocabulary.

Small Town America. Nocturnal knocks on our doors, whispered "Hi, someone in the bar said you're in the movie…?" In the motel bar, Newman was introducing me to single malt Scotch, when a man and woman came to our table. The husband smiled, "Mr. Newman, it's my wife's fortieth birthday and she wanted to meet you."

Graciously Newman said, "Forty. Well, I know what that's like, I've been there."

"So for her present I wanted to give her *you*!"

The husband shoved his wife toward Newman and ran out of the bar. She stood with a shy smile on her face. Paul squirmed. I jumped up, "How about a dance?" I pulled the woman to the dance floor while Newman scooted out. I don't believe that America is rife with weirdos, but I do believe that a movie company draws them out of their holes.

Stuart Rosenberg, John McLiam and half of Harry Dean Stanton on *Cool Hand Luke*.

The dailies were set up in a room at the motel, and it was like a BYOB party. Conrad Hall was the cameraman and the film had a wonderful texture to it. Rosenberg's angles were fresh and though each of us might have found fault in our own performances, we found none in each other's. Wayne Rogers looked to me. We nodded. "This is one we're gonna be proud of."

Robert Mitchum had been cast opposite Newman, but the rumor was he took a hike a few weeks prior to shooting and was replaced with George Kennedy, which to my way of thinking was a blessing for the picture. However, all through the shooting, Kennedy was certain that Rosenberg didn't like him. "He never talks to me. Never says I'm doing a good job. Ignores me. Am I terrible?" I told him that I'd overheard an actor go up to Rosenberg and ask him why he never said, "Good job" or complimented the actor after a take.

"George, you know what Stuart told him? He said, 'I say *print*, don't I?'" Kennedy may have felt terrible then, but he felt a lot better after he won an Academy Award for that performance.

The movie was sneak-previewed in 1967 at a theater near UCLA. When Newman's name came on the screen, the packed house screamed in anticipation. The movie was a blast creatively, critically and commercially. The composer Lalo Schifrin and Kennedy got Oscars and Newman and screenwriters Donn Pearce and Frank Pierson were nominated. Rosenberg was nominated for a Directors Guild award. Nineteen years later, I had the fun of directing Wayne in the title role of *One Terrific Guy*, a movie for television which brought him a slide of terrific reviews.

With my *Luke* money, I again tried to buy my li'l red house and again the owner

Wayne Rogers also pointed a lot as a financial expert on Fox News! Here we're together again on the set of *One Terrific Guy*, nearly two decades after we worked together in *Cool Hand Luke*.

refused. No worthwhile play was in the offing. What with my summer commutes to Los Angeles and three movies, I had become known to some Los Angeles casting people and producers. Maybe I could make a living there. Not a slam-dunk decision to make. For over ten years I had meaningful times in New York, artistically, personally and professionally. There was a spirit of support from the classes, the Actors Studio, the actors, the fans of the theater and my friends. The house on the hill had hosted many creative surges and discoveries, wounds and pleasures. Would a move be another journey with worthwhile rewards? If I could make a decent living in California, then being able to afford a good life for a someday family and children would be reward enough. Children as yet unborn.

22

Hello, Hollywood...
Hello, Anyone There?

When I left my little red house for California, Josh Logan's desperate "We have got to have a hit" had made me more of an agnostic than a supplicant to the Holier Than Thou Theater. "Got to have a hit" seemed to demean my belief in actor as artist. So many of us devoted hours of our lives trying to enjoin our talents and techniques to convince ourselves and audiences that we can finesse all styles of acting. Polonius presented our challenges to us: "...either for tragedy, comedy, history, pastoral, pastoral-comical, historical-pastoral, tragical-historical, tragical, comical-historical-pastoral, scene individable, or poem unlimited. Seneca cannot be too heavy, nor Plautus too light."

A bit beyond Sense Memory.

Using the *Cool Hand Luke* money, I left the little red house in the dying days of 1966 and nestled into a three-bedroom house in a zoned-for-horses street in Burbank. I had no credit rating to qualify for a mortgage loan, but thanks to the negotiating persuasiveness of Wayne Rogers, the owner carried my mortgage payments for $200 a month. No Hudson River view or wild raspberries, but a grapevine, kumquat tree (whatever a kumquat is), orange tree and avocado tree. The only odd element was the realtor's bumper sticker, "Do Not Recognize Red China."

On the first day of 1967, I got a call from Dennis Weaver. "A decent man." You don't hear that much in this part of the country, or in politics. Dennis Weaver deserves that appellation. He was the salt of the earth, and his wife Gerry the pepper. In 1965 he had been the driving force in establishing a West Coast Actors Studio. I got to know him while directing him at the Studio in a play I wrote. Another group of those wonderful for-free Actors Studio actors joined Weaver, Lesley Warren (again), Lane Bradbury, Michael Conrad, Peggy McKay, Martin Landau, Barbara Bain, Joanne Linville... Treasures, every one.

Anyway, on Day One of 1967 he asked me if I could come over to his house and read a movie he was going to do in the Philippines. It was set in World War II and Weaver would be playing a ne'er-do-well plotting to steal some Japanese gold. I sat in his den and read it. My summary to Weaver: "It's shit."

"Well, I know *that*. Have any ideas?"

A few came to mind and he went straight to the telephone. "I've got the writer to re-do the script." He was talking to the producer, Keith Larsen, whose wife, Vera Miles, was to co-star. Weaver was flying to the Philippines in three weeks and that was my deadline. Larsen offered Writers Guild minimum, $1,800, which I accepted. I had never written a screenplay so I grabbed my *Luke* script to study the format. With a beat-up portable type-

Me and Dennis Weaver. A fine actor, and a decent man.

writer and on onionskin paper I started the rewrite from page one, modeling Weaver's character on a few Bogart roles ("I stick my neck out for nobody!!"). The existential loner with hidden morals and beliefs. I got to work.

Two weeks into the screenplay, Poppa had a stroke. Theo flew to Oklahoma City from St. Louis, Jim from New York, and I from Los Angeles. Poppa was in a coma. Mom was quiet but hopeful. We could do nothing but wait. One evening I was in our small kitchen writing, trying to meet my deadline, when the hospital called. We rushed to St. Anthony's hospital. Too late. We took turns holding his hand and talking to him. There in that hospital room, I spoke what I had felt all my life, but had never told him, that I loved him. As a family we didn't say "I love you" to each other daily, we didn't have to. My father was an exuberant man, passionate, hot-headed, funny, intelligent, uneducated and honest. Hundreds of people passed in and out of his life, hundreds came to his funeral to show their respect for the Chicken Fry King, to say, "Goodbye, Jimmy." People loved him.

As I was leaving the house for the airport, Mom put her hands softly on my arms and looked at me with seldom-seen tears in her eyes. "Lou, did I ever tell you … that I love you?" And she hugged me goodbye.

The day before Weaver's flight to the Philippines, I gave him the wrinkled onionskin pages of *Mission Batangas*, no scene numbers, no carbon copies, and off he went. The first of February he called from Manila: "Listen, we can't blow up a bridge like in the script and other stuff. Suppose you could come over? You'd be doing me a favor, too, if you'd travel with Gerry. She's coming." Weaver's wife Gerry is one of the best traveling partners there is. Fun, good storyteller and a good heart. We landed in Tokyo for a layover. It was cold and as we walked from the airplane to the terminal I shivered. "You warm enough, Gerry? There's a little nip in the air." Until she slugged my arm, I didn't realize what I'd said.

The Filipino crew was hired at a flat fee for the entire picture. The sound mixer got $500 for the *picture*. If it went a month or two months, or three months, still $500. Talk about non-union.

They were shooting in a small village and I walked about trying to get a feel of the rhythms and characteristics of the Filipinos, much as I would as an actor. In my meanderings I saw children with the telltale pattern of ringworm in their shaved heads. Some of the little boys wore no pants, their penises infected and scabrous. I talked with a man who spoke English about their diets, which included a preponderance of white rice. I said, "Eat the brown rice, it has many more vitamins and fiber. It's healthier, better for your children."

He looked at me. "If we ate brown rice, we be no better than pigs."

With filming completed, we all returned to Los Angeles. Keith Larsen suggested that I send my screenplay version to the Writers Guild for a screen credit arbitration. I did not know what that was, but, son of a gun, the WGA granted me a solo writing credit, and to this day the laser disc label of *Mission Batangas* says "Screenplay by Lewis Antonio."

Fresh from the Philippines, I was offered the part of an Armenian immigrant in a Western TV series, *The Road West*, starring Barry Sullivan and Andrew Prine. In my heart I dedicated my performance to my father, the little immigrant. Opposite me was Cloris Leachman. I locked and rocked in the part and knew it. After one particularly intricate scene, Cloris asked me with a smirk, "Are you going to play it that way?"

I didn't answer her. She

Rewriting in my office in the Philippines.

went to the director Paul Henreid, who had been a movie star in the '40s. To name just two of many, *Casablanca* and *Now Voyager*.

"Paul, are you going to let him play it that way?" Leachman smirked.

"Yes, why not?"

"Well, it's so obvious!"

Henreid came to me. "It's just right, Lou, don't change it."

He knew Leachman was trying to undermine my performance. He had acted opposite Bette Davis.

Lesley Anne Warren asked if

Left: **With Cloris Leachman; no embrace considered.** *Below:* **Celebrating at the Sands. Clockwise from left: Jon Peters, Lesley Anne Warren, Jane Elliot, Rudy Tartaglia, Lane Bradbury and me.**

I would go to Las Vegas with her and her fiancé Jon Peters. May 13, 1967, a black limousine pulled to my curb, the driver opened the limo door and Warren's friend Jane Elliot was inside dressed up and pretty. Then I met the husband-to-be and his best man-to-be, Rudy Tartaglia, a husky, somber and quiet young man silently sitting in the front seat with the driver. Dressed in a white suit, Peters was energetic, attractive and bristling with charm. In the three-hour trip to Las Vegas, we drank champagne, told stories and got hair tips from Peters. ("Never rub-dry your hair with a towel, take the towel and squeeze the water out.")

Waiting for us in front of the Sands Hotel was its publicity manager, reporters, lotsa smiles, lotsa hustle. Our group was escorted to the penthouse. Peters pulled me aside. "Lou, would you be my best man?"

"What? Jon, you said Rudy..."

"It's fine with him. Will you do it?"

"Jon, it seems—"

"Rudy is for it. Come on."

"Well, okay, yeah, I guess so..."

I didn't understand why I was cast as his best man, until he escorted me down the row of reporters.

"And this is my best man Lou Antonio, co-starring with Paul Newman in *Cool Hand Luke*. Hi, this is Lou Antonio, my best man, co-starring with Paul Newman in *Cool Hand Luke*. Hello..."

Peters was Hollywood-nimble, quick and sniffing a future. He found one.

I hadn't been in California six months when Estelle Parsons called from New York. She was going to do a Tennessee Williams play on Broadway called *The Seven Descents of Myrtle* and wanted me to be in it. There were two temptations, acting with Parsons again and being directed by José Quintero. Parsons sent me the play.

The characters were strong, but I felt the play was not. I hadn't been settled in Burbank for even a year and wasn't keen on going back to New York for a play that I felt would not propel me creatively or professionally. I declined. Though Parsons was nominated for a Tony, it closed after 29 performances.

A provocative two-person play to be done at the 1967 Berkshire Theatre Festival in Stockbridge, Massachusetts, came my way. Written by Lewis John Carlino, it was called *The Exercise*. I would also have right of first refusal if the play went to Broadway. Best of all, I would be playing opposite Anne Jackson. The characters are two actors rehearsing a play that have to experience and act damn near *everything*. Love, hate, birthing (Annie), being birthed (me), murder, sex and whatever et ceteras are left.

The parts and moments were a continual challenge and we got one of the most sage pieces of advice I'd ever been given. Eli Wallach, Jackson's husband, said to us, "Don't try to be brilliant." I gotta repeat that in italics, *"Don't try to be brilliant."* In other words, just do the work.

However, the director Alfred Ryder was an actor and wanted an Alfred Ryder performance. We were too far apart as personalities and as actors. He was 20 years older, a bit of a boozer, physically weak, theatrical, humorless and distracted. He also tried to get Jackson to play it as his ex-wife Kim Stanley might have played it. Annie would have none of it.

Eli Wallach offered words of wisdom.

Stockbridge is an art haven. William Gibson (*Two for the Seesaw*) and the conductor Eric Leinsdorf had places there and Arthur Penn was in residence. Al Pacino did *Does the Tiger Wear a Necktie* and Frank Langella was doing his first *Dracula*, Viveca Lindfors was in *The Merchant of Venice*. I stayed at the estate of Beatrice Straight and her husband Peter Cookson, a few minutes out of Stockbridge. They'd had a five-acre lake dug on their property, and I would whip around in their motorboat yelling my lines. Between that and working on an exciting script with an exciting actress, I was having a terrific summer. And the reviews...

"*The Exercise* was a sellout for the length of its run. Anne Jackson and Lou Antonio were hailed for their performances."—*New York Times*

"Lou Antonio is the actor. Bluff, boyish, commonsensical and funny."—*Boston Globe*

"Both Antonio and Miss Jackson come through with a scintillating performance exhibiting every skill in the actor's kit."—John LaFontana, *Springfield Union*

I returned to Burbank, anticipating that Broadway call. A few weeks later, over a drink with fellow actor James Farentino, he mentioned that he had been sent a script of *The Exercise* with an offer. He was surprised that I hadn't known about it. So was I. Because of my "right of first refusal," they were contractually obligated to offer it to me or they could be sued. My agent called. They made a sham offer of $350 a week. My last Broadway salary was $1,000. Someone didn't want me, and that salary un-offer was the suit-free way out. I'd been done in and didn't know why.

Stephen Joyce was hired to play my part. One night while they were in previews, Annie

Top: In *The Exercise*, with Anne Jackson. *Bottom:* My last hurrah on the stage was a fine one. But it was time to say goodbye (Lane Bradbury, pictured).

called me from New York. "Keep a bag packed. I'm not saying anything, Lou, but keep a bag packed."

That's the last I heard from anyone about it. I unpacked my bag. At a party a year or so later, I pushed Ryder into a kitchen corner. "It wasn't me!" he wailed. "It was Oliver and Lyn [the producers]."

"But why? No one has ever told me why."

"They just didn't want you."

That was not a cleansing answer and, remembering our creative clashes at Stockbridge, probably not an honest one. The Broadway production opened in April 1968 and closed in less than a week. Even though it was a failure, it would have been worth recreating that complex character and acting with Anne Jackson.

After 13 years and 80 plays, *The Exercise* was my last stage performance. Theater was the solid foundation of whatever I would continue to seek and to build upon. I felt my acting experience was incomplete when I left New York; the great roles that were still ahead of me would never be tested. For better or worse, what I carry from those years will always be a part of me. I'll change one word from that tired line that TV cops always say to a victim's survivor: "I'm sorry for *my* loss."

PART TWO

Hollywood

Sometimes Ah'm Up, Sometimes Ah'm Down, oh, Yes, Lawd
Sometimes Ah'm Almost to da' Ground
Oh, Yes

—("Nobody Knows the Trouble I've Seen")

From treading the boards to a clapper board...

23

Shatner, a Bear, a Nun

I am not in Grandview any more. The show biz twister had sucked me up and dumped me in Burbank.

My previous bucks-in-the-bucket summers had calloused my fears of freeways, earthquakes, drought, mudslides, lung-blackening air and angry traffic. I was not cowed by the move, but as I unboxed my books I knew full well that being in show business *anywhere* guaranteed gaps of insecurity and unemployment.

Hollywood is flirtatious and friendly to the young and promising. Interesting roles were available and one that lured me was cuttingly anti-racist and me in tights. It was a *Star Trek* episode, "Let That Be Your Last Battlefield." Lokai, my character, was half white, half black, while Bele, Frank Gorshin's character, was half black, half white. That is, my right side was white, Gorshin's was black, and the dialogue was purple. We had one scene with an explosive argument between Gorshin and me. All Captain Kirk (Bill Shatner) had to do was throw in an occasional platitude of maybe two lines.

Gorshin and I were doing a two-shot with Shatner off-camera. The scene was going well, Shatner forgot his line, made a joke and the camera was cut. Take two, emotions were sparking, and again Shatner screwed up, laughed it off, leaving Gorshin and me with our guts hanging out.

During take three, Shatner again screwed us and tried to be funny. The director, Jud Taylor, came down hard on Shatner: "Two actors trying their best, you're hurting their performances and how damned unprofessional you are!" Shatner grandly exited the stage, proclaiming, "No one talks to me like that in front of my crew." The crew and cast sat around waiting for his return. An hour later, Shatner came back to the set, not a word or apology to anyone. We did our scene with Shatner reciting his off-camera lines so perfunctorily that Gorshin and I would have been better off without him. Poor Jud Taylor, a good guy and a good director, had to look at his wristwatch and print the take. I think this might be why.

Some weeks later, I was being directed by Ralph Senensky on a Burt Reynolds series, *Dan August*. My role was of an addicted, one-legged, nutsy war veteran. My guy had a page-long wacko monologue and after take one I knew I could do it better, but Ralph said "print." I gave him our signal for another take, but he called out the next set-up to the crew. With one leg strapped to the back of my thigh, I started hopping over to him. He moved away from me, I hopped over half of the sound stage chasing him. The panicked a.d. yelled "Lunch!" As the crew left the stage, Ralph walked over to me. I leaned into my crutch.

"Ralph, I gave you our signal, I can do it a lot better. Just one more."

He looked at me for a beat, then: "Lou, I was directing a *Star Trek* last season, and got

Star Trek's "Let This Be Your Last Battlefield," with myself, Nichelle Nichols and Bill Shatner.

half a day behind. They fired me, spread the word. No one would hire me. This is my first episode in a year."

*   *   *

I had written a screenplay from the play I directed at the Actors Studio West. A wise writer named Howard Rodman read my screenplay and advised, "Sell it, then walk away from it or they'll break your heart." Universal offered what I thought was too modest a price for it, $50,000. I asked someone how *I* could get to direct my movie.

"Direct something. A television show or something."

Oh, okay.

In 1968, after *Mission Batangas*, Dennis Weaver was doing the successful TV series *Gentle Ben* in Florida. He played a game warden with a wife, son and Ben, a bear. He asked me if I wanted to try directing one. Oh, yes, verily.

Weaver thought it might help if I acted in one first. "Kinda get the feel of the show," he said.

The acting part was easy, but preparing to direct led to sleepless Miami nights. Blocking in the theater is spatially simple. Upstage, downstage, right, left, center and limited spots in between. The audience looks at it from one place. For the camera there are 360 degrees of them, *plus* the camera moving, camera moving at different speeds, different heights and with different lenses! As an actor, my prep was mostly psychological, character choices, voice, physicality, subtext, emotion, place and time. Tell all that to a bear named Ben, hopefully gentle. A strong plot element in the story included Ben in some wrestling sequences. A wrestling bear? They don't teach Bear Directing at the Actors Studio. Now as a virgin film director I was pushed into answering the first question on my first day of shooting. The cameraman's "What's your first set-up?"

My first day directing.

No problem. Just an escaping panther running through 200 screaming extras in a carnival midway! Nowhere in directing books is there a "How to Direct Panthers in a Crowd."

Says I (with conjured confidence):

"Up high, see the whole thing."

"A 35, okay?"

"Yeah, right! A 35. Right."

Then I said it, my very first "Action!"

Extras screamed, the stunt men and animal handlers did their duty, as did a well-trained escaping panther. Weaver was hopping around, directing the extras, giving me all the support he could and still doing his acting chores.

My assistant director nudged me: "Lou, ya got it. Say 'cut.'" "*Cut! Print!*" says I.

Weaver was always fighting to better the series from scripts to casting. He got the producers to grudgingly raise the guest star salaries to attract a higher level of actors. I think the producers picked that panther episode for me as a way to lay out to Weaver, "See, we brought one of your guys down here and he screwed up. So that's it, we will run this series our way."

With Weaver's help and hustle, I finished on schedule and was offered two more episodes. Because of my meager knowledge of the mechanics of production, I was not at ease directing, and, well, finishing the day's work seemed to be the major objective. The stress outweighed any creative reward. As an actor, no matter how bad the script, how stupid the director, once you're on stage or on your mark, the actor is in his creative circle and there is nothing between impulse and expression. As a director there is *everything* between: a schedule, a late prop, no prop, a late actor, a bad actor, a drunk actor, network notes, producer notes, weather, camera problems, an airplane or a bear that won't take direction. That's a partial list.

I guess adversity is good for you, I don't know, ask Nietzsche. I was in my first day of prep for the second *Gentle Ben* when I got a telephone call from a nurse at St. Anthony's

hospital in Oklahoma City. Mom had just had a heart attack. I flew out of Miami that afternoon, not bothering to take my script with me. Theo and Jim were by Mom's bed in intensive
care. This was a year and a half after Poppa died and my brothers thought that Mom literally
had suffered a broken heart. Weaver called to find out how she was, and would I be coming
back? He said he could direct the first day's shoot if that helped.

Mom and my brothers talked about it. My sweet mother took my hand and said she'd
just worry about me if I stayed. Theo and Jim shooed me away. I flew back to Florida barely
remembering what my script was about, much less having any idea of how to shoot it.

I got there in time for the six a.m. call and was driven to my location, a swamp. The
animal *du jour* was an alligator. Albert Salmi, an excellent Actors Studio actor, was the
guest star. That was good news. The bad news was that he'd injured his ankle playing tennis
and had an awful limp that the character should not have. How to hide it? I had to invent
some sleight of hand. Salmi would take a step out of his scene, cut, action, one step into
his next scene, no walking, thus, no limping. Mostly standing still Salmi breezed through
it.

At night I was so exhausted that I could barely read the next day's scenes, much less
plan them. Every day it was the same, make it up on the spot, fall asleep at night, wing it

Let's see, where should I put the alligator…

again the next day. Amongst mosquitoes, slithery things, alligators and a lame actor, I'd scan a scene, take a deep breath and say, "Put the camera here." My second show.

Working with the actors was easy, but not knowing the technical short cuts of directing shoved a lot of pressure into those long hours. Thanks to the crew and the actors, a disaster was avoided. Finishing that episode did give me a measure of trust in my directorial self. I don't mean I was suddenly this top-notch director, but I carried a bucket of confidence away from it, Nietzsche got another notch on *his* belt, and Mom lived to be 92.

I did not like directing. The emphasis was on the budget and not on quality or an unconventional interpretation of a scene. A phrase I later came to despise from some producers and crew members was, "It's only television."

Gentle Ben was a definite success in the ratings and "The Smiling Cobra," Jim Aubrey, president of CBS, was suffering mocking sneers from NBC and ABC for the "lowbrow" programming of his *Petticoat Junction* and *Beverly Hillbillies* hits. Nielsen envy, CBS was bigger.

To woo his colleagues' respect, Aubrey decided that his half-hour so-called trailer trash hits were undermining what he wanted his reputation to be. A few months later, from the warm heart of show biz, *Gentle Ben's* demise was announced in the trade papers. That's how Dennis Weaver learned his series was cancelled, from *Variety*.

I went back to acting.

That year at the Actors Studio West, I formed an evening acting class. The emphasis was on acting exercises rather than scene study. Sally Field was starring in a television series, *The Flying Nun*, and the show was creatively frustrating for her. She wanted to extend her range, find a technique, she wanted respect. She came to my evening exercise class with determination and courage to delve into the Method. Her first night in class, I constructed a sense memory exercise for the group. "You are all in a bar, make it whatever bar you know, or invent one, no speaking, only behavior and responding to the other customers. I'll whisper each of you a sense memory to work on." To Field: "Pick a time when you were extremely cold. Find one spot on your body that was the coldest and try to recreate that, and, Sally, don't act the cold. Just try recreating it."

I turned from the stage and as I started to sit down, I looked up. Field's nose was red and runny, her eyes watery. Before my ass hit the chair, she had it.

Field asked me to direct an episode of *The Flying Nun*. With reluctance I met her producer Jon Epstein, and with reluctance he gave me a single episode. Epstein was wary of the new kid. As well he should have been, as proven by my very first Hollywood camera set-up. Farrah Fawcett, this sparkling, fresh-faced Texas youngster was in a two-piece bathing suit in a swimming pool scene. The cameraman asked where I wanted the camera and his assistant handed me the parallax viewfinder to show them my shot. I squatted low and lifted the prehistoric viewfinder up to my eye.

"See, we're down here shooting up and as Farrah walks by the pool we pan off her to the guy with the beach ball. Okay?"

It was silent on the set. I looked up and saw the crew frowning at me. Some averted their eyes. The camera assistant leaned over, took the viewfinder from my hands, turned it around and said quietly, "Mr. Antonio, you're looking through the wrong end of the finder."

My first shot in Hollywood. Mr. Antonio wanted to be at the bottom of the pool.

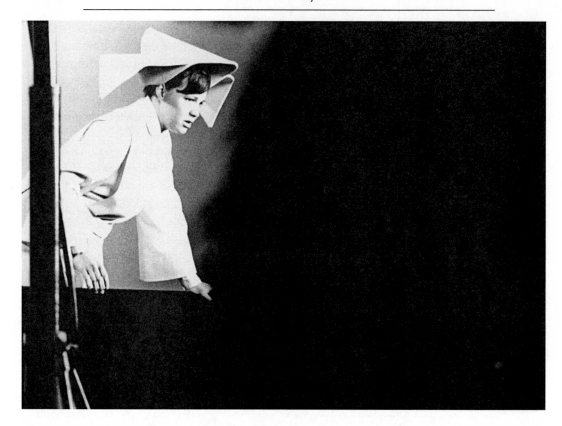

Sally Field's talent still keeps her afloat.

Epstein came to set on my second day of the three-day schedule. He had just seen my first day's dailies. As he approached me, I asked, "So am I fired?"

"No, I'd like you to do two more this season."

Screen Gems was a tight-fisted organization and carved into every director's head was its credo "On Time and On Budget." Break either of those commandments and the director never worked for Screen Gems again. It was the same at Universal, which had over 20 series on the air. Directors got work if they were "fast and good." Notice which adjective is first.

After another *Nun*, Screen Gems hired me to direct, hot diggity, my first one-hour show, *Here Come the Brides*, a six-day Western. Joan Blondell, Bobby Sherman, David Soul, horses and mud. Nailed it. On time and on budget. Great. Next they booked me for a half-hour comedy, *Nancy*, with two charming young leads, Renée Jarrett and John Fink, and Academy Award winner Celeste Holm. Overflowing with ideas of how to fix the script, I strode into the office of the series creator-producer and writer of my episode, Sidney Sheldon. Surely my notes would save his script. After all, I had directed *three* episodes of Hollywood television, and what could this old guy possibly know about my young 20-ish characters? He must have been like *50*. Effusive in my insights, I expounded on how to "save your script." As I rattled on, I noticed a short shelf on a lonely wall holding some sort of naked guy thing. I peered more closely at the statue. Naked guy was Oscar! I squinted at the plaque.—Best Screenplay *The Bachelor and the Bobby Soxer*. An Academy Award! My mouth couldn't move. I looked around his office. Oh, me, leather-bound copies and plaques telling me this Sheldon fellow had created and written *I Dream of Jeannie*, *The Patty Duke Show* and oh, good grief, another naked guy, a co-screenplay Oscar for *Easter Parade*. My effusion deflated, I thanked Mr. Sheldon for his time and shuffled out. A gracious man, he kindly had foregone the opportunity, and the right, to pierce my bloat with Oscar Wilde's "I am not young enough to know everything."

24

Jerry Lewis to Coppola

"Sometimes the enemy is us."

—Walt Kelly

In 1969, a Studio member was friends with Jerry Lewis and she invited me to watch him direct and act in a movie at Warner Brothers called *Which Way to the Front?* He had a new tool that she thought I'd be interested in. (Producers call special equipment "toys," directors call them "tools.") Never mind the tool, I was excited about meeting Jerry Lewis! Back in younger days I was nuts about Martin and Lewis movies. When I was in junior high they came through Oklahoma City with their stage show, a *Hellzapoppin*-type craziness, running through the audience, yelling, joking with the audience. I'd never seen anything like it. So of course, let's go watch Jerry Lewis.

The first scene I watched was a Nazi car chase on the Warners back lot. While the actor Lewis was playing a fake German soldier, the director Lewis yelled *cut*, jumped out of the car and hurried over to the new tool, a playback of the shot on a videotape monitor. What a deal, I thought! He made a few corrections with the placement of the camera, did another take, reviewed it on the cool tool and printed it. Lewis and I were introduced and I was surprised at how cordial he was and that he knew my work. "How do you direct, Lou, from storyboards?"

"No, sir, I block it and then set the camera."

"But that's wrong. Let me show you."

His script was filled with diagrams and camera placements and little dotted lines.

"And here, read a few pages of this." In the back of his script, there must have been at least 100 pages with the title *Jerry Lewis, on Film*, or something like that. I read not only how he directed, but how *everyone* should direct. It was thorough as hell, filled with dense theories of directing theatrical motion pictures. Good stuff, good grief. I doubted I could ever understand or learn all of that. I wasn't even sure *what* I was supposed to learn.

They finished outside and went on a sound stage to rehearse the next scene, which was between Lewis and Sid Miller, a comic actor with years of experience from vaudeville on. As they rehearsed, Lewis exploded. "You call that funny? You wouldn't know funny if it fell on you!" Lewis tossed his cigarette lighter high into the air.

"Don't anybody look for it, it's only gold. I've got a hundred of 'em."

He continued his attack on Sid Miller, who stood silently nodding. Would humiliation help an actor find his funny bone? I didn't know. There is some insight in "Never meet the person you admire." I left.

Directing had been exciting because it was a crash course, and every day was a test.

You passed or you flunked, but you learned. As an actor I'd never had much pressure, even on opening nights. After the Screen Gems directing, I happily returned to acting and teaching at the Studio. Raquel Welch joined us. She carried so much movie star baggage that it had to be shed to get to her talent. First things first. Welch on stage alone, I shouted commands at her, not letting her think or act.

Roll on the floor.

Do the hoochie coochie and sing "Silent Night."

Be a baby learning to walk.

Be a monkey, a cow, a man.

Stuff like that. She did them without a flinch. In class she started applying some of our techniques playing Portia in a scene from *The Merchant of Venice*. Her truth quotient jumped. She understood and appreciated that she was there to *work*, not to be idolized or be a wet dream.

In 1969, Strasberg opened his privately operated Strasberg Institute in Los Angeles and he asked me to teach a beginning acting class. I agreed to do it for one semester. After one of his New York classes, an actor might typically ask Strasberg, "When I was working on the two sense memories simultaneously, music and the taste of bourbon, I couldn't hold both at the same time, I'd usually lose the music. What was I doing wrong?" Stuff like that. After about two weeks at the Institute, a young James Dean wannabe asked if he could see me after class. Of course, says I.

"Mr. Antonio, I was wondering…"

"Yes?"

"Would you look at my composite and pick out the best picture for my 8 × 10?"

An 8 × 10? I lit into him: "To get a job? You don't even know where the switch is, much less have a key to start the car. If by chance you got the motor started, would you know how to steer, shift, know where you're even headed or how to get there?!"

So many, so impatient. To quote William Saroyan, "No foundation, all the way down the line…"

On the way home that night, I kept thinking about the young actor. Of course he believes he's ready for Hollywood. He thinks that to be a *good* actor is not a prerequisite to a career. Why couldn't he be on a series? He's seen the likes of Larry Wilcox, Lee Majors, Dennis Cole playing leads on TV series. After all, he didn't come to Hollywood to be an actor, he came to Hollywood to be a star.

East was different from West. New York actors had a certain cachet in the '50s and '60s, especially ones that had been on Broadway. Our goal was not so much flying the agent's flag of "Get your face on camera," but rather in gaining skills and confidence from acting every day, working on scenes in apartments, on park benches, in subways, and sometimes on a stage in front of an actual paying audience. Learning from those breathing, coughing, laughing, crying, bored, expectant people reacting to us, and we to them. Actors and audience sharing time and space.

We theater snobs, however, were also grounded by the nagging reality of rent, food, drink, classes. Our West Coast brethren had much to teach us. Once I was acting in a TV show at Universal and I got a call from an actor asking me to get him a drive-on pass so he could have lunch with me in the Universal commissary. I didn't know the actor particularly well, but I got him a drive-on. He rubbernecked and table-hopped with charm and energy, playing the room, never touching his tuna fish sandwich. As we walked out, with his sandwich bagged, he thanked me. "What for?" I asked.

"Commissaries are a great place to be seen. A casting person, a director, a producer might see you, and it might remind them you'd be right for a part. Same deal for parties."

The execution of his determination made good sense. Dollars and sense.

The likes of Harrison Ford made even more dollar sense. Ford was on the Charlie Rose PBS show to promote his latest $100 million movie. After the standard film clip and small talk, Rose tried to draw out of Ford the suppressed, hidden artist that supposedly ferments in every star. Rose kept prodding Harrison, whose movies had easily grossed over a billion dollars, with questions like, "If a small meaningful movie were offered to you, you know, for no money, something meaningful, wouldn't you want to do a film like that?" Ford looked him square in the eye and replied, "Charlie, I make my *living* as an actor."

Rose shuffled his notes and changed the subject.

Bob Booker and George Foster, who wrote and produced the 1962 comedy album *The First Family*, which sold over seven million albums, were producing a musical for Warner Brothers in 1969. Originally the lead role was offered to Donald Sutherland, but for some reason when he passed they hired me, me the Method Guy, for a far-out comedy lead. Good thing they never asked Preminger or Amateur for a reference.

The plot of *The Phynx* concerned a young Albanian prince who loves old Hollywood and has kidnapped some former movie stars, who he holds captive in Albania. The U.S.

"More stars than in the heavens" are in *The Phynx*.

My hair, Larry Hankin and Ultra Violet, with an unidentified actress in the background.

Super Secret Agency, bossed by Mike Kellin, divines that the only way to rescue the stars is to form a rock 'n' roll band—the Phynx—and get them invited by the prince to perform.

A few of the 25 kidnapped stars of yore: Butterfly McQueen, Ruby Keeler, Colonel Sanders, Martha Raye, Dorothy Lamour, Johnny Weissmuller, Joan Blondell, the Lone Ranger and Tonto, Edgar Bergen and Charlie McCarthy, Ed Sullivan. They'd all had their days of wine and roses and they seemed delighted to be back on a sound stage. I was in the midst of nostalgia and motion picture history, memories, stories, warm and cozy and funny. It was a mix of actors of then and *now.* Of the now generation was Larry Hankin from Chicago's Second City doing a hilarious parody of record producer Phil Spector. Playing his foot-massaging assistant was the French-born beauty Ultra Violet of Andy Warhol fame. Kellin, Ultra and I were rehearsing a scene in a mixing booth watching the Phynx run a song.

The three of us stood there being lit while Mademoiselle Violet stared at the brightly colored knobs on the mixing board. Then she very softly said, "Look at dose knobs. I want to suck every one of dem." Mike and I froze and broke into a sweat at the same time.

As much fun as it was to make, it was hardly a career booster. The only time *The Phynx* played in a theater was when previewed in Orange County. Well, no, a friend said she may have seen *The Phynx* in Mexico, but she wasn't sure. It could have been the water.

Then came a call to test for the part of Sonny in Francis Ford Coppola's *The Godfather* at his place in San Francisco. As I was waiting to audition, Coppola came out of a reading to answer a phone call, apparently from James Caan. "Jimmy," he whispered, "just relax. I have to go through all this for Paramount. You, Al and Bobby will be doing it. Relax."

Coppola had me and Adam Roarke (auditioning for the Pacino part) improvise on 16mm film. All my Sonny prep was for naught; he had me improv the part of the other brother, Fredo. Coppola set up the improv: "Lou, you are now a big cheese at this hotel in Vegas and showing your brother the room that you've got for him. Impress him."

An actor couldn't have asked for a better audience than Coppola. During the take, he would laugh as I jabbered about my heart-shaped Jacuzzi, girls with big tits, I don't know what I said, but he was enjoying it. A week later, Coppola and his casting director Fred Roos called me at home. Maybe because I somewhat physically resembled Brando, they offered me Fredo. I was now settled in California. Roos told me the deal. I was to pay my own way back to New York, pay my own living expenses, and the salary offered was SAG scale, $1100 a week minus 250 dollars withholding. I was resistant.

"Francis, paying my own way, I'd literally *lose* money on what you're offering."

"But, Lou, everyone is working for less. Marlon's salary is deferred, Jimmy, Al, Duvall, all below their quotes."

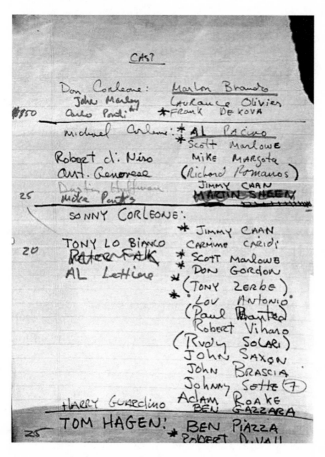

Early cast list for *The Godfather* enshrined at the Coppola winery in Geyserville, California.

"Guys, Fredo is not a high-profile part. We're trying to have a baby, there's a problem and the doctor bills are mounting. I've just started directing and it's worth more for me to learn about directing than play Fredo. Financially and personally, I can't afford your offer. But thank you."

The offer didn't seem a fair one, and once more I had not foreseen what the film might bring to me in the future between Coppola, Paramount, playing Brando's son, calling attention to my acting… My decision never gave me night sweats, and there's no way to determine if the role would have brought me back to Broadway or films in important parts. One aspect of my decision that I regret is missing the experience of working with Coppola and that incredible group of actors in a film masterpiece.

I never got a call to audition for another Coppola movie. But I do drink his wines.

Coppola's restlessness and creative reserves have not dwindled. In June of 2016 Coppola invested his time and money into a "different way of shooting." In July of 2016 Coppola put together an experimental project at UCLA quite unlike the filmmaking norm of Hollywood. With sets and green screen he rehearsed a twenty page scene for several weeks with twenty-five actors, a full crew, fifty cameras and shot those twenty pages once, like an opening night on Broadway. No added coverage, no "Cut. One more." The coverage was done with selected angles from carefully hidden cameras. Okay, Birdman is being revered by moviemakers for its extended no-coverage scenes. But Coppola seems to be going beyond that. He had done the experiment a year before in Oklahoma City with a different group of actors. As he learns the bad and the beautiful from each adventure he will eventually solve the problems. Here is another newbie. That singular Opening Night was somehow simultaneously viewed in selected homes, a few classrooms, by some professionals, and hell, maybe a bar or two. Did he rent a satellite or what? My sources do not know. We wish Francis Coppola success, and hopefully we all will be the audience of his daring and talent.

A Mixed Bag

Trying to think positively, I theorized that the move to California had been the right decision. Even though I wasn't earning a lot of money, employment was steadier than in the theater, and I was learning this directing stuff. At that time in television, directors were the lowest paid of the creative teams. For the director, a half-hour episode paid $1,300, a one-hour episode $3,000. Yes, a guest star on most hour episodes got $2,500, but that was for only six days, whereas the director's job required 15 days. Fortunately, guest shots still came my way.

Back in my New York days, we Broadway-ites sneered at the seven-year contracts demanded by television series. I was one of them. When a Hollywood producer named Dick Dorso wanted me for the lead in a series pilot, I smiled benignly and turned him down. After all, I was of *the theeatuh*. Now was I of Hollywood? Oh, well, artistic considerations were seldom fretted over in television, whereas learning about directing film was compelling.

The motion picture producer-director Roger Corman was attending my acting classes at the Actors Studio. He'd directed 50 movies, and produced probably that many, yet here he was attending an acting class. A quiet, middle-aged man, he craved to know about this working-with-actors business. He asked me to direct a movie he was producing called *Boxcar Bertha* with Barbara Hershey, David Carradine and Shelley Winters. A movie to direct! I was between agents, therefore, the two of us negotiated. He named a salary. "But, Roger, I'm DGA and that's below DGA minimum."

"Oh, I don't even know what that is." Corman knows the price of the slice of bologna in his caterer's sandwich. On a Corman set? One slice.

"Tell you what, Roger, I'll do it for rock bottom scale. Ten thousand for the shoot, and three thousand for pre- and post-production."

"Lou, do you know who got their start with me? Coppola, Bogdanovich, Robert Towne, Curtis Harrington…"

"Look, Roger, hopefully my wife and I are going to have a baby. For that long a commitment, what, six months? I'm just asking for another $1,000 to get me through the year."

Corman and I never agreed on terms.

Boxcar Bertha was released the next year, directed by a young unknown director named Martin Scorsese. So now Corman probably adds Scorsese to the list of, "Do you know who got their start with me?"

*   *   *

The Actors Studio had been renting the El Centro Dance Studio in Hollywood for our sessions in 1965, but a new owner wanted us out. We looked all over Hollywood for a space,

The Actors Studio West.

to no avail. I got a call from an actress, Cay Forester, saying she had heard of our situation. She told me that her husband Carl Schaeffer was superintendent of the Los Angeles Parks and Recreation Department, which controlled the use of the William S. Hart estate in Hollywood. It was an old wooden two-story house one block south of Sunset Boulevard. Forester pointed out that it was available. We met at their home in Toluca Lake.

Schaeffer got right to the point. He was businesslike, but not unfriendly. We drove to the house for a look. It was a bit shabby in appearance, and it had a garage. Hell, the Greeks used to do it outdoors, so "Yes!" With Schaeffer's City Hall connections, we got the estate with a lease of one dollar a year. To do the house repairs and turn the garage into a small theater would take a lot of work, ingenuity and money. The New York Actors Studio would not send a dollar to help. We were on our own. We reconvened most of the bunch from the Dennis Weaver meeting and elected Jack Garfein executive director at our new digs.

We had to go into a lot of pockets to turn that garage into a theater and to fix up and clean up the house. That first year, there were about 70 Studio members on the West Coast and in a year or so the joint was jumping with scene sessions and exercise classes. Eventually a director's unit was added and a playwright's unit headed by William Inge.

In 1971, after being on the executive committee for five years, I succeeded Lonny Chapman (who had replaced Garfein) as executive director. We were in trouble. Our lease was expiring and other acting organizations were competing to grab our theater and house. Cay Forester, now a member, set up a meeting between me and Sam Yorty, the rather right wing mayor of Los Angeles. The purpose of the meeting was to convince Hizzoner to extend our lease.

Dennis Weaver, Roscoe Lee Browne, me. Our hands clenched in prayer for funds.

Ah, but Lou Antonio was unknown to him, I needed someone with celebrity value to go with me. Bill Traylor, an active member, suggested Academy Award winner Lee Grant, who was on screen everywhere in *Plaza Suite*. Great idea, but…

"Uh, Bill, you know how far to the right Yorty is and, well, Lee was blacklisted in the '50s. Is that gonna kill us?"

"I dunno, let's see."

The three of us drove to have lunch with Mayor Yorty in his private dining room at City Hall. Three thespians, a mayor and his assistant, Mr. Rodriguez. Yorty was a short fella, 62, trim and easy to talk to. Taylor and I spoke briefly to Hizzoner about the importance of the Actors Studio to the Los Angeles artistic community. Traylor and I shut up when we heard Grant coo, "Sam, how do you keep such a cute figure?" Yorty puffed up an inch taller and espoused the physical virtues of swimming every day. Grant put her considerable female attributes to advantage and finally Mayor Yorty said to his assistant, "You know, these seem like nice people. Let's give them what they want."

Driving back to the Studio, we were jubilant. I said, "Lee, you were brilliant. You had Sam eating out of your hand!" She said, "Oh, Sam just wants to fuck a Commie."

Jon Epstein was now at Universal producing an hour drama, *Owen Marshall, Counselor at Law*, starring Arthur Hill, and he asked me to direct one of the episodes. On my first day of filming, with a six-day schedule, I had ten pages to shoot with two moves to exterior locations and then back to the Universal sound stage for one scene. A killer day, as you will see. Lee Majors, a regular on the show, was in the first scene and not there. Calls were made, no conclusion. No way I could wait for him and still get the day's work done. The first sequence was Hill, reacting to the actor who wasn't there. Uber-professional that he was, we filmed his close-ups with the script supervisor reading Majors' dialogue. Majors came to the set 45 minutes late and furious that his contract dispute with Universal wasn't going his way.

I looked at my watch and dropped some coverage to get to our next location in nearby Toluca Lake. If I didn't bring this sucker in on time, I might never direct for Universal again, and they had 20 series on the air. The scene, staged to overlook the lake, was with Lee and a nice actor, Kathryn Hays. Either Lee truly didn't know his lines or he was purposely screwing Universal again. His dilemma was dumped on my wristwatch and on Hays, who kept her mind right and dealt well with the scene and with Majors. Then back to the studio in another hurry.

On the *Owen Marshall* office set, it seemed as if I just might get the day's work done. Yay! While rehearsing the last scene of the day with Hill and Joan Darling, I heard a thump from 15 feet up on a catwalk. An electrician was slumped over, his eyes closed. I got the actors off the set and the studio nurse came immediately. She went up the ladder in her starchy white uniform and looked helplessly at the fallen man. A studio fireman arrived, looked up at the nurse and quietly asked, "What have you got?" She looked bewildered.

"Do you have a pulse?" he whispered.

No answer.

Frustrated, he climbed the ladder. I saw the fireman's white hand holding the fallen electrician's black wrist, checking for a pulse. He looked down at his partner and shook his head. I called Epstein: "Jon, we're in Owen's office and a crew member just died. Everyone's pretty upset. Why don't we wrap?"

"It's 20 'til six, shoot 'til six. It'll keep everyone's mind busy."

Without relief or elation, I finished the day's work wondering if this first day at Universal was a forecast of directing days to come.

As an inexperienced director, I was absorbing the techniques and language of film. I started calling the Universal lot "The Campus" because I was learning so much from top-notch cameramen, editors, sound mixers, dolly grips, prop masters, special effects, set designers, costumers, makeup, assistant directors, other directors. Every crew person I asked a question would take the time to answer.

I was strong and in good shape so I wondered why at the end of a directing day I was so tired. I sensed it wasn't solely the intense stress of a daily 10- to 12-page shoot crammed into a six-day schedule. Curious, I wore a pedometer on my ankle one 12-hour day. Seven miles.

While I was directing a TV movie, a student from Vassar was doing a study on how many questions a director was asked in a day's shoot. I guessed 200. "Not even close," she said. "Seven hundred."

To slog away on a script honestly and openly with a writer is a two-on-the-seesaw treat. Michael Gleason had been a Broadway stage manager in New York and got his Hollywood break as a writer with an episode of *My Favorite Martian* entitled "Boo Boo's Dilemma," co-written with Bill Blinn. I'm sure it's in your library of classics. One of the things that's beneficial for me as a director is to hole up with the writer, the two of us reading the script aloud, my mining the script with questions about character, motivation, structure and plot. That's what Gleason and I did on a *McCloud* script.

I would prep during the day, locations, casting, wardrobe, stunts, special effects, equipment concerns, etc., and then late into the night with Gleason, drink some Scotch, smoke some cigarettes, pace, improvise "what ifs," drink some Scotch, home by midnight. I loved it. Gleason is a stimulating writer to hash and clash with. Egos buried, discussions, disagreements, but never toward any end other than a better script. A favorite story of Gleason's: At the beginning of one such session, I entered with the penetrating critique of, "This scene? It's kaka."

On another *McCloud* we were lucky enough to grab Lee J. Cobb, who had immortalized Willy Loman in *Death of a Salesman*, Johnny Friendly in *On the Waterfront* and loads of

Me with Dennis Weaver as McCloud.

other memorable performances. We had him for one day's work of eight pages. His part was of a Mafia don (only we couldn't use the "M" word due to pressure from an Italian anti-defamation organization). I took for granted that an actor of Cobb's caliber and experience would waltz through it. No, he was nervous and needed more than just a few quick TV rehearsals. "Could we do another rehearsal, kid? I'm just in Philadelphia."

His concept of the role was of a bitter, sour man, which weighed down his scenes with Dennis Weaver and Brad Dillman playing his second in command. After several rehearsals we still couldn't get out of Philadelphia. I was perhaps being too reticent in giving direction to Lee J. Cobb. Finally I said to him, and I might get one in the Bridge Burners for it, "Lee, it's all there. I just want to suggest one thing. Do it this time without the *lemon* in your mouth. Take out the lemon."

He looked hard at me. Threw his head back and laughed. "Oh, I get it, kid. I get it."

He sailed the rest of the day with a smile and a shoeshine and we finished so early he said to me, "Jesus, kid, if I'd known it was gonna go this fast, I'd have taken another job for the afternoon." He was well-liked.

Up to this point, you can see that I made career decisions that were not so much ill-considered as *not* considered, e.g., Corman, e.g., Coppola. Oh, did I mention this e.g.?: the *Children of the Corn* motion picture, the first one? The movie was offered to me straight out. After I read it, I told my dreamboat agents, Laurie and Amy, that I would not direct a film about children killing children and children killing adults. Smart. I believe the *three* movies of kids just being kids were all box office hits. I never had a career plan, a calculation, a strategy. It seems long-held artistic beliefs underscored my decisions, not career. I had briefly discussed these opportunities with my agents, but I made the final decision. A mistake. "He who represents himself has a fool for a lawyer." Coppola, Corman, *Corn*. I coulda been a contender.

Plus this one that happened in the late '60s, before the books, television and the Internet flooded us with the subject. I wrote a comedy about a father and daughter having a one-time sexual encounter and not being devastated from it. A comedy, you say? Yes.

Newman read it and returned it with a, "Lou, you know I've got a daughter. I can't do it." Walter Matthau read it and said, "I can't do anything like this. Men have daughters."

Richard Shepherd, a partner in Jack Lemmon's company, read it. We had a Malibu meeting. As we walked the beach, Shepherd told me that Lemmon would be interested in doing the part if I would make one change in the script: instead of the daughter, make it the stepdaughter. How righteous I became in the sands of Malibu. The Artist Aria soared out of me. "No! That would change the whole meaning of the story! That we are all categorized and put into pigeonholes by society, the Bible, politics and therefore the law. Father, daughter, mother, son, priests, sister, brother. Those are labels, pigeonholes, not people!" Shepherd listened patiently and quietly said, "Lou, that would still remain inherent in the script. Jack just wants her to be his stepdaughter."

If I'd only had a brain.

Brother Jim said, heck, I should shoot it in French with subtitles. Americans could soothe themselves with, "Hey, it's not us, it's those decadent French." Well, Louis Malle did well with his incest winner *Le Souffle au Coeur* (*Murmurs of the Heart*). It received a 1973 Academy Award nomination for Best Screenplay.

Perhaps I should have put my Artistic High Horse out to pasture? I don't know.

26

Who Has the Power,
Who Has the Pain?

Owen Marshall was a moderately successful lawyer show, running from 1971 to 1974. Staffing:

1. David Victor sold the show to the ABC network. He was an executive producer at Universal; you never saw him.

2. Jon Epstein was the producer who ran the day-to-day operation, from budget to scripts to casting, and with his associate producer oversaw the post-production chores of scoring and editing.

3. A story editor worked with the assigned freelance writers on the stories and did many rewrites by himself.

That was it. Three producers, but really only one, Epstein. (A quick 20-year flash-forward to Christmas 1994: The *Chicago Hope* producers give swell jackets to the cast and crew. Having been raised right by my momma, I sent 13 thank you notes to the producers, ten of whom were writers, most of whom I'd never met.)

To the frustration of *real* producers, the producer credit has lost its meaning, which has always been bereft of definition anyway. Good writers are so necessary that agents negotiate that title and a money bump, substantially elevating the cost of a series. Thus ten writer-producers are born. Premature births for most. With almost all series having a huge writing staff, the freelance writer in Hollywood is having a tough time landing an assignment. The Writers Guild rule is that at least three episodes per series have to be written by non-staff writers after the first season. Gee. Three. Out of 22. Will Congress sell it as an anti–minimum wage weapon?

I believe it was Richard Levinson and Bill Link who impregnated the writer with their power seed. They were a successful writing and producing team. In three decades their heavy hammers brought us 13 seasons of *Columbo* and 12 years of *Murder She Wrote* from Universal plus *Mannix*, eight years from Paramount. Their respected and prize-winning television movies brought in audiences, awards and bucks for the studios and networks. Levinson even hit Broadway in 1983, writing the book for the musical *Merlin*. Steven Bochco learned from them when he was a fledging writer at Universal. David Kelley learned from Bochco on *L.A. Law*. The only time the trickle-down theory has worked.

One-hour episode directors are given little authority these days. Casting in previous eras, we'd say to the producers, "Oh, I've got an actor who'll be good in that part." That was that. Hired. Now an experienced actor, no matter how minuscule the role, has to audition.

In a *Boston Legal* there was a silent bit of a middle-age secretary who sees a body and screams. That's all, a scream. Actresses had to drive 20 miles in an hour of traffic-filled freeways to the Manhattan Beach Studios to do a scream. The casting company, the producers, the guard at the gate knew actors who could have done the part drive unseen.

Every three years the Directors Guild contract with the Alliance of Motion Picture and Television Producers (AMPTP) expires and is re-negotiated. For three such negotiations, I was on the Creative Rights Committee, headed by the masterful Elliot Silverstein. At one such negotiation in the '70s, the hour-episode directors wanted a mandatory rule that seemed inarguably practical. On the first day of the director's seven-day preparation, there should be a script. Not too much to ask for, one would think. In some instances, a script would be two or three days late, sometimes *five*, yet the seven-day prep stayed inviolate, the start date remaining unmovable. Suffering from this: the director and every department involved (casting, wardrobe, locations, props, transportation, special effects, art department, etc.). One night in the contract negotiation, Sid Sheinberg, then head of Universal, countered the mandatory script-ready ruling with, "But you know, sometimes the writer gets stuck, writer's block, maybe needs a day or two to solve the problem. That's just the way it is with writers."

I was prompted to respond. "Sid, look at it this way then. I'm in the middle of a shoot, 90 people waiting for me to give them a set-up. Waiting, waiting. Deep sigh, I say, 'Nah, I've got director's block. Everyone go home, I'll work it out in a day or two.' Does the director get the same leeway as the writer?"

Sheinberg, a shrewd and always fair negotiator, got the point and we got the ruling. Which to this day is conveniently not enforced. Why? Because the fine is $2,670 for every day the script is late and for the director to report it to the Guild is always having to say you'll be sorry. Which a top director learned on a hit series. The script was three days late, the director dutifully reported it to the DGA. A minor executive of the writer-creator's production company cajoled him with, "Come on, we're family here. We want you to do a lot more of our series with us." The director adhered to the rule, was paid, and henceforth has never directed for that writer's company again. I just checked with the DGA to see if the rule is still in effect. The late-script penalty is now so complicated, almost indecipherable, that it is hardly ever attempted.

One evening for the 1979 negotiations, I arrived early at the AMPTP office. Also early was the president of 20th Century Fox, Alan Hirschfield, good-looking, forties, slim, hair with just a touch of gray, blue jeans and loafers, no socks. We were the only two in the room and wary of one another. He eyed me.

"You're from Oklahoma City, right?"

Suspiciously: "Yeah…"

"You went to OU, didn't you?"

Reluctantly: "Yeah…"

"I saw you in some plays there. I was in law school."

"Oh!"

"And wasn't your dad Jimmy the Greek? Had the Lafayette café?"

"You went to Central High?"

"No, I went to Classen [our archrivals]. But we'd drive over for one of your dad's chicken fries at lunch time."

"Hell, I probably served you. I worked there during the lunch hour. Poppa called you guys the Boulevard Boys."

The president of 20th Century Fox used to eat at Poppa's.

As Steven Wright said, "It's a small world, but I wouldn't want to paint it."

27

Natwick and Hayes Up, Garner on Deck

In 1973, Geoffrey Fisher, head of casting at Universal, asked me if I wanted to act in a new series as a regular. It was an *offer*, he said; I wouldn't have to read for it. The series was four 90-minute episodes called *The Snoop Sisters* starring Helen Hayes and Mildred Natwick. I'd been in two plays with Natwick, but I'd never met Miss Hayes. (Though one evening when she was away on location I did do the dance with her house guest on the living room sofa in her Nyack house.)

To act with those two would be a double dip I had to taste! Plus, I now had two daughters. Eighteen months after Elkins came beaming into my life, Angelique arrived to keep her company. I had wanted a family and now I felt in my bones I had validated my move to California.

Art Carney had played the Snoop Sisters' chauffeur in the original television movie, driving them about in a tank of a 1936 Lincoln. On location in New York City, I practiced driving the stiff and heavy '36 Lincoln through Manhattan traffic while the ladies were in the back seat running lines. The term "iron butterfly" meant nothing to me until I overheard the following rehearsal:

Ms. Hayes (worriedly): "Oh, Millie, those three lines just don't seem right for your character."

Sweet Millie: "No?"

Ms. Hayes (for the greater good): "But, the scene needs them so why don't I just take them. All right?"

Sweet Millie: "Well, yes, I suppose so."

In 20 minutes, Hayes had snatched half of Natwick's dialogue. Float like a butterfly, sting like a bee.

One time she teased me about my Method preparations before a scene. "But, Miss Hayes, I see you do *your* preparation before your scenes."

"What, no. What preparation? I don't—"

"Well, yes, ma'am, you do. Before every entrance you cross yourself."

She called upon a Higher Source than I with my lesser deities, Stanislavski and Strasberg.

Being around Ms. Hayes was a treat. One night I watched a TV adaptation of an F. Scott Fitzgerald short story, "Last of the Belles." I mentioned it to her the next morning and she said, "Ah, Scottie!" and launched into a couple of fascinating stories about Fitzgerald. One morning I threw my line into the water baited with Hemingway's *The Old Man and the Sea*. She grabbed it: "Ah, Ernie … he'd get drunk with Charlie [her husband] and

Mildred Natwick and Helen Hayes as the Snoop Sisters, and me as their chauffeur.

sleep on our couch." I couldn't resist catching a little literary or filmdom tidbit every day. She knew everybody!

Talk about working with the pros! She and Natwick were immaculate in their preparedness and on-set attitude. Natwick, 68, had received an Oscar nomination for *Barefoot in the Park* and an Emmy for *The Snoop Sisters*. Hayes, 81, had two Oscars and nine Emmy nominations, They were so easy to act with, there to do their chores with no fuss, investing their characters with skills gleaned from many years of experience and living. They never left the set except to go to the rest room.

For one episode we actually had Daniel Mann as director. I say "actually" because he was a first-class motion picture director, *BUtterfield 8*, *The Rose Tattoo*, to name a few, plus *Come Back, Little Sheba* on Broadway and on film. Directors with such achievements were not easily found in television at that time. We did a scene that was supposed to have some humor in it and I went for it. Our producer Leonard Stern kept emphasizing the comedy and Mann saw me step into the Funny Trap. He came up to me: "Let's do it again, Lou. You were pushing." He was so right! No big deal, he related to the actor that simply and I needed it. Today most directors go for the shot and not the life in the shot, mainly because they don't know squat about what actors do. To slightly misquote one of the current hot directors, Michael Bay, "Nothing excites me more than to come up with a camera angle no one has ever done before." Bay and his disciples are indeed alchemists, they transform lenses, explo-

```
 ┌────────────────────────────────────────────────────────────────┐
 │  uu u                              Telegram                     │
 │  western union                                                 │
 └────────────────────────────────────────────────────────────────┘

       HDA142(1850)(1-043396A101002)PD 04/11/74 1846
 TLX NBC NYK
 ZCZC 013 PD NEWYORKNY
 PMS LOU ANTONIO
 1316 MORINGSIDE DRIVE
 BURBANK CA


 I W
 XXX
 DEAR HELEN
 I WANTED YOU TO HEAR THIS BEFORE YOU READ IT IN THE NEWSPAPERS.
 I AM VERY SORRY THAT I HAVE TO PASS ALONG THE NEWS ABOUT THE
 CANCELLATION OF "SNOOP SISTERS". WE ALL HAD HIGH HOPES FOR IT,
 BUT I THINK THE WORD IS "ONWARD" AND THERE IS ALWAYS ANOTHER
 SHOW. YOU WERE MOST COOPERATIVE AND I SEND YOU MY BEST WISHES FOR
 THE FUTURE, AND HOPE ALL YOUR SHOWS ARE BIG HITS. WARMEST

 SF-1201 (R5-69)
```

```
 ┌────────────────────────────────────────────────────────────────┐
 │  uu u                              Telegram                     │
 │  western union                                                 │
 └────────────────────────────────────────────────────────────────┘


 PERSONAL REGARDS.
      DAVID TEBET VICE PRESIDENT  TALENT
      NBC TELEVISION NETWORK
```

My Snoops dismissal, by telegram. I didn't take it personally.

sions, computer generated images, sound, fire and fury into box office gold. The Snoops had no such riches. The payoff was paper. Delivered to my house, it read:

I wonder if Dear Helen got my "Dear Lou" (or did they send one…?).

After the demise of *The Snoop Sisters*, I stayed at Universal and directed, receiving another dose of good fortune by directing James Garner, a fellow Oklahoman. We met in 1975 when I directed the first episode of a new show called *The Rockford Files*. He was a walking tutorial on film acting and deportment. Well, more limping than walking. That hitch in his gait you noticed over the years was from a knee that was devoid of cartilage, but not of pain. Yet he put in the long hours without dogging it or pulling back physically. And what proficiency he had as a driver. Occasionally he'd get bored or a bit cranky and I'd say something like, "Jim, instead of just driving straight to the bad guys, why don't we do a cut where we see you've missed a turn and you jam a 180? Does that work for you?" He was as good as any stunt driver and after the perfect 180-degree spin he'd be sunny and cheery the rest of the day. Totally loyal to his crew and his good friend and stand-in Louie Delgado, he made the demanding 14-hour days bearable with his courtesy, humor, skills and contributions. At the end of the day, he and Delgado would be in his dressing room kibitzing and playing backgammon while I'd have a Scotch. Garner was not a drinker and Delgado and I would hear him brushing his teeth with an appreciative "Damn, this toothpaste tastes good!" If you get my drift.

At the season's end wrap party, it was noted that in the 22 episodes filmed that first season, Garner had been in every scene but one!

Episode television is grueling, and not only for the viewers. A 60- to 80-hour work week can take its toll, in a lot of ways. Concurrent with *The Rockford Files*, another Universal series, *Switch*, was lagging in the ratings and the head of Universal TV, Frank Price, called its producer Glen Larson and told him to get a *Rockford* script and study it. Stephen J. Cannell, the creator of *Rockford*, gave Larson a copy of one they'd already filmed. Garner got a call from *Switch*'s star Robert Wagner. "Jim, I'm reading my next script and it's like one of yours I just watched."

Larson Larceny Number One: Larson's *Switch* script essentially *was* the *Rockford Files* script with little more than the character names and page numbers changed. Cannell was set to go to the Writers Guild when Price said, "Let's keep it in-house." Then there was Larson Larceny Number Two: He created the series *Las Vegas* and wrote the musical theme himself, suspiciously akin to composer Mike Post's innovative and popular *Rockford Files* theme. One night as Garner was leaving the lot, he saw Larson and confronted him. Words were exchanged and Garner hit Larson with a quick chop to the jaw. Larson ran to the guard station, locked himself in and called the sheriff. The next day's gossip went something like this:

"Hey, there's good news and bad news about Garner and Larson."

"Yeah, what's that?"

"The good news is Garner hit Larson. The bad news is, he only hit him once."

Thirty years later I was working with a more mellow Garner on *First Monday*, an ineffectual series about the Supreme Court. The script was a stinker, but I could not resist that cast: Garner, Charlie Durning, Joe

James Garner in bronze, as Bret Maverick, in Norman, Oklahoma. He was what Robert Burns would have called a "man o' independent mind."

Montegna, James Karen, Gail Strickland, Joe Flanigan, Lyman Ward, all playing in the Supreme Court sandbox. One evening Garner was sitting outside the sound stage having a smoke and we were chatting. "You know, Lou, yesterday was the first day in 30 years that I didn't have any pain."

"Good Lord, Jim, then take it easy. You're putting in 15-hour days on this show. Quit this madness. Retire."

"No, I like being on a set. I love it. I'll never quit it."

For over 50 years we were the recipients of that love. And he of ours.

28

Classes at Universal U

Being on the Universal campus and doing hour-long episodes was my directing curriculum prior to graduate school. It was there that I met the director John Badham, who was being noticed for his strong work; we younger guys all knew he was on his way. With his quiet talent, he had a fresh way of seeing a scene, a moment, and offbeat casting which I found insightful and correctly tilted. Badham was offered a MOW (movie of the week) in 1975, *Someone I Touched*. He declined, and recommended me. I was hired! Badham graduated to *Saturday Night Fever*, *WarGames*, *Bird on a Wire*, *Short Circuit* and a dozen more.

In *Someone I Touched*, a woman (Cloris Leachman) becomes infected with a venereal disease by her unfaithful husband (Kenneth Mars). It was a 90-minute movie with a meager ten-day shooting schedule and I needed a *cum laude* cast to get me through it. Leachman was always punctual, every day 45 minutes late. The basis for her daily excuses were, "Had to make breakfast for my children," "Had to run out for oatmeal," "Burned their eggs and had to start over." The headline was always "Breakfast to Blame!"

We overcame Leachman's truancy thanks to the discipline and talents I enlisted from the Actors Studio. So thanks, Peggy Feury, Allyn Ann McLerie, James Olson, Fred Sadoff and Glynnis O'Connor, whose real-life mom, Lenka Peterson, played her mother in the show. Peterson had a leading role in *The Girls of Summer* when I was assistant stage manager 18 years earlier.

The cast and the James Henerson script were lauded and the movie did well with critics and audiences. *Variety* called my contribution "refreshingly straightforward direction." Badham munificently thrust me into MOWs and thanks to him, except for a few rotten apples now and then, it was a long and fruitful ride.

After my MOW, I wasn't (nose in the air) "doing hours any more." I was directing only 90-minute or two-hour programs. When offered a one-hour episode of *Delvecchio*, it was too tempting to turn down. There were talents that lured me: Judd Hirsch, the lead, producers William Sackheim, Bochco and prominently, the Oscar-winning cameraman Russ Metty. Metty had shot over a hundred movies, *Spartacus*, *The Misfits*, *Touch of Evil* and *Bringing Up Baby*, to name just a few. I laid out a busy four-page master shot that included Hirsch quickly going from his dad's multi-mirrored barber shop into a back room and then re-entering the shop. Four pages, the camera always moving. What with those damn mirror reflections I fully expected Metty to suggest I shoot it in cuts.

Apologetically I said, "Look, Russ, we're on a six-day shoot, if it's too stupid or will take too long to light, just tell me and I'll simplify it."

"It'll be okay."

He never left his chair as he whispered to his gaffer, pointing out where and what lights to hang. Once the whispering ended, we had the set in half an hour. It looked good, Hirsch and his dad Leonard Cimino were terrific, and I had watched a director of photoghraphy quietly do his calling. Like in college, some classes a director just has to take.

In 1972, Leonard Nimoy was preparing his first directing effort, an episode of *Night Gallery*, Universal's spooky series. When he asked me to play a small role in it, I jumped at the chance to be in his directorial debut. Lesley Anne Warren played a vampire and maybe I got bitten in the neck, I hope by her, but I don't remember. I do remember the calm and assurance Nimoy quietly exhibited throughout the shoot. He only had three days to film it and every minute counted, so what did this first-time director have to deal with on his first day of filming? A visit to the set by Secretary of State Henry Kissinger.

With Secret Service men trailing him, precious minutes were pissed away by introductions, mindless small talk, questions about the show, and Kissinger trying to impress Warren. Resourceful and nimble, Nimoy came in on time and with a gentle directorial hand helped the actors and the script with proficiency and confidence. He pushed out of his director's blocks in good form, later helming some excellent motion pictures. ("Helming": from the Greek *Helmet*, protection from bullshit thrown at the director.)

Ah, those old demons Schedule and Budget nip at a director's heels on every job. Aaron Spelling hired me a lot as an actor and *once* as a director for his series *The Rookies*. The guest lead, Theresa Graves, was in a hit comedy show, *Laugh-In*, and had never acted in drama, but they wanted "a name." It's called Stunt Casting. During prep, I would go to her apartment after work and coach her. I convinced myself that she'd be okay. Denial. On my first day of shooting, she was in a four-page scene, almost half the day's work, and I staged it with a lot of movement, requiring only about two close-ups for coverage. She was better when she was moving. After two and a half hours of rehearsal, the actress was still shaky and at 11 I still hadn't printed a take. Catastrophic enough for the production manager to bully onto the set with a full-voiced, "Why aren't you rolling?!"

Innocently: "Oh, you want me to roll? Okay." I threw myself onto the floor and rolled some 50 feet across the sound stage. I came up dusty and dirty. "Okay, I've rolled. Now what do you want me to do?"

He never came to the set again. I never directed for Spelling again. That is one example as how my actor's training of "impulse to expression" always seemed to be at ON. I needed an OFF switch.

29

Rabbi Problems,
Rich Man Problems

One of the funniest actors in existence was Art Carney, and I wish I had a print of his every take from *Lannigan's Rabbi*, a two-hour pilot I directed for Universal.

Stuart Margolin (Angel in *The Rockford Files*) was Rabbi Small, Janet Margolin was his wife and Lorraine Gary played a suspected murderer (before her *Jaws* role). Carney's character, Lannigan, a detective helping the rabbi solve a case, is making crepes. We had real batter and a real stove and Carney went at it. Everything that could go wrong did. The batter bubbled over onto his shoes, he flipped the crepe, it stuck to the pan, he fought bravely, all the while popping fresh strawberries into his mouth and doing his dialogue. I kept the camera going and the crew was trying so hard to hold in their laughter, I thought there was going to be a group hernia. There are treasures among the tripe in this profession. I just wanted to mention one.

The sour part was that the pilot went to series, but without Margolin. I called Epstein, our producer. "What the hell is going on? This is nonsense! Stuart's wonderful!"

"You don't have to tell *me*. I agree. It's the network. They say he looks too Jewish."

Did NBC really fear the country would react with an "Oh, my god, Maud, a Jew! Quick, turn off the TV."

I got a call from Margolin. "Lou, did you think I wasn't any good, is that why I'm not doing the series?"

"Good God, no!" Then I got it, the phone call from the real rat, whoever it was, had escaped Margolin's question by making *me* the bad guy. "Stuart, this is the awful truth of it. The network thinks you look too Jewish. And I'm not kidding, they want to cast an actor with blue eyes and 'blondish hair.' Some lamebrain at NBC concluded that America would better 'relate to a younger *blue-eyed* Jew.'" Quote, unquote.

Blue eyes they got, in a mediocre actor who lacked everything that Margolin has: talent, comic charm, sensitivity, likability, mischief and believability. The series dropped four one-hour bombs. All duds. Though I had not the power, Margolin had been convinced I was the culprit. A network executive had laid out a self-protecting deflection that Antonio did the deed, not NBC. Succeeding *Rockford* specials were done without me.

The first television mini-series, an innovation of Barry Diller, was from Irwin Shaw's novel *Rich Man, Poor Man*, in 1976. The series' popularity convinced ABC and Universal that a second year should be scheduled. It started with a two-hour opener that I was to direct, my faves Michael Gleason and Jon Epstein to produce.

The original season had sprung Nick Nolte into a movie career and a replacement had

to be found. Epstein asked me to direct some screen tests. Brother Jim called and said that Sandra Seacat, a member of the Actors Studio, wondered if I could get her boyfriend Mickey Rourke a test for the part. I'd never heard of him, but I trusted Seacat's judgment and said I'd slip him in. He flew in from New York. This quiet and introspective actor came onto the set and introduced himself to me in a head-ducking James Dean manner. We did as many

Top: **With my daughter Elkin and Art Carney on** *Lannigan's Rabbi. Bottom:* **Rock Hudson, me and Jon Epstein, one of the best producers ever.**

takes as I could stuff into the 30 minutes I had made time for. He was honest and skilled, but at that time I suspect his looks and persona were going to be too unique for the formulaic look of television. He didn't get the part. Jim called me and said that Rourke apologized, that he had been tense and tired from his flight, and that some time he'd like to "Show Lou that I was a better actor than that." Well, Rourke has proved to the world the truth of that.

A director's dilemma. Part of the job.

Peter Strauss was returning to his previous season's role for the two-hour opener. We were shooting the last scene of the day at the Van Nuys airport between James Carroll Jordan (Billy Abbott) and the actress portraying his Mom. I only had about twenty minutes to shoot this last two-page scene. I staged it and the actors nailed it so well I could get the scene in one setup. The cameraman said he could light it in ten minutes. By golly, the set was ready in ten and the actors were brought in. Time for two takes. Only we never got even one. Take one—"Mom" stumbles, wobbles, has a dazed look. She could hardly stand up. Cut. I saw her boyfriend holding this giant bottle of I guess smelling salts under her nose and she was taking heavy inhalations. Okay, maybe that would do it. Take two—she couldn't get through two lines. Cut. We had to wrap. Epstein came over to me. "What was that?" he asked me. "No one can get that drunk in ten minutes." We never found out.

The next day the actress asked me how much time she had before her scene because "it helps my acting to have some sex, so if I could have five minutes."

"Take *ten*!!" I insisted.

If the crew doesn't like you, well, read on—filming in a wooded area on Universal's back lot, the actress, in character, is lying on the ground dying after a helicopter crash. I noticed the crew veering around her prone body as they worked. I asked one of the guys why the detour.

"She's lying in poison oak." And no one told her.

Ah, he was probably joking.

I printed a master of the scene, and was ready to punch in for a close up. An angry itch spread on "Mom" and she was ambulanced off to the dispensary. Didn't see her again until her itch had subsided, the last day of her contract. We had to film the needed close-up of the death scene a week later on a sound stage. At one-thirty in a.m. time. Unfortunately the actress had watched her dailies and now her death scene had become a DEATH SCENE. Oh, no, and oh, woe. I talked to her; "Simpler. She's weak as hell, no strength, she's dying. Simpler." She'd nod and on the next take it was just as grotesque. Peter Strauss was patiently doing his lines off camera for her, though he and the actress disliked one another so much that she ate garlic before their love scenes. It got to be two in the morning, I was failing miserably. "More *less*," I urged. She had a Teflon brain, none of it stuck. By god, she was going to EXPIRE. BIG!! I called the executive producer Michael Gleason in his office.

"She won't die!"

He came down to the stage and talked with her softly and patiently. I caught snatches of "…we're still shooting at two in the morning to accommodate your stop clause…. I will shut down the company now unless you die the way the director wants … you will be in breach of your own contract, caused by you. Universal could sue." It's bountiful when producer and director hold hands and pray.

Gleason the Good. She expired quickly, and quietly.

30

Dog and Cat Are Neutered

In the theater, a play closes; in television, a show is canceled. On Broadway, it's the lack of an audience, in TV not always. I offer you *Gentle Ben*'s demise. In 1976 I was directing an episode of *McMillan and Wife* when I got a call to go to ABC on a Saturday afternoon and screen test for a role in a new series pilot. There were five gals competing for the role of a young police detective and four guys for the older cop. They were to be a team called *Dog and Cat*. I did my test and the producer Larry Gordon asked if I'd stay and assist a few other actresses with their tests. All the women were cute and good (one whispering to me, "I'm dating Joe Namath"). But then in comes Kim Basinger, this stunner with the freshness of inexperience and exuding 23-year-old exuberance.

Kim and I were cast in the pilot. It sold. We started filming the following year. An active actor is a well-oiled instrument and work is a definite rust inhibitor. I hadn't acted in a year, and the first few episodes, the rust was flying off me like hail. Tetanus shots for the crew were considered. The tone of *Dog and Cat* was light-hearted exchanges between Kim and me in tightly plotted stories. Though Kim had acted some, she had hardly any training or technique, but underneath her drop-dead beauty and Southern accent she held the screen with a natural and youthful erotic quality. People wanted to watch her. Our time slot was Saturday night against Carol Burnett's show on CBS and *Saturday Night Movie* on NBC. Two ratings winners. We clobbered them every week. One reviewer liked the show and noted Basinger's beauty and, well, categorized me as "veteran Lou Antonio." I said to brother Jim, "Veteran?! I'm 34 years old, how am I a veteran?!"

Dog and Cat was a hit, no doubt about it. People and the press were clambering all over Kim. I was enjoying acting again. Basinger, free-spirited, a quick learner with a big laugh, brought vitality to the set. One scene I still remember, I'm at my police desk, Basinger enters wearing a clinging evening gown, her nipples prominent. I ad libbed, "Is it cold in here or are you just happy to see me?"

In those days, that question never hit the air waves. Today a reference to a nipple wouldn't cause a ripple.

Top Ten though we were, odd notes started coming down from ABC during filming. For example: Gun drawn, I was chasing the bad guy (Alex Rocco). I heard, "Cut, cut!" A panting production assistant had just handed the director a slip of paper. He looked at it incredulously. "Uh, Lou, you're not allowed to point your gun at the bad guys any more."

The 1977 Congress was threatening the networks with censorship due to violence on television. The president of ABC, Fred Pierce, was facing Congress, America's thermometer of morality. Apparently TV had a fever. Whereas *Dog and Cat* was winning its sprints, it

had no track record beyond six episodes. Pierce had two mildly violent shows that had been proven hits for several years, *Starsky and Hutch* and *Baretta*. To appease the Inquisition, Pierce did his patriotic duty as a responsible network president. To ward off the virus infecting the morals of America, he threw *Dog and Cat* into the pound and locked the cage. The gun guys continued to kill.

In 1930, motion pictures were restricted by a self-imposed "code" to protect itself from the aforesaid U.S. Congress. It was called the Hays Code, aka the Production Code. Here are a few of the rules in effect from 1930 to 1968. Take your time, today it could be a *Saturday Night Live* sketch.

Left: **The beautiful Cat (Kim Basinger) and the Dog.** *Below:* **Title card from *Dog and Cat*.**

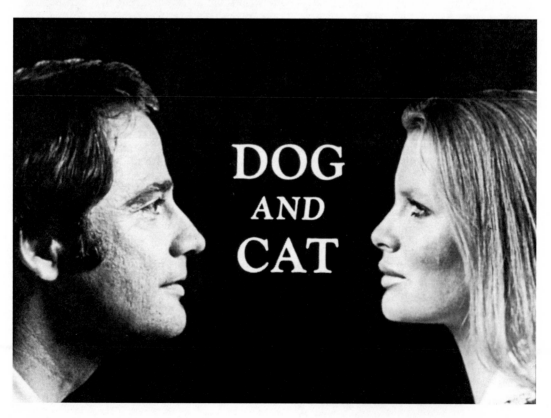

Congress's Ten Commandments

No picture shall be produced that will lower the moral standards of those who see it.

Excessive and lustful kissing, lustful embraces, suggestive posture and gesture, are not to be shown.

In general, passion should so be treated that these scenes do not stimulate the lower and baser element.

Brutal killings are not to be presented in detail.

Illegal drug traffic should never be presented.

Miscegenation (sex relationships between the white and black races) is forbidden.

Pointed profanity (this includes the words, God, Lord, Jesus, Christ, unless used reverently), Hell, S.O.B., damn, Gawd, or every other profane or vulgar expression, however used, is forbidden.

Complete nudity is never permitted. This includes nudity in fact or in silhouette, or any lecherous or licentious notice thereof by other characters in the picture.

Dances which emphasize indecent movements are to be regarded as obscene.

Ministers of religion in their character as ministers of religion should not be used as comic characters or as villains.

As you can see, most of the above have been transferred to an old rules home. However, in television, a married couple were never to be seen sharing a bed. Always two single beds in evidence. There were occasional isolated instance of cohabitation, but in the early '70s that twin bed restriction just sort of wandered away. Today, well, December of 2015 in an episode of *The Good Wife* the wife says to her husband, "You wanna get laid?" Along the way:

• **1990**: In the interest of commerce and capitalism, violence mostly got a hall pass. The networks were still skittish about addressing sexuality, particularly undressing. That year I directed Jaclyn Smith in a TV movie, *Lies Before Kisses*. A word, a current politically incorrect word, about Jaclyn Smith, she's a lady. Combined with her basic honesty, she has a face that is natural and inviting. Invariably when I was setting a size for her close-ups I'd hear myself saying to the dolly grip, "Closer, move in closer." She draws the camera in to her.

Though as an actor she can reveal her emotions in a heartbeat, not all reveals are easy for her. In our TV movie there was a scripted front room sit-and-talk scene with her leading man Nick Mancuso. Though using the dialogue exactly as scripted, I put Smith in the shower for the first half, and in bed seducing Mancuso the second half. On the bed, Mancuso's well-honed back was a kiss away from Smith. "Go ahead, Jac, show me how you'd do it." She damn near blushed, but ever the professional, she whispered to me, "No, show me." Oh, swell, the MOW must go on. So there I was in front of a smirking crew kissing and caressing Nick Mancuso's naked back. I don't know how Mancuso took it, but I was in the crew's pocket the rest of the day. When Smith did the scene, however, they became quiet and attentive. Heterosexual wimps.

Here's an addendum on the morality of the times and what some actors had to face. In 1980 and '81, the HIV-AIDS epidemic finally had captured the public's attention and infused the acting profession. In 1988, Jaclyn signed to star in a television mini-series, *The*

Me and Jaclyn Smith, on the set of *Lies Before Kisses* (1990).

Bourne Identity, opposite Richard Chamberlain, a popular television leading man. Their characters had love scenes to do. To act freely and openly in their scenes, they knew there had to be personal trust and no apprehension. Chamberlain offered that prior to filming, he and Jaclyn should meet and provide written results of their HIV-AIDS test. Both were negative. Filming began.

Ah, the lava-like change in television's protection of America's morality. A few years later, in the Henry Thomas–Jason Bateman–Michael Biehn TV movie *A Taste for Killing*, I filmed a woman in a slip straddling Thomas. She smiles down at him with sensual, slight movements of her body, so slight it could have been breathing. Early the next morning I got a call from Barbara Fisher, the head of Universal cable which was producing the show. She had just viewed the dailies and ordered me to cut the scene. "But why? You don't see anything. She's wearing a slip!"

"She's *moving!*"

- **1992:** A short scene in an early *NYPD Blue* has Detective Sipowitz and his fiancée discussing a problem. The dialogue included heretofore banned nouns such as "asshole" (three) and "prick" (one). The actor got one "asshole," the actress got a "prick" and two "assholes." Plus we got a bit of breast, a dose of derrière and ABC got ratings.
- **2011:** From the *New York Times* review of *2 Broke Girls*: "[A] teenager named Tessa is appalled by another girl who is thrilled that a pair of absurdly tiny shorts will show off her belly ring. 'You know what else it shows off?' says teenybopper Tessa. 'Your vagina.'"

Whitney Cummings, who was writing her own comedy for NBC, said, "I think our tolerance for what is edgy is changing. If one day passes without me writing any more vagina jokes, my career is blown." She said jokingly, "Vagina jokes paid for my house."

Requiescat in pace, pu pas.

31

Cappelletti, Sand and Subways

Jerry McNeeley, ex-professor at Wisconsin University, was a TV writer-producer when he watched the 1973 Heisman Trophy broadcast. Penn State's John Cappelletti was the recipient and in accepting the award he movingly dedicated it to his little brother Joey, who was dying of leukemia. Touched, McNeeley thought, "That might make a TV movie." It did.

Mary Tyler Moore's company, MTM, produced it for CBS, which for a change did not demand TV stars. I offered Kazan the part of the father. He gracefully declined. A youthful Mark Harmon, two years after quarterbacking at UCLA, auditioned. Excellent, but not enough bulk for a Penn State running back. Casting the parents, we got Geraldine Page and Gerald O'Loughlin, whom I knew from the Actors Studio. For Cappelletti we scored heavily with Marc Singer, fresh out of Actors Conservatory Theatre, first-timer Steve Guttenberg, Linda Kelsey, Kathleen Beller and Jeff Lynas as Joey.

Every day of the 18-day shoot was brimful with expectation and dedication from the cast and crew. Wouldn't you know that the day Cappelletti visited the set, we shot the scene when Joey asks his brother John, "Do I have cancer?"

"...Yes."

I didn't dare look at Cappelletti, I so wanted to get it right. The next day, Cappelletti went to watch the rushes. McNeeley told me what happened. The roomful of viewers wept. Cappelletti quietly went to McNeely:

"Why did you have to do it so well?"

The actors were wonderful. Even with the tight schedule, after Page had knocked a scene out of the park, I'd do more takes just to see what she'd come up with next. Nuggets of gold sometimes hide until uncovered by a mistake or an accident, which is why an actor should never stop a scene. Example: Cappelletti has just won the Heisman Trophy and telephones from school to tell his family, Joey talks a bit with John and turns to give Mom the telephone. He accidentally smacks her hard on the forehead with the phone. Page takes the phone in one hand and gingerly feels her forehead with the other while continuing the scene. Page, with her discipline and theater background, didn't drop out of character or the scene. No cutting of the camera for gag reel jokes, apologies or scatological laments. It's in the picture, true, funny and effective.

With nearly every sports page in America plugging the picture, 51 percent of America's television sets were watching *Something for Joey*. It was nominated for a Golden Globe, won a Humanitas Award, and McNeely and I were nominated for Emmys. A Japanese producer wanted to acquire the picture for a theatrical release in Japan. For the rights they

John Cappelletti, me and Marc Singer on set during filming of *Something for Joey*.

offered either $50,000 or 15 percent of the gross. MTM took the cash. In a season that included a James Bond movie and a Spielberg picture, *Joey* was the fifth highest grossing motion picture in Japan. Oh, ye of little faith? Yearly I was compelled to tease Grant Tinker and his partner Arthur Price about the sale of *Joey*.

Tinker was a swell guy, educated and classy, with a sly humor. One lunch hour he,

MTM's vice-president Stu Erwin and I were returning from lunch in my big old dirty 1971 Chevy truck, the three of us in the front seat, the only seat, Tinker at the window. At a stop light, a Porsche convertible stopped next to us on the passenger side. A snazzy hotshot executive greeted Tinker, who was about four feet higher up than the low-riding Porsche. With the hotshot craning his neck upward, they chatted until the light changed and we drove back toward the studio. After a block or two, Tinker said to Erwin, "You know, Stu, what with all the work Lou did in pitching that pilot, maybe we ought to give him a small bonus. Like $5,000." A beat of silence, then he added with only a touch of grump, "Help him buy a *car*..."

While the town was still talking about *Joey*, the Disney people handed me five motion picture scripts and told me to pick the one I wanted to direct. They were all generic comedies with the same three or four writers' names on every one of them. Not a good sign. Then another script was offered to me by indie producer Martin Jurow, who had produced Hollywood movies such as *Terms of Endearment*, *The Pink Panther* and *Breakfast at Tiffany's*. He had a small movie he was preparing to shoot in Austin, Texas, about a University of Texas football running back who lost his leg to cancer. It was a true story and a good script. I met with Jurow and actress Anne Archer at her house in Beverly Hills. Archer was to play the love interest of Freddie Steinmark, the young football player. We auditioned actors and immediately cast Dennis Weaver's son Rob as Freddie.

My directing agent at the time, Marty Shapiro, advised against my going to Texas until the contracts were in place, but I was too excited by the project. I packed and went to Austin. Coach Darrell Royal, who had played quarterback at OU with my cousin Dee Andros, could not have been more friendly or cooperative. My cameraman Bruce Surtees and I scouted the campus for locations, I started auditioning students from the drama department, watched film of Freddie in his gridiron glory. I was convinced we would make a poignant, powerful film. A completion bond man came to town to look at the budget and the end cost of the movie. For a fee, these completion bond companies will financially guarantee the completion of a movie once they sign on. I had the movie in my mind. I could see it, hear it, feel the heart of it.

After doing his math over the script, schedule and budget, the guarantor guy informed Jurow that his crew was too spare and needed a couple of extra grips, electricians and some other expenses that he felt were required to finish the film on budget. Jurow could not come up with the added costs. He canceled the picture.

Shapiro telephoned me an "I told you so." That was that. I went to Jurow's motel room for at least some remuneration for my airfares, apartment and car rental. He turned to his wife: "Dear, we owe Lou *something*. Do you have any cash on you?"

Yessiree, Bob, I got something from Dear all right ... $38, cash.

Movie-less, I returned to Burbank. It was June of 1976.

The next year, Steve Gethers gifted television with a script about a deaf stuntwoman, Kitty O'Neil. CBS again granted me freedom in casting and with her company producing it, Stockard Channing stunningly played Kitty. Fortune upon fortune, Colleen Dewhurst agreed to play Kitty's mother and was nominated for an Emmy. Another talent feast came along: James Farentino, Edward Albert, Brian Dennehy. My two daughters, Elkin (five) and Angelique (three and a half) played Kitty at different ages as a child. Although Elkin has blue eyes and Angelique has brown, no one noticed that as she got older, Kitty's eyes changed color.

Working with those actors and that script was dear to me. Being immersed in a pool of *unselfish* and committed talent lifted me into an aura of relaxed creative intensity. As with *Joey*, I was in the midst of an ensemble of actors that paid homage to the script through their artistry and hard work.

Silent Victory: The Kitty O'Neil Story was another ratings whopper, and received nominations. After having been nominated for Emmys two years in a row, *Joey* and *Kitty*, I lifted from hour series to pilots and TV movies for the next 17 years. It was great, like being a movie director, picking my cameraman, composer and crew, establishing the look and style of the picture, overseeing set design, color coordinating sets and costumes, interviewing every crew member who had daily contact with the actors, such as hair, makeup, wardrobe, props and sound. We rehearsed two or three days prior to filming, and the movie went on the air with at least 98 percent of my edit staying untouched. Though not leisurely, the 18- to 20-day schedules were usually sufficient for the required 96 minutes of broadcast time. Your math is right, 24 minutes of commercials. Nowadays in a one hour episode, there's 17 minutes of products whizzing by your face. If your remote's not working.

I got to go play in a big sandbox called Malibu. In the sand and partial ruins of a massive fire we shot the four-hour ABC mini-series *Breaking Up Is Hard to Do* (1979). It was sort of a male soap opera based on six real-life show business men whose marriages and relationships were in trouble. Friends, they all decide to share a beach house for the summer. The cast was resplendent with TV stars: Billy Crystal, Robert Conrad, Bonnie Franklin,

Billy Crystal, me, Tony Musante's back, on the set of *Breaking Up Is Hard to Do*.

Tony Musante, Ted Bessell, David Odgen Stiers, Susan Sullivan and Jeff Conaway, an actor who had departed his hit series *Taxi* in an ill-advised attempt to achieve stardom on his own. Conaway's flight fluttered and fell. Be careful, success can kill a career.

This was Crystal's first important dramatic role. He went for it clean, no joke-protection. In one scene, after being badgered by Conrad's character, Crystal's guy finally flips out and starts punching the drunk and unresisting Conrad. Cameras are rolling, it's looking good and then, whoops, *pow*, Crystal smacks Conrad on the nose. A bit of blood. Crystal broke out of the scene.

"Oh, jeez, Bob, I'm sorry. Are you all right? I'm so sorry."

"Damn, Billy, don't stop," said the bleeding Conrad, "it's goin' good."

I had been told that Conrad would

With Bob Conrad on *Breaking Up Is Hard to Do*.

be difficult, but I found him cooperative and an attentive actor. In his machismo core, he saw direction more as a challenge than a craft.

"Bob, when you see the girl, add not only the attraction, but maybe a bit of finally meeting the person you've secretly admired only from afar."

"I can do that."

And he did.

We're Fighting Back was the most difficult shoot I'd ever had. It was an MOW about why and how the Guardian Angels were formed in 1978. Even though the group's organizer Curtis Sliwa had been paid $30,000 for the rights, I quote the following from the *New York Times*, December 16, 1980:

Film Makers Sued on Guardian Angels

…Curtis Sliwa, the leader of the Guardian Angels, a volunteer group of youths, asked a court to award him five million dollars in damages and to stop a film company from making it a TV movie of his life.

Mr. Sliwa, in his suit filed in State Supreme Court in Manhattan, contended that the film was based on a "materially false, fabricated, and misleading script" that falsely depicted him and the Angels as "vigilantes" seeking revenge.

He brought the suit against Highgate Pictures, Inc., a subsidiary of the Learning Corporation of America, 1350 Avenue of the Americas. The suit charges breach of a contract made with Mr. Sliwa last June first.

Deep pockets can be tempting to pick, and CBS Legal was nervous as hell, but it and Highgate Pictures pushed on. Casting for Morgan Casey, the renamed Sliwa character, was yielding us nothing. All those fine New York actors and we couldn't find our man. One lunch hour I was walking off my frustration in midtown Manhattan. I spotted a guy walking on 57th Street. The way he moved, his hair, you just knew he was an actor. I trotted up beside him. Yep, a strong handsome face.

"Excuse me."

He looks at me like I'm cruising him and slows down but keeps on walking.

"Look, I'm directing a television movie and if you're an actor you might just be right for the lead."

Now he stops, "Yeah, I'm an actor."

"Great, if you—"

"Call my agent. I don't think he wants me to do television. I just finished a movie."

"Right, right. What's your name?"

A bit skittish, he took a few steps away from me.

I persist, "Really, this is legit. It's the lead and it's a pilot for CBS and would shoot here in—"

"I think I'm just gonna do movies."

Off he went. Damn.

I rushed back to the office and told my producer Linda Gottlieb about him. We started our star search in the Academy Players casting book.

"That's him!"

Gottlieb looked up at me. "Well, nice try, Lou. That's Peter Gallagher. He just did the lead in *The Idolmaker*. Taylor Hackford beat you to him."

We ended up with some stellar actors: Ellen Barkin, crooked smile and perfect figure, Joe Morton, articulate and concerned, Paul McCrane, intense and appealing, Stephen Lang, self-effacing and strong and, in a smaller role, Phylicia Rashad, who later won many Emmys on *The Bill Cosby Show*. Gallagher eventually did do television: *The O.C.* from 2003 to 2007. Now he can afford to do theater, and he does.

Shooting nights in the subway was unpleasant and unhealthy. Inhaling the stale air and the steel dust from the tracks took the juice out of the crew, rendering them even pokier than usual. I had a large tank of oxygen brought down to give their brains some nourishment. Most didn't use it. Maybe one or two. Wasn't manly.

We'd finish at eight or nine in the morning. I'd emerge from our subterranean dungeon into the South Bronx air, breathe, cough, spit and wake up my driver in the front seat of the station wagon. "Yeah, okay," he'd mumble. "Let me just get a beer and we'll scat."

The stress was so intense that every day of filming I was excreting blood. I wasn't getting much of anything from Kevin Mahon as Sliwa. It wasn't his fault. His only acting experience had been the fighter that De Niro almost kills in the ring in *Raging Bull*. Mahon had had a few pro fights and was a nice young man, but he was green and scared. The network found him somewhere and did not go beyond his looks for the role. In one scene he's supposed to chew out his group. It was an important scene and I was behind schedule. I had him pound my open hands, then "Action!" I couldn't get any inner life from him. Again, not his fault, put me in a ring for the first time and I'd be helpless. Finally the producer, John Quill, looked at his watch and said, "Just one more take." He was pulling the plug.

It started to drizzle. The one-more take was no better. I stood there wet and defeated, tears rolling down my face. Quill came over to me: "Let me see what I can do, Lou." The next week he juggled and finagled and I got to reshoot the scene later in the schedule. It was acceptable.

The movie aired on April 28, 1981, got good ratings, eleventh for the week with a 34 share, and some positive reviews. Judith Crist of *TV Guide* said it had "[a] talented cast and deft direction[,] grit, guts, and a kind of ending we all root for."

However, it was broadcast with this on-screen, sue-safety disclaimer:

The persons, organizations and events depicted in this film are fictitious and are not intended as a factual portrayal of any person, persons or group.

32

Trashing Trash
with Rock Hudson

After working in a black hole in the Bronx, I needed to be among pretty people doing pretty things. I was ready to trade subway steel dust for the sweet smog of Los Angeles. Before *We're Fighting Back* hit the airwaves, *The Starmaker* came along, a four-hour mini-series produced by Johnny Carson's company. The script was mediocre, but at least it was set in Hollywood, where indeed there are pretty people doing pretty ugly things. Every star offered the lead turned it down. The head of NBC casting, Joel Thurm, was trying to get some serious "Attaboys" from the NBC brass and ate up days of our short prep period by submitting the script to the likes of Michael Caine, Albert Finney and Kevin Kline. Fine, live in Never Never Land, but time was flying by while Thurm waited for their agents to stop laughing and give him a "no."

A few years earlier, on my first *McMillan and Wife*, I went into Rock Hudson's motor home to talk about an upcoming scene. I hadn't knocked and he was standing there wearing only a protuberant pair of jockey shorts. I caught sight of his groinal area and blurted, "Jeezus, no wonder you're a star!"

Thank goodness he didn't take it as a talent slam, he just choked up laughing. I believed Rock Hudson would bring a lot of Hollywood to the part and we made an offer. We had laughed together a lot over the years and now we were talking about a script.

We met for lunch and drinks. I hoped the drinks would cloud his judgment. "It's not going to be trash is it, Lou?"

"It's Hollywood. So let's go for realistic trash. Okay?"

A couple more Scotches cinched it.

That was mid–January. It usually takes about half a year to get a four-hour mini on the air. The airdates were in April. We had less than three months to serve up *The Starmaker* to 25 million viewers.

Ronald Reagan had just been elected president and his daughter Patti Davis was to audition for the starlet part. Right before her arrival, Joel Thurm ordered us: "Read her, then cast her." Accompanied by two Secret Service men, Ms. Davis arrived wearing a snug sweater, her bust line asserting she was indeed starlet material. She was quiet, unpretentious, nervous, nice, her reading simple and honest. The character, however, was complex, nuanced and needed an actress with chops. What she must have been going through, the daughter of the president of the United States having to audition for a television part and thoroughly cognizant as to why. Obviously Thurm wanted her as a ratings booster. I had run into this before. A fresh young exec at ABC insisted I cast a young singer-celebrity for a lead dramatic role in an *Owen Marshall*. I explained to him that it was a demanding part and the boy had never acted a day in his life.

The ambitious exec said, "It is my job to get viewers. Cast him."

"But he'll kill the episode."

"See that he doesn't."

"But you are making that impossible."

"I am doing my job. Do yours."

He hung up.

I had to tell *Starmaker* producers David Debin and Peter Locke to find another director because Ms. Davis was not ready for the role. Debin and Locke fussed some with Thurm and NBC and we proceeded to read other actresses.

Lord, what a procession of potential starlets ensued! Each one arrived for her reading in a magnificent set of wheels, Mercedes, Porsche, BMW. I asked Debin how on earth these young unknowns could afford those fine cars while I was driving a small Honda. "Lou, come on, you're paying alimony, private schools for your girls, and by the way, is the term still 'sugar daddies'?"

One elegant and talented young actress knocked us out, but her manager wanted $40,000 for her services. Locke was incredulous: "Who the hell is Michelle Pfeiffer? I never heard of her."

No starlet, and we had to start shooting in a week. Melanie Griffith entered our lives like a fresh breath of polluted air. A bit of a pudge, squeaky voice, and a ton of talent, she was our girl.

With Rock Hudson on *The Starmaker*.

Quick story set-up: Movie director Rock divorces star Suzanne Pleshette, marries Melanie, makes her a star (aha, *The Starmaker*...), she cracks up, has an affair, Rock and her lover have a fight.

Hudson was 6'4". I couldn't have him whipping a wimp, but from all the big fellas that auditioned, only one stood out, Fred Dryer, a tight end for the Los Angeles Rams. He was suffering from negotiation concussions with Rams owner Georgia Frontière. Though he had never acted professionally, he was a lean 6'5", good-looking, and had been studying with Nina Foch, an excellent actress and teacher.

The prep was perking along. Our location manager, the flamboyant C. Robert Holloway, got us into homes in Bel Air and Beverly Hills whose doors were usually slammed shut on film folks. Every shooting site was above ground, with sunny skies, no cold and dark cement to light. Smog seemed sissy stuff. Holloway really scored when we needed a bedroom for a huff-and-puff with the pretty Suzanne Pleshette and studly Jack Scalia. He snagged the ex–Mrs. Dean Martin's bedroom. *Youch!* Mirrors, mirrors everywhere. On walls, closets and, well, sure, the ceiling. Yes, indeedy. Pretty people doing pretty things.

While my director of photography Charlie Correll was lighting a scene, Hudson started telling me a joke about a guy getting ready to jump off the Golden Gate Bridge. I panicked. Was he really telling me *that* joke? Rock Hudson cannot tell me *that* joke!

"So the man saves the guy from jumping and asks him, 'Why do you want to kill yourself?' The guy says, 'See that building over there, I designed that building, but does anyone say that I'm a great architect? No.'"

The smile on my face was frozen.

"'And see the wharf area there? I conceived that whole restructuring, but does anyone call me a great city planner? No.' [pause] 'But suck one little cock...'"

He roared and I did too, out of hysterical relief.

After my first trip to Hollywood, back in 1960, I stopped off in Oklahoma City to visit my folks, including brother Theo and his wife Louise, the archetypal mid–America movie fan. She wanted all the latest. "Tell me about Rock Hudson and Tony Perkins. They're such dolls."

"Well, Louise, from what I heard out there, your guys are homosexuals."

Long pause, then: "Oh, I don't believe men even do that!"

Hudson, who was constantly trying to improve as an actor, was immersed in Uta Hagen's book. Fred Lerner, a terrific stunt coordinator, set up the fight, with Rock ending up atop Dryer pounding the crap out him. The first take was okay, Hollywood convincing, but...

"Rock, when my marriage busted up I was going to this shrink and one day I came in really hurting and she handed me a tennis racquet and said, 'Hit the sofa,' and I did. I hit it and hit it, and all kinds of stuff started pouring out of me. You wanna try something like that? I'll stack three pillows next to camera, no Dryer, and you just beat the hell out of the pillows and let's see if something happens. Okay? Want to try it?"

"Sure."

The camera operator laid on the floor holding the Ariflex. Hudson started hitting the pillows. Harder, harder. It was starting to happen, his anger, hurt, frustration, his humiliation pouring out. *Wham, wham,* his eyes were tearing, *wham,* I heard a *crack* and, "Oh, shit!" He straightened and held up a limp and bleeding hand. He had hit the camera and broken his right hand. A piece of his flesh was hanging off the camera box.

He came back from the doctor with his hand in a cast. A removable cast. Against the doctor's advice, Rock had insisted on it so we wouldn't have to find ways to hide the cast in his scenes. Shooting continued. A few weeks later, he went back to have the hand checked. The doctor told him that because of that removable cast, his hand hadn't set correctly and the doc would have to break it and reset it. He injected the hand with Novocain and smashed it with a hammer. Another "Oh, shit!" The Novocain didn't take. Hudson came back to finish his day's work. In a removable cast.

With dreck, you can be creative. Check that—With dreck, you *have* to be creative. Here are a few examples of dreck polishing on *The Starmaker*.

The Scene: Hudson is having Griffith photographed for the studio publicity department. I work on it the night before we're to shoot it. Hey! I get on the telephone to the art department, "Do you suppose you could hustle up some of that white paper that photographers use as backdrops? Yeah, and white chairs and tables. Paint the floor white. Everything white. Except Rock's camera."

To wardrobe: "Do you have anything for Rock and Melanie that's all white? Yeah, white everything. Shoes, pants, hat."

To makeup: "Make Melanie stylishly pale tomorrow. The only splash of color we'll see are her dark red lips and blue eyes."

To the cameraman: "Charlie, how do you get that kind of glow when folks are in white? Can we do some of that tomorrow?"

They all did all of it.

Everybody had input. Impulse to expression. Maybe we get our cinematic genes from the old one-reeler hustlers. (Or from Roger Corman?) Before the creatively challenged were allowed to slither out into our sun, the most fun, yes, was from the hip, on the fly. Run, action, print, "over here" can pump fresh juice into an oft-squeezed tale. It is crucial what a cameraman like Charlie Correll and a good crew can give a director: freedom.

33

Give Thy Thoughts
No Tongue

My Bridge Burners. I should carry a fire extinguisher.

In 1982, after Grant Tinker departed MTM to take over programming at NBC, I was hired by MTM to direct the first episode of a new hospital series called *St. Elsewhere*. It had been pre-sold without a pilot. Bruce Paltrow, the executive producer, was on a publicity tour plugging the first movie he had directed, *A Little Sex*. MTM had produced the picture, and while I was prepping they screened it for all MTM employees. At the end of the picture, the silence was deafening, not one hand clapping. Outside the screening room, MTM vice-president Stu Erwin asked me what I thought. My Bridge Burners ignited. "Well, as a director, Bruce is a helluva used car salesman." Little did I know that Bethany Rooney, Paltrow's secretary, was passing by. The MTM audience was not alone in its apathy. Janet Maslin of *The New York Times* said, "[T]here have been plenty of funny movies about philandering, and this might well have been one of them. In this case, what's wrong is the sour, charmless manner in which the story is presented."

The next day I got a long distance call from Paltrow. "I hear you didn't like my picture." After a scene or project in workshops, classes or just in bull sessions, there were always discussions of "the work." You know, camera, performances, story. I started a similar exchange with Paltrow, we said goodbye and I thought no more about it.

We gathered an outstanding cast for *St. Elsewhere* and started shooting. I was enjoying the writing and the actors, but after the first day's dailies, Paltrow and the writers came to the set with such attitude that the cast labeled them the Doom and Gloom Group. Then came a second day note from Paltrow: "Not grainy enough." (He wanted to copy Bochco's *Hill Street Blues* look.) "You jump from one size to another." The cameraman was fired and his replacement was a "grainy stuff" Emmy winner. Late night calls from Erwin: "Can't you make Joe Sommer [the hospital chief of staff] harder, tougher?"

"Stu, the way he's written and why he was hired was for his compassionate quality, not for a hard-case asshole."

Josef Sommer was fired.

I'd been shooting maybe three or four days when Paltrow came onto the set, called a halt to the work and sent everyone home. I was officially fired a few days later. That evening I was having drinks with Erwin, a really good guy, and Michael Gleason. They told me about a few of the immediate rumors that "someone" had spread: "Lou's a drunk." "Right after he was fired, he went into makeup and put on blackface." It was mean. Mark Tinker was the only producer who called and expressed his sympathies. From the cast, William

Daniels and Paltrow's friend Norman Lloyd, the wisest of actors, called and wanted to know what this was all about. I had no answer.

Thomas Carter, who had acted and directed on Paltrow's 1978 series *The White Shadow*, was hired to replace me. A good director, but four days later, guess who replaced Carter? Right, Bruce Paltrow, in violation of the Directors Guild rule that no producer of a project may hire him or herself as director.

Okay, fast-forward: Eight years later, there was new management at MTM and Michael Gleason had a pilot he wanted me to direct for them. The New Boys there fought the idea because, after all, hadn't MTM fired Antonio from a project? (Positives are quickly forgotten and replaced by never-forgotten negatives.) Arthur Price, one of the owners of MTM from its inception, was still there. He told the New Boys, "Oh, yeah, but that wasn't Lou's fault."

I got the pilot, but I was forever blacklisted by all of the writers from the Paltrow group who went on to produce their own series. Eventually I learned that Bethany Rooney, Paltrow's secretary, had heard my exchange with Erwin and quickly long-distanced Paltrow my "used car salesman" aside. Why Rooney thought that would cheer her boss up, I'll never know.

I should have heeded the old World War II poster, "Loose Lips Sink Ships." Our enemies were defined in those days, we knew who the bad guys were. Lots of show biz folks are Iago-adept. A hug, "I miss you," a lunch, "luv you" are just a few of the easily applied faces (feces?) these days. Daily salute Uncle Sam's credo.

34

Patty, Ricky, Sugar, Booze

"Has Lou lost it?" Bill Self, president of CBS movies, asked my Creative Artist agent. I had been offered a CBS movie, *Something So Right*, only it had conflicted with *St. Else-where*. Well, no conflict now, and the producers Steve Tisch and Jon Avnet assured Mills that they still wanted me. When they called Creative Artists to restate their offer, Paula Wagner, ever the faithful agent, countered with, "Lou's a good director, but you should hire Jud Taylor to direct it." Tisch and Avnet insisted I be hired, and again Wagner continued to push Taylor. Tisch and Avnet said no and Wagner shut up and made my deal. Years later, I mentioned it to Taylor, he thought a minute and said, "Oh, I remember. I'd told CAA that I was unhappy with the agency and I was going to leave them. Guess she was trying to get me a job so I would stay." Agents can kiss you or kill you and both at the same time. I left the agency, as did Wagner, but not because of me. She became Tom Cruise's partner.

Written by Shelley List and Jonathan Estrin, *Something So Right* was to star Patty Duke as the single mom of troubled 12-year-old Ricky Schroder. A friend suggests that the Big Brother organization might help and they send a gallumpy nightclub owner who becomes Ricky's Big Brother. Conflicts between Mom and Ricky, the guy and Ricky, Mom and the guy, the music pumps into a happy ending.

The part of Duke's son was a natural for a natural like Schroder (he's Rick now). Several stand-up comics were suggested for the nightclub owner (that stunt casting thing again), but we were intent on casting an actor. I knew and had directed a man who seemed the opposite of what our part required, James Farentino, who had played the sexy stunt-man husband to Stockard Channing's deaf stuntwoman in *Silent Victory: The Kitty O'Neil Story*.

Steve and Jon weren't quite as incredulous at the suggestion as was the network, which was pushing Chad Everett. He wanted the part rewritten so he could play his guitar and sing a song. As much as Farentino strutted and wowed the ladies, there was a rooted sweetness in his nature that our character needed. We got him.

To make Farentino gallumpy, we thinned his thick crop of hair as if he were balding, and padded his upper torso to fatten up his sleek physique. When we filmed his first scene, something was off: his walk. It was still his cock-of-the-walk swagger. "Jimmy, maybe just one thing. The walk, maybe a kind of waddle. Like maybe he's just done a big dump in his pants. Wanna try that, see if it works for you?"

Farentino has courage, he waddled and it was perfect. Boredom is not kind to actors. One day Farentino was scheduled on a location shoot for the first scene of the day and the last scene of the day. Not smart. He subdued the interval of boredom with vodka. Two

Me spying on Patty Duke, Ricky Schroder and James Farentino, as directors are wont to do.

locations and ten hours later, he and Duke had a *Tom Jones* sexual-subtext dinner scene. Eating with fingers, drinking wine, plenty of sex signals, the scene was funny, bawdy and touching. A year later, I was talking to Farentino about how good he was in it.

"You know," he said, "I was so bombed I don't remember doing that scene."

The dangers of boredom and booze. But some still do their day's work. George C. Scott referred to himself as a functioning alcoholic. Richard Burton once told me he did a film with Lee Marvin called *The Klansman* and that he hadn't the faintest memory of it. Yet by heart he could recite Shakespearean monologues, poems by Hardy, scenes from *The Historical Historie of Dr. Faustus*, quoting both Faustus *and* Mephistopheles.

There was another addiction to deal with: sugar. Right before our lunch break, I rehearsed a two-page scene with Schroder, Farentino and Duke and they were excellent. After lunch, disaster. Schroder could not remember his lines. Sobbing, he ran to another room. I stroked. Patty, with two sons, consoled. Farentino, with a son of nine, cajoled. None of us won him back. It was a mystery, this absolutely perfect actor had fallen apart. We switched to a scene that Ricky wasn't in. I went to the caterer. "What did Ricky have for lunch?" Ricky had asked for and gotten an entire roll of those uncooked chocolate chip cookies that you bake. One pound of cookies. And a Coke. A sugar crash. A few hours later, we went back to Ricky's scene. Not a hitch. I asked Mrs. Schroder about Ricky's daily eating habits. One habit made me wince: He consumed six to eight Cokes a day. I gave Mrs. Schroder my copy of *Sugar Blues*. Later that year I went to visit my little guy on his new series *Silver Spoons*. He ran over to me: "I only drink two Cokes a day now!"

35

I Got Plenty of Nothing

Staring at my bedroom ceiling one morning, an idea for a movie meandered into my head: This thirtysomething guy loves his wife, wants to have a child, wife is too involved in her life of politics and power. He goes to the symphony alone, meets a violinist and they fall for each other, have a sweet affair, she becomes the mother-to-be of his child. His wife gets pregnant at about the same time.

I wrote a two-page synopsis and started throwing my pitch to incipient movie moguls, starting at MGM with an exec named Chris. I arrived for our after-lunch meeting. Chris was sprawled on a sofa, her assistant leaning back in his chair. Three empty beer bottles were on the coffee table. Seems as if I didn't have perfect pitch. With half-closed eyes, they mumbled a thank you. My next mogul was also a woman, Paula Weinstein at Fox. She was polite and professional, and turned it down. My third pitch was to a young man, Robert Lawrence, a junior executive at Columbia. He was interested, took it to his superior and Columbia optioned it. Hot off of *Tootsie*, they wanted Larry Gelbart to write it and that didn't happen.

This is what *did* happen. My contract stated that I was to produce and direct the picture. First chore, hire a writer. Columbia and agents were flooding me with screenplays. As I didn't have an office, they were stacking up in a corner of my bedroom to a height of, I just had to measure it, 58 inches, two inches shy of five feet. One that held me was the script of a movie I'd seen that Scorsese directed with De Niro and Jerry Lewis, *The King of Comedy*. It was funny, odd, rather dark, with well-drawn characters. Just what my movie needed. Columbia flew out the writer Paul Zimmerman from Bucks County, Pennsylvania, and in slick Hollywood fashion we hashed out a story outline in two days at his hotel, the Bel Air. We took *Micki and Maude* in for a three o'clock with Robert Lawrence and Frank Price, the big boss of Columbia. Zimmerman and I alternated doing the pitch, with Price sometimes tossing in, literally, the likes of…

"Like *Captain's Paradise*."

Then some more story and the likes of…

"Like *A Touch of Class*."

I'm thinking, "Oh, swell, is he mocking us?" Then I caught on that his references were either compliments or that he wanted our story to go along those lines. He kept canceling the rest of his appointments until finally at about five o'clock he said, "Let's get a woman's opinion."

A woman? In pops Bambi or Amy or Debbie, I don't know, a cigarette in one hand and wearing a peasant blouse showing her perkies. She looked as if she just hit 21. I encapsulated the story for her. She took a deep drag. "I hate your lead character."

Zimmerman and I were surprised. "Why?"

"Well, he obviously hates his wife so why should we like him?"

"He *loves* his wife," Zimmerman insisted.

She lights up a cigarette, the first one still burning in the ashtray.

"How can a man love his wife if he's having an affair with another woman?"

I looked at Price, who though married had a bit of a rogue rep. "Frank, you know that a man can love his wife deeply and still have an affair. True?"

He looked silently at me, poker-faced. Perky had a cigarette in each hand; her distaste for me was distracting her addiction. She left.

Price gave us a go-ahead. In evening light, Zimmerman and I paced the Columbia parking lot.

"I don't know, Lou…"

"Come on, Paul, we can do the *Captain's Paradise* thing and then cut it out before we shoot it."

"No, I mean I don't know if I want to work for a company that listens to a Bambi-Amy-Debbie. I'll have to think about it."

"Is it because she's a woman?"

"God, no. I don't care what gender brains are. Coulda been Bob, Arnold or Don. But 'a *woman's* point of view' we did not get."

(Years later, February of 2015, Perky was the successful head of Sony Pictures until she got scorched when some of her inflammatory e-mails were hacked and became public. The Internet was her Bridge Burner.)

Zimmerman called me two days later from Pennsylvania and said no.

Back to reading scripts. Another one grabbed me, *Geniuses*, an Off Broadway play by Jonathan Reynolds about a writer brought to the Philippines by Coppola to do some work on *Apocalypse Now*. It was goofy and funny and the characters were believable and sharp. Reynolds was hired.

Now a star was needed. The nominees are…

Warren Beatty? Nah, this guy has to be naive, not a seducer.

Robin Williams? Oh, come on.

Alan Alda? Perfect! He could squash a chihuahua with a manhole cover and still be lovable.

He turned us down, didn't think his female fans would want to see him in a role like that.

Dudley Moore? Even more perfect!

The good news is he took it! The bad news is he had director approval and disapproved me. Wouldn't meet me or look at my work. His movies from 1982 through 1984, *Six Weeks*, *Romantic Comedy*, *Lovesick* and *Best Defense*, were all flops. His career was in the toilet, and he was in a panic. My career was strong then, but to movie people *television* isn't a career, it's *TV*. I felt as if my child was being kidnapped.

Take a chew and forget it. Okay, I'm no longer the director, but as producer it was my job to select a director. A dozen submissions, none rang my chimes until Blake Edwards was dropped into the hat. How could I turn down a talent like that? Edwards had directed *10*, Moore's last success five years ago, a millennium in Hollywood. Edwards was set on a Monday. On Tuesday I called Lawrence of Columbia. Neither he nor anyone at Columbia ever returned my calls, ever.

"Lou who?"

But not ignored. Columbia wanted me to give up my profit participation and my executive producer credit. "In exchange for what?" I asked my agent. "In exchange for nothing." my agent answered. I turned them down. Frank Price was replaced with ex-agent Guy McElwaine. I got a letter from McElwaine while I was directing an HBO movie in Toronto. If I didn't "accede to their requests," I just might find it difficult to get hired in Hollywood.

A person I barely knew had been asked to call me and tell me that Blake Edwards' producer Jonathan Krane was a nice guy, so would I give up my producer's credit? A mellow "Screw you" aired its way west. Well, those slicks can turn a "no" into an "oh, yeah?" Worldwide, the on-screen credit reads

Executive Producer:
Jonathan Krane

Krane's credit goes off and up comes a blank screen. A few beats of silence, then a lonely—

Lou Antonio

Over the next few months, several people said to me, "I saw your name on a movie last night, but it didn't say what you did on it."

36

Legends

Elizabeth Taylor limped into my life in 1983. She'd just returned from her "peace mission" to Israel. As she recovered from a car accident in the Holy Land, newspapers across the world front-paged her smiling gamely, neck in a brace, she in a wheelchair. Taylor had many accidents in her life. Some were life-threatening, some were marriages.

I was to direct her in an HBO movie in Toronto, *Nobody Makes Me Cry*, based on a novel by Shelley List. For three weeks I scouted locations, auditioned Canadian actors, chose key crew personnel. The writer-producers, List and Jonathan Estrin, were snortin' at the gate, ready to go, when, whoops, the movie's insurance company wouldn't insure Ms. Taylor. Neck brace. Wheelchair. Peace mission pictures. She was out. HBO placed our heads under the Cancellation Guillotine. Unless we could find a star to replace her, the blade would drop. We immediately suggested Colleen Dewhurst for their approval. We got—

"No."

Okay, how about Geraldine Page?

"No."

Okay, how about—

"Either get us a star or forget about it. Like Ann-Margret or Mary Tyler Moore."

Carol Burnett wanted to do the co-starring part, wasn't that enough? Not enough for HBO. They (or *it*) demanded *two* stars. *Movie* stars. HBO proclaimed itself "Bigger Than TV" but movie stars knew their close-ups would get smaller on HBO.

These days, though, as you have noticed, quite a few stars don't believe that size matters.

Ann-Margret turned us down. I think even Kim Novak said no. The late night pizza meetings were clogging our arteries and our hopes. Despair.

A phone call. Elizabeth Taylor's agents had made a deal with the insurance company: For the first three days of any Elizabeth Taylor illness or incapacity that halted production, *Taylor* would have to pay $70,000 a day.

She wasn't on her *Cleopatra* salary any more. Though television, this gig was important to Taylor, it could prove she was fit enough, emotionally and physically, to work. (Later I learned that friends such as Robert Wagner had guaranteed any loss.) She was bailed out. Carol Burnett signed on and the snow fell on some cold and happy people in Toronto.

That's the kind of man Wagner is. I had the good fortune to work with him on *This Gun for Hire*, the Movie of the Week version of the 1942 movie. I like it when a good guy or gal gets wonderful reviews. And R.J. got 'em.

The scary part of working with Taylor, actually working *without* her, was my having

As you can see, directing Robert Wagner is low-stress.

to choose her wardrobe in her absence. What with the delays, there was no time for the usual pre-production costume designs and fittings.

Taylor and I had never met nor had a chance to discuss her character, and I hadn't the faintest notion of what kind of a person she was, what made her laugh, what moved her, what size ego she wore. Judy Gelman, a top-grade Toronto costumer, dragged me from shop to shop as I selected Taylor's entire wardrobe. A week later there she was, Elizabeth Taylor, in her Toronto hotel room thoughtfully and silently regarding my pickings item by item. Quietly she examined the clothes, touching and studying the dresses, coats, shoes, handbags, scarves, hats and gloves. I, who suddenly felt like the young, taste-free Okie that I had sought to grow beyond, was sweating out Elizabeth Taylor's approval or dismissal of her wardrobe. Which in a *Hollywood* sense meant approval or dismissal of *me*.

The Canadian producer Bob Cooper, List, Estrin and I stood quietly hyperventilating, awaiting her thumbs up or thumbs down. For me it was more than a wardrobe test, it was "Did she and I see the character the same way?" If she hated the wardrobe, I had chosen for her, would she trust my directorial choices, my style, my taste? It wasn't about fabric or color any more, it was about me.

She turned to me. "This." She touched a belt, my stomach tightened. "Maybe something a bit wider." And that was that. I had earned a plaque in the Transvestite Hall of Fame!

On our second day of rehearsal, Taylor and I were having lunch, I mining a bit to find little nuggets that I could use in working with her. Her character had come from meager circumstances and was now being proposed to by a wealthy man she didn't love. Should she marry him and so forth.

"You remember, Elizabeth, how we all started out poor, scrapping just for the rent? Remember those days? Well, you see, if—"

She looked at me quizzically. "Lou … I never had those days. I was never poor."

Oh, swell. I had read her credits, I should have read movie magazines.

The first day of filming, the actors had the normal first day flutters. Me too. Elizabeth had worked with the greatest artisans in the industry and here she was doing this low-budget Toronto TV quickie in 21 days. She was nervous, a twitch under her left eye. Rather than closing up and playing it safe, she was diving in. She wanted to be good.

"Elizabeth, let's try it this way…" Bingo, it was there. Open, vulnerable, absorbing direction, doing her job without ego or a need for pampering.

As my visual guide I was using

Elizabeth Taylor and me.

the paintings of Thomas Eakins, muted colors, classic composition. The first day's dailies would tell me and my cameraman, François Protat, if we got it. After the screening room lights went up, the producers bunched and François and I buzzed quietly about our work. Bob Cooper cleared his throat: "We think the film is too dark. It should be brighter."

The Greek in me is always too near my mouth. I leaped up and started the artist's aria. "*No!* You want this movie lit like some goddamn Aaron Spelling *Charlie's Angels*, so bright that you have to squint. I won't do it!"

"Well, like that shot of Elizabeth in the front room, she was too dark."

"Damn right. The woman doesn't know what her life is, who she is, she's literally hiding her fear from Carol."

Cooper looked to my cameraman for support. "François," dripping with subtext, "don't you think it should be brighter?"

That put François in a spot. Was his job on the line? He was staring up at me with a peculiar expression on his winter-pale face. He gestured toward me. "Theez man, theez man … he *inspire* me!"

No more talk of Brighter. Protat made beautiful film.

Burnett and Taylor? Instant friends. Not an ounce of pretension in either one of them. At lunch, instead of going to their dressing rooms, they watched soap operas, giggling and gossiping. However, there were differences in their work habits. Burnett (dubbed C.B.) was always on time. E.T. was not. Once there, she was ready to work, but to the cast or crew, never an apology for being late.

Barbara Tyson, Elizabeth Taylor, Carol Burnett (Elizabeth, stop texting!).

Early in the schedule we had a particularly difficult day to shoot. This killer day was in a chic shopping mall. Every shot was designed for the Steadicam camera, whose operator, unfortunately, was an incompetent screw-up, but you see, his daddy owned the Steadicam. Taylor was 45 minutes late, and what with her tardiness and the idiot operator I dropped as many shots as I got. Every minute lost was quality lost. The next day might be even more schedule-afflicting. It was in the Toronto train station. We had hustled a train, *but only for an exact and limited space of time*. There could be no waiting for Elizabeth or we'd never get the day's work done. I went up to her as she was leaving the mall.

"Elizabeth, tomorrow you have to be on time. Now what do you need? Do you need another makeup person, another hair person? What do you need?"

"What do I need?" She took my hand and sashayed me to a pricey suede shop in the mall. Pointing at a suede suit, she said, "I need *that*."

My face dissolved from scarlet to corpse-white. "Uh, what color? And what size?"

She smiled, "Oh, you pick the color, and they'll know my size."

Nine hundred dollars later, I took a ribboned boxed bribe to her hotel suite. She was most gracious, her secretary made me a Jackson (Jack Daniels) and soda. E.T. thanked me for the gift, we chatted and sipped our booze. Glory, glory, the next day she was two minutes early and we got wonderful film and completed the day's work on time. The following day she was 45 minutes late. The suede suit only lasted one day. (Jay Benson, a television producer, called me several years later. "You worked with Elizabeth Taylor, right? What the hell is this clause in her contract that she gets a *present* every day?")

Well into the shoot, we were preparing the last scene of the day when her secretary whispered something to her. Taylor walked to a corner of the room, sat in silence and cried. The assistant director called for the actors and she rose stiffly and went to her mark.

"Elizabeth." I stood closely to her. "What?"

She dropped her head, "Tennessee died."

I wrapped my arms around her and she sagged against me. She wept. She and Tennessee Williams had been close friends. "Do you want to go home now?" I asked.

She said she would do the scene. She stopped crying, did the master and then it was time for her close-ups. "What are you going to do?" she asked.

"What do you mean?"

"Look at me, my eyes are all puffy and red. The close-up will see it. It's not right for the scene."

I called over the cameraman and the producers. "Now tell me straight, François, is there any way we can light her close-up without the swelling showing?"

The producers leaned in anxiously, visions of dollars dancing in their heads. Protat took a beat and studied Taylor's swollen face. "No."

We shot the close-up on another day, in a different location. Vanity? Hardly. In a later scene, her character awakens hung over and stares into the early morning mirror wondering if she is going to keep pissing away her life or survive. I used one of those beveled mirrors so that I could get about six different angles and sizes in one camera move ending in an *extreme close-up*. I asked her how she would feel about doing the shot with absolutely no makeup. A dangerous question to ask a star.

She shrugged, "She wouldn't have any on."

When I saw her scrubbed face, with its clear skin, an occasional freckle, those green eyes (they didn't look purple to me), lordie, she was innocence personified. Until the camera rolled, a hangover and failure haunted her eyes, her face sagged. Burnett whispered to me, "If they carved me in marble, I couldn't have skin that smooth."

The two of them had such total trust in one another. Neither one tried taking the front seat in a scene, and neither one minded taking the back seat. They granted each other total freedom. Throw what you want, I'll catch it.

Later in the script, Taylor tries to commit suicide, fails, and is lying on the floor as Burnett rushes in, goes to her and cradles her head in her arms. I had two cameras going. The first take was terrific, but out of focus! Performances are secondary to the merciless mechanics of film.

In the second take, the two of them were just imitating take one and it was empty. The third take clicked, tears and remorse from Taylor, tears and relief from C.B. The scene as written was finished. With a signal to the crew to keep the cameras rolling, I said, "Cut." The ladies' tears turned into laughter, and then they both got quiet, thoughtful. Something personal infused each of them, something private.

Taylor's character worked part time in a bookstore. After a martini lunch she's a bit drunk, the customers are getting on her nerves, she explodes and tells them off. That's the way it was written. Taylor was playing it fine, but to end the scene it needed a banger. "Eliz-

Above: **Carol, you were way off your mark!**
Left: **Burnett and Taylor, Giving, Taking, Trusting.**

abeth, make up something at the end, you know, curl that little old lady's blue hair. Say whatever you want."

She nodded. Next take, Taylor railed at them, groped a beat, hunched over, then spewed out to an aghast blue-rinsed extra, "You, you *asshole!*" Excited, I turned to Estrin and List, the writer-producers: "Can we say that? We can say that on cable, can't we? This isn't network so it's all right, isn't it?"

They were smiling. "Don't change a syllable," Estrin said.

Carol Burnett makes your day seem better. First day of rehearsal, I didn't know squat about her personal life or what kind of person was in that consummate performer. I'd been divorced a couple of years and she was much fresher from hers, therefore, we had a mutual reference point to draw from. Burnett has the ability and courage to bring not just her comedic impulses to a role, but also her sensitivity, pain and hurt. She is sexy, sharp, susceptible and kind. Which worried one of the producers.

Marion Rees, a tasteful and savvy producer, was concerned that Burnett wasn't showing enough of her "funny stuff, what makes her Carol Burnett." That's exactly what I wanted to keep away from. She kept her performance multifaceted and honest and Rees fretful.

After all those cold days of desperately scrambling for a star, the movie was broadcast on HBO. *Variety*'s tone called it "shrewdly and unsparingly produced. Taylor … digs into the role without reservation and shows off a self-pitying, spoiled, drunken woman with all the character's blemishes. Burnett, handed a less flashy role as a bed-hopping mother … delineates the woman with superb craftsmanship…. These ladies have earned their high-toned reputations and can still deliver the goods."

Burnett was nominated by the American Cinema Editors for Best Actress. I wasn't invited to the awards dinner; I must have burned an HBO bridge. Burnett won. I'm told she graciously thanked "my director, Lou Antonio." No, no, no, Carol, thank *you*.

Appropriately, the title became *Between Friends*.

E.T. and Burton
on Broadway

In April of 1983, a job came to me in a most un–Burbank way. I was having a small dinner party and the telephone rang.

Little Girl Voice: "Hello, Lou, it's Elizabeth."

She was starring in Noël Coward's *Private Lives*, which was trying out in Boston. Milton Katselas, the director, had been fired. Was I interested in taking over, she asked?

"Elizabeth, jeez, why don't you ask Mike Nichols, or Gene Saks, or Michael Blakemore, you know, one of *those* guys?"

"Well, we did, but they all said no."

I took the red-eye to Boston and caught their last matinee. It was not good. Taylor and Burton were clunky. The show had no fun, energy, pace or sexuality. Afterwards, Taylor, producer Zev Buffman and I met for a drink. They asked me what I thought.

"I can help it, but I can't save it."

They spoke quietly together, then: "Okay, help it."

You just knew the New York critics would pound it, and being informed that Katselas' contract guaranteed him sole director's billing, thus denying me a Broadway directing credit, it certainly was not a career boost. But as one of life's little bonuses, I couldn't resist.

My first rehearsal was a few days later on the company's return to New York. A new director not only has a disquieting effect on the actors, but, well, when the new guy is a *television* director, "*Harummph!*" I didn't make a speech about myself, the play or what it needed. All I said was, "Let's take it from the top."

Taylor's character isn't in the first scene so she was given a later call. John Cullum was the other man in the play, Kathryn Walker the other woman and Helena Carroll played the maid. Of the five cast members, I knew only Taylor and Cullum.

Burton was pleasant but seemed not at all interested in his performance. In that first rehearsal, I suggested that when he was alone on his balcony he might do a bit of something romantic with his scarf. Sort of a honeymoon thing.

"Like what, dear boy?"

"Make it your dance partner, a few turns. Whatever."

He did and it was good. During a break, Cullum and I chatted a bit then he leaned in and said quietly, "Gielgud directed Richard in the Rosencrantz and Guildenstern scene and made it beautifully touching and really heartbreaking. Richard did it that one time in rehearsal and never again. You know how perverse he can be." The dance bit was never to return. Never ever had I imagined myself and Sir John joined by a director's dilemma.

In that first-day-rehearsal, Burton advised me, "Later on in the act, when Elizabeth shoots me the bird, well, they didn't do that in the '20s. Suppose you could get her to drop it? It's anachronistic."

Taylor arrived and we rehearsed up to the spot of "the bird."

"Elizabeth," I said, "I understand they didn't do that gesture in this era. Let's try something else."

"Oh, no, that always gets a laugh. We should keep it, shouldn't we, Richard?"

"Oh, yes, dear. Absolutely."

Just a dollop of I'll-get-rid-of-this-*TV*-boy. He underestimated her affection for me. I wasn't fired.

Cullum was not happy. Walker used a funny voice and played it like Betty Boop. Carroll was doing the maid as if she were in a Cockney music hall. Too many disparate acting styles. I told Cullum that there were two virile leading men up there, so let's try to find some contrast in the two characters. On Broadway, Cullum had done *Hamlet* and *Camelot* with Burton, received Tony Awards for *Shenandoah* and *On the Twentieth Century*. He is such a helluva fine actor and theater person that he understood what I was suggesting and went to work on it immediately.

Zev Buffman laid down a couple of restrictive caveats: no new blocking for Taylor and no new costumes. I could see that the wardrobe dictum was probably financial, but no re-blocking? "That would just make Elizabeth less confident," he insisted.

I cut a rain effect in Act Two, but with the staging mostly in a locked box, the lighting, sound, performances, pacing, pieces of business were all I could attend to. On second thought, that seems plenty.

What I saw on the stage in Boston were two aging, sexless actors going for laughs through charm and celebrity. Love and sex pretty much support the plot, such as it is, and both were absent. There was definitely a need to instill some sexual fizz.

Burton and I were sitting together during a break and I asked him a question or two about the *Cleopatra* days when he and Taylor fell in love. The man could mesmerize you with a story and he enjoyed telling them. He called Taylor over to clarify a point and they got into this animated conversation of "No, first you..." "But, darling, the togas and sandals..." They were getting a kick out of reliving those stormy and passionate days. Good.

"And there Elizabeth and I were in her room stark naked and that little Fisher man is pounding on the door, 'I know you're in there, open the door!'"

"So what'd you do?"

They looked at one another and smiled.

"Well, dear boy, we did not open the door and we went on about our business."

At one point in the play, she is lying next to him on the sofa. I suggested to Burton that perhaps he might try running his hand over her breast while he was saying his lines. They did it that evening and the house roared. He kept that one in.

They told me Yacht Stories, Emerald Stories, Gstaad Stories, and the more they dug up the past, the more fun they had, and the sexier they became on stage. They seemed to get younger.

Rehearsals were two hours a day, barely time for individual scene work much less a run-through. No matter the budget or size of a production, large or small, problems large and small must be solved.

There was a short dance with Burton and Taylor in the play. Done skillfully with pliant actors, it can be hilarious and usually a show-stopper. In the 1999 British National Theatre production, I saw ex-dancer Juliet Stevenson do it and the audience went wild. Not so with our two. The dance was creaky and clumsy. I tried stylized movements in place rather than dance steps.

"Richard, if you hold her in a dip there and then—"

"Can't do it, dear boy. The old back, you know."

"Uh, okay, then just two quick snaps of the head on the beat and—"

"Can't do it, bad neck, rather stiff."

"Uh, huh. Okay, Elizabeth, just half a turn upstage then a snappy look over your down right shoulder."

"I've got a bad neck, too. Remember when I came back from Israel and the accident?"

"Uh-huh. Okay, can you lean back at the waist? And Richard can circle you with his hand on your back."

"Oh, I wish I could, but I have a bad disc in my lower back."

"Well then..." A Jack Benny pause. "Why don't we try it *without* the dance?"

Previews started. By upping the energy and pacing, we had lost about eight minutes running time. Cullum was creating an interesting character. Walker was doing her same stuff. ("But that got a laugh in Boston." Oh, the curse of that age-old deflection of direction.) Carroll, playing the maid, was still doing non-stop cornball shtick. Here I was trying to bring her to the level of the rest of the cast and she was whining to Bufman that I was ruining her performance. I asked Bufman if the Coward estate would allow us to cut the maid's part completely. While he pondered the legalities, Carroll brought her performance down considerably.

Taylor was able to take notes in a way I probably never would have been capable of as an actor. Before curtain, I'd go into her dressing room while she was doing her makeup and give her notes for the first act, line readings, business, shorten that pause, etc. On stage she'd nail every note. After the first act I'd go to her dressing room and give her notes for the second act. Again, *wham!*, never missed a one. Sometimes I'd give her at least 20 suggestions! The problem being, two days later I found myself having to repeat the same notes. If she got a proper laugh, she'd mug it up and go for a bigger (albeit cheaper) laugh the next performance.

"But I got a laugh doing it that way."

"Getting a laugh doesn't mean it helps the play. Cullum could fall over the rail or drop his pants and get a laugh, but the bit would put a dent in the play."

She didn't quite trust the notion that sometimes more is too much, but I got an "Oh, all right."

At one rehearsal I suggested to Burton that he find something that would motivate their idea of running off together. He was just saying the words. Without a reality behind the action, it seemed a writer's trick. He said to me, "No, Lou, don't look for subtext, there is none with Noël." Yet in the next afternoon's rehearsal, he actually deigned to take some direction. That evening's preview played so beautifully that Bufman rushed over to me in the lobby and said, "My God, you've saved it!"

Yeah, I saved it *once*. We never got that performance again. That's the beauty of film: You only have to get it once and it's there forever.

All in all I had only about 12 to 14 hours of rehearsals, but managed to cut 17 minutes playing time, which helped it but didn't save it.

The opening night performance was solid, if not sparkling, and the atmosphere in the theater was one of friendly enthusiasm (well, except from the critics). Taylor's dressing room, painted mauve, was filled with purple roses, telegrams and gifts. I gave her a flask of Opium perfume, she gave me an inscribed Cartier watch. Al Pacino came into her dressing room, no "tell" on his face. He chatted, hugged her and left quickly. Austin Pendleton went to her. In her Broadway debut he had directed her in a highly praised performance of *The Little Foxes*. His face seemed strained. A guy can't just start giving notes on a night of room-filled purple roses. He smiled at her, confusion and sympathy in his eyes.

The party at Tavern on the Green was a blast. Elizabeth's invitations instructed "tails and tiaras." The Beautiful People packed the restaurant. They had no interest in the critics' reactions, they were happy to be there, *mingling*. Mary Tyler Moore entered, we chatted a bit and she said, "Wait. I just read your name somewhere."

"Well, yes, it was in the program tonight. 'Production supervised by...?'"

"Oh, yes. Well, see, I was right."

The best food, the best drink, the best dancers, singers, actors, producers, directors, playwrights. All the show folk categories represented and smiling. I left early and joined John Cullum and Kathryn Walker at a small, crowded midtown bar. The three of us nodded and lifted our glasses high: "They're gonna kill us."

The critics slammed the production, the audiences loved the stars. It was scheduled for a limited run and it sold out every one of its 12 previews and 63 performances. On the road it was equally successful, an event for theatergoers and fans.

An event for me as well. Not a particularly creative one, but even though the plot may have been familiar, the characters were fascinating.

While it was playing in Los Angeles, Zev Buffman and I had the notion of making a movie of it on a sound stage. We had only a window of eight days to film it because of the schedules of Taylor and Burton. The play's set designer, David Mitchell, was brought in from New York and we found two adjoining sound stages on which to build our sets.

LUNT-FONTANNE THEATRE

UNDER THE DIRECTION OF THE MESSRS. NEDERLANDER

THE Elizabeth THEATRE GROUP

ZEV BUFMAN & ELIZABETH TAYLOR

Present

ELIZABETH RICHARD TAYLOR BURTON

in

NOEL COWARD'S
PRIVATE LIVES

also starring

JOHN CULLUM   KATHRYN WALKER

and

HELENA CARROLL

Settings Designed by	Costumes Designed by	Lighting Designed by
DAVID MITCHELL	THEONI V. ALDREDGE	THARON MUSSER

Additional Music by
STANLEY SILVERMAN

Sound by	Casting by	Hair by
JACK MANN	SHIRLEY RICH	MICHAEL KRISTON

Production Stage Manager	General Management
PATRICK HORRIGAN	ALEXANDER MORR

Production Supervised by

LOU ANTONIO

Directed by

MILTON KATSELAS

The Producers and Theatre Management are Members of
The League of New York Theatres and Producers, Inc.

JUNE   20

See? There's my name. Down toward the bottom. Squint. See?

Though Bufman and I admired Taylor's theatre discipline, we were wary of her motion picture habits. Her tardiness could sink the project's extremely gaunt schedule. I suggested French hours: start at noon, no lunch break, food available all day, wrap at eight. Punctuality would be no problem for Elizabeth and she bought the idea completely, as did Burton and the rest of the cast. Hot dog, on our way! We only had to get permission from Screen Actors Guild, the International Brotherhood of Teamsters and the International Association of Theatrical and Screen Employees. Every one of the unions said "*No.*" Their reasoning was that French Hours would deprive the actors (SAG), Teamsters (IBT) and crew (IATSE) from grabbing overtime. They denied us the pleasure of Taylor and Burton together again. Burton died less than a year later, in August of 1984.

38

Lee Remick, North and South

Back in Burbank, Warner Brothers hired me to direct a TV movie in New York. *A Good Sport* was a romantic comedy along the lines of Tracy-Hepburn movies with Ralph Waite as a hard-drinking sports reporter and Lee Remick as a beautiful fashion editor. Complications … happy ending. It was a last-minute green light and instead of the usual fifteen days of preparation I had eight. Waite's production company was producing it.

Michael Norrel, an ex-actor from the TV series *Emergency*, had been hired to do rewrites on Arnold Margolin's original teleplay. On television movies I always ask the network exec for a copy of the original script, before they "improved" it. Margolin's original was better than what I was handed by the network. With Norrel among us, Remick, Waite and I kept replacing the rewritten passages with material from Margolin's original. To his credit, Norrel agreed and jumped in to help.

Waite, who played Poppa Walton on *The Waltons*, is an actor whose sole purpose was to do as well as he can with no power position attached. If he couldn't nail a scene, he'd finally say, "Do it for me, Lou, show me."

He was an interesting man. Prior to his being admitted to the Actors Studio, he had spent three years at the Yale Divinity School and then became a Presbyterian minister. Keep that calling in mind.

Flashback: We were both in *Cool Hand Luke* and late one night on location in Stockton I returned to the company's motel and went to the bar. It had closed, the lights were up and the guys were finishing their last drink. Across the room, Waite stood up, not too steadily, and shouted, "Lou!" Weaving toward me, he started disrobing. By the time he was two feet in front of me, he was grinning broadly and stark naked! It's good to have a history with your actor.

Waite had been sober for eight years by the time we did *A Good Sport*. In a Greenwich Village bar we had a scene in which he does his dialogue and tosses down a straight shot. During the take, he raises the glass to toss down the shot. The booze was about an inch from his lips when he stopped and said, "This is real whiskey." I cut. The prop man was cringing with embarrassment. I asked Waite what would have happened had he downed that first shot of alcohol in eight years. He looked at me and shook his head. "I don't know, I just don't know."

Lee Remick loved direction, welcomed it. In this, our first of three television movies together, she told me that when she was doing Kazan's *A Face in the Crowd*, her debut film, he asked her to think of some personal and painfully sad event in her life before a particular scene. She told him that never worked for her. Her system (like Katina Paxinou's) was to

On the set of *Rearview Mirror*, a Southern thriller with Lee Remick.

be the character and the emotion would happen. She was smart, funny, beautiful, genuine, full of enjoyment and good cheer. As was the public's reaction to the movie:

> "[This] telefilm turns into a delight. ...Remick and Waite demonstrate a solid talent for lightweight comedy touches...."—*Variety*
>
> "A blithely engaging contemporary romantic comedy.... Arnold Margolin's script is witty, sophisticated and delightfully reminiscent of Tracy-Hepburn teamings..."—*Hollywood Reporter.*

A year later, my second movie with Remick, NBC's *Rearview Mirror*, was a scary woman-in-jeopardy thriller by Lorenzo Semple who wrote *Never Say Never Again* (Sean Connery's last appearance as James Bond), *The Parallax View* and *Three Days of the Condor*. Our movie was set in the South Carolina countryside outside a hot and humid Charleston. Michael Beck is terrifying as a sadistic escaped convict who captures, toys with, and humiliates Remick, ultimately threatening to kill her. *Variety* praised him: "Michael Beck was too real as the crazed convict..." What actor wouldn't somersault over "too real"? And a gentler man you'll never meet.

Tony Musante, who had been in *Breaking Up Is Hard to Do*, played a New York cop transferred south to help the local sheriff rescue Remick. Brother Jim was the sheriff. Acting with Jim, an experienced and respected pro, or directing him is always great because we have so many specifics in our lives that we can use as a creative short-hand. Jim might suggest something like, "Hey, remember that gesture Poppa would do when he couldn't think of the right word in English? Maybe something like that?" Or I'd say, "Try the moment like Uncle Nick might do it. You know, how he'd never look at you when he was talking about himself." Some directors hire the same actors over and over because their creative familiarity is imbued with trust. Kazan, Frankenheimer, Ford, Soderberg, Apatow come to mind. Jim, however, says the only reason I hire him is so I can tell him what to do.

Shooting on location lifts a film. Everyday, at-home distractions are diminished. No taking the car in for a lube, cleaning the house, fixing a stopped-up toilet, getting your teeth cleaned. There is little to absorb your concentration except the job at hand, and finding a good restaurant and wine shop. Except I prefer my own cooking so I always get an apartment or a house, wherever there's a kitchen. At the end of the day's shooting, some of the crew and actors would bring bread and wine, I'd cook and we'd laugh, tell stories. With her ever-ebullient nature, Lee would proclaim, "It doesn't get any better than this!"

Yet another advantage of location shooting is that you can wing it with no network nitwit coming on set to dampen the day. There was a three-page sit-and-talk scene between the Southern sheriff (brother Jim) and the New York detective transplant (Musante). I asked them if they would mind rehearsing their scene while I took 15 minutes to shoot some exterior angles of the police station.

"Only instead of being at the table," I suggested, "see if you can start up there at the top of the stairs, improvising something as you come down the stairs, then end up at Jim's desk on the first floor. And, oh, throw in something to button the scene." I came back, they were ready to shoot. They came down the stairs, story points intact, and at the desk, Musante handed Jim a cold piece of pizza. Jim sniffed it. "'Stead of yore people's pizza thang, shoulda gotten us some Southern fried chicken, somethin' reliable." Not a biggie, but a chuckle, and those few added lines gave the script a better transition into the following scene. From time to time, actors, serendipity and locations are treasures to plunder.

39

Peter the Great,
Dunaway Less

A two-hour pilot script from Universal written by Peter Fischer, Bill Linke and Richard Levinson was sent to me. It was called *Murder She Wrote* and it was just right. I called Fischer and told him how much I liked it and asked if the role of the lady author had been cast. He said Jean Stapleton and my heart sank. She was wrong for that woman. With regrets I signed on for a MOW. Wouldn't you know, Ms. Stapleton dropped out and Angela Lansbury was hired. And I was in Greenwich Village shooting a television movie trying to justify Art over Residuals. Also, I waved aloha to the pilot of *Magnum P.I.* starring Tom Selleck. I'd done two pilots with Selleck. He was wonderful to work with and I liked him a lot. It was difficult to say no, but I simply did not want to work with producers Glen Larson and Don Bellisario. Larson had done the Copycat caper on a *Rockford Files* script, and Bellisario's reputation as a meddling demagogue preceded him, so bye-bye, *Magnum P.I.* And to 12 years of *Murder*'s royalties and residuals and *Magnum*'s eight; collectively I could have opened my mailbox to 20 years of smiles. A plan, a plan, my kingdom for a plan. Or a crystal ball.

Several months after *Rearview Mirror*, Warner Brothers Television gave me a present, an Agatha Christie mystery, *13 at Dinner* with Peter Ustinov as Hercule Poirot, a character he'd played in *Death on the Nile* (1978) and *Evil Under the Sun* (1982). Ah, my seductive friend, location. It was to be filmed in London. Alan Shayne, head of Warner Television, wanted Faye Dunaway to play dual roles of the actress-villain and her lookalike nightclub comic. "Alan," I said, "Bernadette Peters would be better. If Dunaway does it, they'll know who the murderer is before the opening credits are over."

"I discovered Faye. I cast her in *Hogan's Goat*, her first play in New York. She will be wonderful."

A television director does not have star approval. In movie and play reviews, word of mouth can bring an audience in. Not so in movies for television. It has got that one night to suck in the viewers. It's that star, and/or the little two-sentence blurb in *TV Guide* that gets 'em to the tube. "Tonight's movie has three fun-loving nuns seducing the Notre Dame football team and suffering humiliation on finding the defensive line and quarterback drunk and naked with their parish priests." Well, okay, maybe you don't need a star for that one.

Dunaway was living in London with her four-year-old son and celebrity photographer husband Terry O'Neil. I called two directors who had worked with her.

1: "Never will I work with her again. After the set's lit, she walks through it looking into a mirror to make sure she's lit right. Drove my cameraman crazy, he wanted to quit."

2: "I never want to work with her again. Doesn't matter what direction you give her, she won't change."

Swell. Two out of two.

Dunaway's career was a bit shaky after three flop pictures in a row, *Wicked Lady* (1983), *Ordeal by Innocence* (1984) and *Supergirl* (1984). Of lesser import, but still a career C-, the rumor of drugs had chilled her heat. She had just signed with my agency, CAA, who assured her they could bring her back. They figured that doing this TV movie and changing her publicist would shine her tarnished image. (Actors hire publicists to hide, disguise, maintain or change an image. Image: "a fabricated object of symbolic value.") If I build me, they will come.

I asked that three things be communicated to Dunaway: (1) no walking the set with a mirror, (2) no talking to the cameraman, (3) no watching dailies.

"Oh, of course, and don't worry, she'll be fine."—the Silver Tongue of Alan Shayne. What, me worry?

Ah, the blessings of the multi-talents of Peter Ustinov. His knowledge, wit, precision, his kindness.

During my early days in New York, I read for *The Last Angry Man*, a movie from a Gerald Greene novel about a crusty, temperamental Brooklyn doctor in a rundown tenement neighborhood. I met with Daniel Mann, the director, and author Greene. (Screenplays are by a writer, novels are by an *author*.) They asked me what I thought of the script. I gave them a critique from the depths of my 22 years. Mann nodded and said, "Uh, huh. Well, thanks, Lou, for coming in."

Joby Baker got the part.

A week later I got a call from Mr. Mann asking me as a favor to read with an actor whom they were considering for the part of the Brooklyn doctor. I put on the suit and the tie and on a chilly Sunday morning walked to the Sherry Netherland Hotel. Another young Lou had read for the movie—Louis Gossett, Jr.—and he was also there to help. He and I were new to all this, and especially to a hotel like the Sherry Netherland.

The actor that Mann was considering was Peter Ustinov. What an acting lesson the two Lous got that day. Over a period of six hours, we got to watch this refined British actor transform himself into a Jewish doctor from Brooklyn. Plus we got a lavish room service lunch for free. During the lunch break, I told Ustinov how taken I was with his Nero in *Qvo Vadis*. "How old were you when you did that part?" I asked him.

"I think I was 25."

Twenty-five! There I was 22 and an unsettling distance from such expertise. Chicken fry, pick it up! On the set of *13 at Dinner* I reminded Ustinov of that first meeting. He didn't remember it. I'll never forget it.

Rose Tobias Shaw was the casting person in London. We had met in New York when she'd cast me in several of my early TV roles. She was now married to a Brit and living in London. During prep, I'd come in every day with enthusiasm about an actor I'd seen perform. "Rose, did you see Clive in the fringe play at—" (Fringe plays are the equivalent of Off Broadway.)

"Oh, I don't see fringe plays."

Next day:

"Did you see Prunella in the West End play called—"

"Oh, I don't go to the theater."

Next day:

"Did you see Nigel last night on television in—?"

"I don't watch television."

Next day:

"I saw an interesting actor in a movie last night. Do you—"

"I don't go to movies."

A London-to-Burbank whine got Alan Shayne over to help me with casting.

Man, those Brits are interesting, and the well-known ones haven't the slightest hesitation about coming in to read or meet. What a parade of performances came before me, and I didn't have to buy a ticket. Natasha, the youngest Richardson-Redgrave daughter, was a marvel, but she threw us over to do Chekhov in Birmingham rep. Stanley Baker's son Glyn read and was cast. Edward Woodward and Frank Finlay came in for Poirot's stuffy sidekick Hastings, as did two-time Tony-nominated Alec McCowen (*Hadrian VII*, *The Philanthropist*). As if at a cocktail party, they were outgoing and relaxed, and held Shayne and me helpless with great stories. There are fine actors all over the world and I get to talk with them, watch them act, and get paid for it.

John Stride and I had done *The Lady of the Camellias* together on Broadway. At his house in London we had a drink and I asked him if he'd read for Hastings. He did. Too young, sexy and attractive for the part. Okay, I asked him then if he would mind playing a small part, the role of a nervous film director: "John, I'll certainly understand if you turn it down. There aren't many lines, but hell, we'll make some up." Stride had starred in his own popular series in the UK three years earlier. A downgrade in his career?

"I'll play it. We'll have some fun."

One actor gave a peculiar twist to a role and Shayne whispered to me, "Read him for Hastings." Shayne has a terrific eye. He was right. Jonathan Cecil was an unforgettable Hastings, an off-center, perfectly polite, perfectly uptight, perfectly eccentric Poirot foil. Ustinov and Cecil unearthed the coincidence that Ustinov had been a pupil of Cecil's father at Oxford.

David Suchet auditioned for the part of Scotland Yard Inspector Japp and sailed with it. Later, during the shoot, he asked my advice about whether he should go back to the Royal Shakespeare Company or stay on in films and television. "It depends on your creative and financial needs," I said. "They are not always compatible, but a career here goes unpunished even when you do radio."

"Well, the money *is* raising its ugly head," he replied.

Toward the end of the shoot, he confided in me, "You didn't know this, but while I was waiting to audition for you, I was also waiting to hear from the doctors if my wife was going to live or die. The National wants me to do Iago, but I don't know…"

Live or die? Iago? Films, television. Jeez.

His wife is fine now. What tickles me is that Suchet went on to great success playing the Poirot character in 24 seasons of that television series, plus continuing his Shakespeare and winning all kinds of prizes.

The first day's dailies were fine. To dilute any hardness, I had Dunaway costumed in soft fabrics of off-whites, pale pinks and pastels, and the cameraman Curtis Clark, a Texan trained in London, lit her beautifully. The artifice of her acting would be right for both characters. Alan Shayne called me from the States, very pleased. And, oh, by the way, "Faye wants to see the dailies."

"No, Alan, that was not the agreement."

The next phone call, from my agent Ron Meyer at CAA: "Lou, isn't it okay if Faye sees the dailies?"

"No."

"Okay. She just wanted me to ask."

In the script's opening scene, Ustinov is being interviewed on a TV chat show. To play the host, we hired David Frost, who'd made his living and reputation from his show interviewing the famous and infamous. I encouraged Ustinov and Frost to improvise whatever they wanted. It went 50–50, that is, Ustinov was quick and funny and Frost was not. Half an hour later I saw Frost sitting next to a man who was scribbling in a small notebook and handing the pages to Frost. I asked my assistant director David Tringham who the guy was.

"Oh, that's Frost's writer. After that last improvisation, David rang him up to get here quick. He's writing some ad libs for David."

A three-page question-and-answer scene (always plenty of those in a murder mystery) had originally been written to play in a restaurant. In my location hunting I came upon a canal. Yes, a canal in London! Brainstorm. I'd have Dunaway as the actress do a morning jog on a path next to the water with Ustinov and Cecil keeping pace in a small motorboat, Cecil at the rudder.

Close-ups can be lonely, as Peter Ustinov discovered.

Benedict Taylor (far left) learns from his elders, Allan Cuthbertson (in hat) and Peter Ustinov.

Lord protect me from the Muse of Shallow Cleverness.

By the time we reached the canal, traversing the midday London traffic had put us two hours behind schedule, and Dunaway was taking forever to get out of her motor home. Tringham dubbed her "Faraway."

But I couldn't wait, the winter sun sticks to its own schedule. I turned to Ustinov: "Peter, this is not fair to you, but do you suppose we could go ahead and shoot your close-up while we're waiting for Faye? I'll have Caroline [the script supervisor] read the offstage lines for you."

"Of course. But I don't want Caroline to do the lines."

"Oh. Well, who? Do you want me to read them?"

"No, I don't want anyone to read them." Ustinov and Cecil got into the boat.

"Peter, I'm not sure I've got this. You don't want *anyone* to do the off-stage cues?"

He nodded. I rolled the camera. The grips towed the boat for a 120-foot dolly shot, Ustinov said his lines, listened to silence, reacted to silence, looked to Cecil, said another line and so on. He played the entire scene honestly and flawlessly with all its nuances! "Print!"

"Peter, I've never seen anything like that in my life. How did you do that?"

He answered quite simply: "When I work on the part in my hotel room, I *rehearse* alone, don't I?"

Faye wasn't really a problem. As she started to relax and gain confidence, I was fairly sure that Shayne and Ron Meyer were feeding her positive reactions from her dailies. And what a perfectionist. One of her two characters is found dead on her bed by Poirot and

Hastings. It was Ustinov and Cecil's scene, all Faye had to do was hold her breath and lie there lifeless for a few seconds. I shot their point of view of her dead body, breath held and lifeless. Good, NAR (No Acting Required). Cut, print. She rose from the bed, hurried over to me and whispered, "Lou, could I have another one?" She wasn't kidding. I said, "No," fearing she might overact dead.

Remember the self-addiction of actors? We had a difficult day ahead of us inside Albert Hall: stunts, Poirot's revealing of the murderer, Dunaway madly playing away at its giant organ, the reveal of the villain, stuff like that. As is my wont, I arrived before most of the crew: 5:30 a.m., pitch black, and cold. Dunaway's call was for five. What's this then? Sitting on the curb outside Dunaway's motor home were her hair and makeup women. They were smoking cigarettes and shivering.

"What are you two doing out here in the cold? Paula, you don't smoke."

"I thought a fag might warm me up."

"But what are you doing sitting out here on the curb?"

The two women looked at each other. Paula said, "We were doing Faye and she told us she wanted to be alone. Says she wanted to listen to music to help her get in the mood of her character, and for us to leave."

Anna, the hairdresser, stood and stepped on her cigarette. "*And* we've taken enough shit from her so we were sitting here thinking, 'Do we quit or not?'"

When good producers must save the day, ours, Neil Hartley, was awakened, hurried over, sorted the whole thing out. Hartley was an American from the South who as a young actor had toured with Tallulah Bankhead. He knew his way around misbehaving actors. In my first Broadway play, *The Good Soup*, he'd been David Merrick's stern and unsmiling stage manager. He'd lived in London for many years as Tony Richardson's producer. Because he knew everyone in town, we got a top-notch crew and stunning visual locations from castles to Albert Hall to the steps of Old Bailey. I know of at least ten subsequent producers that I've worked with whom I wish could have shadowed Hartley, learning how a bona fide producer can enhance a production. Hartley protected the director, not his own ass.

Dunaway was good in both roles and on set never a problem. She held to our agreements and was always prepared and responsive to suggestions. I think it helped that we had touchstones we could share: Kazan, our theater time in New York, a few mutual theater friends. It was sad to see that she didn't laugh much, but she was there to prove to her new agents that she would be worth having as a client. She accomplished that.

Years later at a Directors Guild screening, she saw me and said to me, "Aren't you one of my old directors?"

"Former," says I.

40

Candice Bergen: Motherhood to Madam

Mayflower Madam (1987) was a resurrection for Candice Bergen. She hadn't acted in two or three years; she put her time to better use, being with her husband Louis Malle and birthing and attending their daughter Chloe.

Robert Halmi, the Mike Todd of television, owned the rights to Sydney Biddle Barrows' *Mayflower Madam*, a successful and scandalous memoir about Barrows as a young Blue Book socialite who created a successful call girl business in New York City, and got caught. Halmi was chasing Bergen for the Madam.

Before motherhood, Bergen had done a piece of TV trash called *Hollywood Wives*, parts one and two. Wary of venturing into tawdry waters again, she was reluctant to accept Halmi's offer to play a madam. I wasn't too hot to dive in either, but I am usually open for an all-expenses-paid trip to damn near anywhere, especially to Manhattan where my art got its start. Bergen and I met there for Halmi to talk us into it.

It takes only a few moments to be captivated by Candice Bergen's wit and intelligence. She was nervous not only about "coming back," but about hitting the airwaves with what had the chance of being a real piece of smelly.

After 30 minutes of paddling ideas back and forth, testing one another as it were, I knew that I wanted to work with her. She committed herself to the project, as did I. Halmi clapped his hands: "Okay, vee got a dill!" (That's Hungarian English for a *deal*, not a pickle.)

I watched hours of talk-show tapes of Sydney Biddle Barrows, the madam. She was one slick chick. Damn, for each interview she'd go through the same drill, same stories, same innuendoes, and as a result I didn't learn one thing about *her*, what she emotionally went through being booted out of the Blue Book, losing friends, her love life, facing her family. I arranged to meet with her in her modest West Side apartment. She was 35, attractive in an understated way, wore a simple beige dress and appeared to be apprehensive about my questioning her.

"What gave you the idea of being a madam?"

"I needed money."

"For what?"

"To live on."

What was she, what was in there? "Sydney, did you ever, out of curiosity or for the money, turn a trick?"

"Absolutely not."

As my questions became personal, the reactions of her family and friends, she'd launch into her meaningless talk show routine.

Maybe she'd open up to Bergen. The three of us were at lunch at Café des Artistes, a polite, quiet, and very expensive restaurant. I had a quick vodka and slipped Bergen my credit card and whispered, "Get into 'girl talk' if you can. I'll leave you two alone."

"Well, I've got a meeting. You two stay and have your lunch."

Barrows jumped in. "Who's paying for it?"

That was one thing I learned about Ms. Barrows.

Speaking of monetary, Atlanta was to double as New York City because Halmi got cheaper crew rates there. Steve Mills, head of the CBS movie division, had misgivings about that. Mills was experienced, smart and right. Rather than try to appease Mills, I had to convince Halmi that three

Top: **Producer Robert Halmi, the Mike Todd of television.** *Bottom:* **The Mayflower Madam, Sydney Biddle Barrows.**

days of exterior scenes should be filmed in Manhattan to intercut with our Atlanta footage. For all its architectural variety, Atlanta had no stoops, no brownstones, no bridges, and no hotel remotely similar to the Plaza, where our closing scene had to take place. Manhattan would boost the budget a bit, but Halmi wasn't about to alienate CBS for a few dollars more. I was told the few dollars became a $40,000 boost.

Production designer Charlie Bennett and I plotted the disguises we'd use to make Atlanta look a little more Manhattan-like. Color correcting the street signs with decals to match New York City's, bright yellow paint jobs on five cars to turn them into New York taxis, hot dog wagons, sidewalk vendors, a fake subway entrance. Henry Bronchstein, straight from the streets of New York, was my assistant director. (He later went to the streets of New Jersey as a producer of *The Sopranos*.) He did a bang-up job recreating the hustle and hurry of Manhattan. Long lenses helped hide Atlanta and I think we did a pretty fair camouflage. Certainly better than the African American-less and sanitary tameness of Toronto so often used as Gotham.

I did a bit of homework on Bergen. Saw a lot of her movies and, wow, what a beauty. Not much range in the acting department when she debuted in *The Group* in 1966, but when you're a gorgeous teenager that's not a requirement for being a movie star. Treat yourself to her and search Netflix for *The Group, The Wind and the Lion, The Sand Pebbles, Getting Straight, Carnal Knowledge, Gandhi*. I also kept reading her book, *Knock on Wood*.

I had trouble figuring out how to address her. "Candice" sat too stiffly on my lips and "Candy" would have made us both spit up. During a telephone conversation, "Bergitz"

Chita Rivera (left) was a hot dancer and hot actor. Note Candice Bergen's concept of courtroom deportment.

jumped out and she laughed. "You've stolen my heart," and that was that, she was Bergitz from then on.

The script still needed help with some of those old standards like character, conflict, humor, resolution. The previous year, Halmi had hired playwright Jeffrey Sweet to rewrite *Pack of Lies*, his Ellen Burstyn–Alan Bates TV movie. Sweet joined us in Atlanta to "punch up" *Mayflower Madam*. He was welcomed with open typewriter.

During prep, Bergen, line producer Ira Halberstadt, Sweet and I would have evening meets in my Atlanta apartment. I'd cook a little pasta, toss a little salad, pour a lot of wine. The script was a bit cold, it needed some fun, some humor. Bergitz jumped up and announced, "You want funny? I'll show you funny. Give me a song to sing!!"

Bergitz had admitted to being rusty and was game for anything. At the end of the movie, the Mayflower Madam is silently watching the debutantes enter the Plaza for their debut, an important event for these young women, as it had been for Barrows. You're only a debutante once. It was an occasion she had attended annually until her notoriety and removal from the Blue Book. Her moment of an era gone, a tinge of remorse, a thread of nostalgia, her future? Not there. Bergen's concentration went south, her involvement zero.

"Bergitz, do you know any foreign language, even a little bit?"

"Uh, some Spanish…"

"Now this may sound nonsensical and insulting, but it's just an acting tool. As you look at the girls, start counting backwards from ten in Spanish. Nothing else, no acting, just—"

"Oh I know about that! Gene Hackman showed me stuff like that. Yes, sure."

It was simple, it was connected, the *story* told the audience what Sidney Biddle Barrows was thinking. Thanks, Gene, a job well done.

Bergen never seemed secure about her acting ability. After a take: "I can't do it any better, that's all I can do with it."

"It's not a question of better, let's just do it differently."

Later: "I don't think I'm good enough for motion pictures. I might be good enough for television. Maybe I should get out of this business."

No psychic she. *Mayflower Madam* was in the top ten for the week, and for her series *Murphy Brown*, she won five Emmys and two Golden Globes. Now in her sexy seventies, she's busy with television, Broadway and *movies*. Considering her perfect profile, here's a Bergitz that came looping out of left field, one that I still puzzle over:

"I hate my nose."

41

Academy Award Winners
and Whiners

In New York, there's the Broadway Show League. Casts of plays and acting groups field teams every summer in Central Park to play for the league championship. On the 1963 Actors Studio team, Jim, who had once turned down a berth in the minors, played third base and I played second base, where a lob to first was short and sufficient. We were up against the Circle in the Square team and George C. Scott, a very competitive man, was their pitcher. I had a good day, two doubles, and we beat 'em.

Next season I was acting on Broadway in *The Ballad of the Sad Café* opposite Colleen Dewhurst, then Scott's wife. They invited me and my girlfriend to their house in Riverdale for supper. Scott wasn't drinking—he didn't consider beer and after-dinner cognac drinking.

The evening didn't start too well. My date had brought her neurotic Afghan hound and we heard a gravel-voiced yell from another room. "That goddamn faggot dog shit on my floor!" Dewhurst whooped and grabbed paper towels.

During dinner, I kidded Scott about the two doubles I got off him that summer. "Bullshit," he said. "No one ever got two doubles off me." A George C. Scott glare. "So you're lookin' in pretty good shape. Got a tough gut, have you?"

Dewhurst, warning him, "George…"

What with running along route 9W and lifting weights before the show, I was fit but not sculpted. "I guess it's okay."

"Colleen pulls those punches in the fight scene. What if she didn't? What would happen?"

Dewhurst, "*G e o r g e…*"

"I'd be okay, I guess."

Scott got up quickly from the table. "Let's see."

I stood up, he reared back and pounded a fist into my stomach. I slid on my butt about 15 feet across the waxed floor. Other than a fist-sized red welt on my tumtum, I showed no signs of his shot.

Dewhurst, sweetly: "So, G.C., does this mean if I nail Lou during the fight, I won't have to worry about him?"

"Yeah, yeah, but stage fights are bullshit. And no one *ever* got two doubles off me!"

When he was sober, G.C. was a quiet, thoughtful, interesting man. His and Dewhurst's relationship has been chronicled, but my favorite tale is when they got divorced in 1965. Their fellow actor and friend Clifton James was heard to mutter, "This divorce will never last."

George C. Scott pitching, me on second base dancing.

They remarried in 1970, appropriately on July Fourth. The second divorce two years later did last.

That was just a bit of our history before I directed George C. in Savannah, Georgia, an intriguing city. I chose it as the location for a two-hour CBS movie entitled *Pals*, a comedy with Don Ameche and Scott playing retired postal clerks who discover an abandoned car with two million dollars in the trunk. It's gangster money and one of the bad guys chases them. As I was leaving for Savannah to prep, the CBS mogulette Larry Strychman called me into his office and issued a stern order: "No rewrites. Not a word is changed unless it comes through my office."

The mogulettes seldom left their thrones to visit an out-of-town location for fear of leaving their tenuous seats of power unprotected. However, for filmmakers, location is a welcome respite from network intruders. Taking advantage of that, here's an example of how we have to hurdle their hubris.

Whenever I found it necessary, I'd approach George C., hold up some pages and, shaking my head, intone, "What do you think of this scene?"

"It's shit," Scott would growl.

I'd rewrite, go to him the next day and hold up the new pages. "What do you think of the scene now?"

"I say let's shoot the damn thing."

The on-set producer, Ira Halberstadt, a cagey New Yorker, would then dutifully call

George C. Scott expounding upon … something.

Strychnine and tell him that Scott would not shoot the scene as written and that Lou was accommodating Scott with a few changes.

George C. had two sane provisions in his contract. Instead of the usual six-day location work week, we did five-day weeks, and only ten-hour days, his call from eight a.m. to six p.m. This clause wasn't star stuff, it was for a practical reason. Scott started drinking vodka with a beer chaser at about ten in the morning. He knew that after six, his performance might begin to waver.

At that time I thought, and I certainly wasn't the only one, that George C. Scott and Marlon Brando were the finest actors in America. Their early work was volatile, original and dangerous. I told him so, he thanked me.

"I want to ask you something, George. Why did we lose you? You and Marlon should be doing the great roles. Where did you go?"

He thought a moment. "I don't know, it's just like, like my pilot light just … went out."

"When? When did that happen?"

"Guess about 11 years ago." (About six years after *Patton.*)

"But look at you. You're still a damn fine actor. You don't dog it or slough it off. Why is that? Pride?"

"Yes, I think it might be. I don't know."

I never asked or learned why the pilot light went out, but I did learn about acting from Scott. Once, between takes, I complimented him on his performance in *The Hustler*, and asked him how he had prepared for it and executed it. He thought a beat. "I played it the way Ben Gazzara would have played it."

That doesn't mean he did an impression of Gazzara. Actors often work from a character image of some kind. Scott's technique was to find one or more aspects of Gazzara that enticed his imagination and propelled him to selective physical movements, attitudes and emotions. It sure as hell worked.

I had directed Don Ameche in an episode of *McCloud* in 1975. At the time he was not exactly at the height of his career. Most of his jobs were in dinner theaters. In fact, the Hollywood casting directory didn't list an agent for him, only a message service. It was a rotten period for a man who had been a movie star in the '30s and '40s. On *McCloud* we had gotten along fine and later I hired him for a Tom Selleck pilot. He did a good job, accommodating, pleasant, and relieved to be taking a break from clanking flatware. Now here we were 12 years later in Savannah, his career rejuvenated by an Academy Award won a year earlier for *Cocoon*. However, he was still not a familiar name to a young Atlanta production assistant.

"There's a call from Los Angeles."

"Who's it for?"

"Dunno. We got some lady here named Donna Meechy?"

Nor did I escape: "We gotta LuAnn Tonio here?"

We had two days of rehearsal in Savannah. Ameche and Sylvia Sidney, playing Scott's mother, antagonized each other on sight. She would smoke and bitch about Ameche, he would come to me complaining about her. Sylvia Sidney had been a movie star in the same era as Ameche. She was 76, crabby, tough, and not in the best of health. She noted of her youthful days as a movie star: "I had great tits. *Still* got 'em."

On the second day of shooting, there was a scene in a parking lot with Scott and Ameche. Scott suggested, "Don, maybe if you moved to this side of the car during that—"

"No."

"See, that way you can stand in front of the license plate and the cop won't see it."

"No. I'll stay where I am."

"Am I missing what you're after here?"

"I don't know if you are or not, I'm not making the cross."

The sun was doing down. Oh, well, I could make it work in the edit. "Okay. Fine. Let's shoot it."

My telephone rang at about ten that night. It was the producer Robert Halmi from New York. (You'll have to do your own Hungarian accent for his dialogue.)

"So what's the matter with you and Don?"

"The matter? Nothing. Just a little blocking problem, but it was insignificant."

"Then why does he want to quit the picture?"

"Quit?! Why? What'd he say?"

"Well, he says George is getting more close-ups than he is."

"He's counting close-ups!?"

Exhaling, I reassured Halmi, "I'll talk to him tomorrow."

The first set-up the next morning was a oner with Ameche and an excellent young

Working out a problem with Don Ameche. Maybe...

actress, Susan Rinell. We rehearsed and blocked the scene. While the crew went to work, I touched him on the elbow and said, "Don, I understand there's a problem. Let's—"

Bing! He jerked his arm away. "There's no problem! I know what you think of me by the close-ups I'm not getting!"

"No, I think you are doing a terrific job and if—"

He started walking away from me, walking backwards and shouting, "I *know* what you think of me. Of my part. Of me as an actor. By the way, you're covering me!"

After lights and sound were ready, he returned to the set. "I am a professional, let's shoot the scene."

We did. Oh, me, he was over the top. O.T.T. as we say in the show biz. "Uh, Don, maybe simpler, a little less."

"*Vocally* or *facially*?"

"Uh ... both."

He did them both a bit more than a little less, but still less. He was a professional.

I must say that I did have admiration for Ameche. He was 78 years old, bright, friendly when he wasn't being testy, and ran an hour a day. To defrost his chill toward me, I wrote a short scene of a 50-yard dash competition with some locals and Ameche in running shorts, to show off his sturdy legs. His character wins the race, and as Ameche realized I was on his side, his tantrums subsided.

When an actor comes in to audition and hands me his or her résumé, I look first at the training and then to the bottom of the résumé at the Special Abilities category. I've seen some doozies. Aside from the usual martial arts, dialects, sports, yoga, languages, horseback and ballet, I've encountered basket weavers, snake handlers, jugglers, fire swallowing, belly-dancers, actors who can bark like dogs, and an actor who "can whistle with my tongue hanging out." In Georgia, one caught my eye: "Wheelchair skills including a wheelie." I cast that actor, Marc Gowan, as the judge in a tax evasion case with Scott and Ameche as the defendants. We shot in a Savannah courtroom, and without telling Scott and Ameche I had a ramp built adjoining the judge's bench. All they could see was an actor sitting up there in a black robe. We rehearsed the scene with the judge announcing his verdict from behind his bench, Scott and Ameche seated at the defendant's table. For the first set-up, I had two cameras on my stars for their reactions and dialogue. Okay, we're filming the first take, they do their dialogue, the judge bangs his gavel, whips down the ramp in his wheelchair, stops in front of Scott and Ameche, does a wheelie, and pronounces, "Not guilty!"

Out of Scott pops, "What the fuck was *that*?"

That was a Special Ability. Print.

In another sequence, Scott was hitting the last two lines of a scene too heavily, flattening the character's comedic flair. We tried it again.

It wasn't right. I went to Scott. He growled at me, "You're not going to give another goddamn acting lesson are you?"

I suggested an adjustment. We tried it again. Three takes go by.

"What the hell's wrong with it?" Scott asked.

"It's still a little too … too Robert Newton."

"Jesus, Lou, you're making me self-conscious."

That stung me. What an awful thing for a director to do. Experienced actors can be as sensitive, apprehensive and unsure as a beginner. A director must never forget that. I apologized. We got the shot.

We moved to another location. Scott was leaning against a porch rail smiling. "I wouldn't be in your shoes for anything," he said.

"What do you mean?"

Nodding toward Ameche and Sidney: "You'll never shut her up, he'll never stop complaining, and I'll get drunk and fall all over you."

He was right on the first two predictions, but not once did he fall all over me. Scott would try anything as an actor. In one sequence, the men are in a Denny's having a sandwich, his mom is napping in their car. Scott looks out the window. The car is gone. His character reacts to his missing mother and runs into the parking lot looking for her. I asked Scott if he was familiar with the Charlie Brown comic strip.

"Love it."

"Okay, you know how Charlie's mouth gets as wide as a river when he's been tricked by Lucy and he yowls? Maybe Charlie Brown when you realize Mom's vanished."

Cameras rolled, George threw back his head and with tears in his eyes and stamping his feet like a kid, he yells full out, "Mmmommmmmm!"

Fearless actors bring tears to *my* eyes.

At ten one morning, I went into his motor home to talk over an upcoming scene. He was alone watching TV. Well, not completely alone. He had a can of Budweiser and a small glass of straight vodka before him.

"You want a beer? A drink?" he asked.

I declined. We talked briefly about the scene and then I indicated the half-gallon of Smirnoff on the table and joked, "You know, George, you can afford it, why don't you get the 100 proof instead of that cheap 80 proof?"

"What, are you crazy? I'd get shit-faced."

The bottle would be empty by six, but he never fluffed a line, never lost his way in a scene, never lost his energy or timing. I was crazy about that man.

42

In to Africa

Hallmark Hall of Fame had a reputation for sponsoring quality television movies. Robert Halmi sent me a script he was producing for them, to be shot in East Africa. Unfortunately, *Face to Face* was not a story of relevance, sensitivity, social significance or quality. It was trying dismally to be a romantic comedy. Twice I said no. The stars it was submitted to said no. The starting date was fast approaching and Halmi called again to say the script had been rewritten and ask me to read the new version.

"Who did the changes?"

"Peter Stone."

Yippee, Peter Stone! *Father Goose* got him an Oscar and aside from his Tony awards, some of his movie credits are *Charade*, *1776* (stage and screen) and *The Taking of Pelham One Two Three*. Sure enough, his dialogue improved the piece immeasurably, but the script was still slight. I was ready to turn it down again.

Brother Jim pointed out, "It's Africa, Lou. When will another offer like Africa come in?"

Location, location, location.

"Hello, Robert. Yes, I'll do it."

I called Peter Stone.

"Peter, you really helped the piece. I wonder if we could talk a minute about the structure of the story. You see I—"

"I won't do structure! I was hired only to redo the dialogue."

"It's just that in the third act—"

"I won't do *structure*. I was hired only to redo the *dialogue*."

Aha. Okay, that was that. On with the MOW.

My friend Peter Bogart, whose father Paul had directed me in several TV shows, had been my assistant director on two MOWs. For the past few years he had been a movie producer on *Blue Lagoon*, *The Rock* and *Ace Ventura, Pet Detective*.

"Peter, I've got a gig. Would you consider going back to a.d.ing?"

"I don't know, Lou, I kinda want to stay where—"

"It's in Africa."

"When do I leave?"

Charlie Correll was now directing television dramas and MOWs, no longer a cameraman. I needed someone with his ease, humor and expertise.

"Charlie, you gotta get back to being a cameraman again."

"I tell ya, I really like this directing thing. I don't know if I'll ever go back."

"I'd really love for you to photograph a thing I'm doing in Africa."

"Well, you know I really should do it once a year, and you're the one this year, pal!"
Location, location, location.

Halmi met me at the Nairobi airport at six in the morning. I was edgy and exhausted
from 24 straight hours of travel. Sleepless, I was picked up at my hotel for a location scout
of Nairobi at ten a.m. Then to the bush to reconnoiter the wilds of Kenya. Six hours out of
Nairobi, I scanned red soil, flat open spaces and sparse vegetation. Hell, we could have shot
this sucker in New Mexico or Texas and hired a junior college basketball team as the Maasai
tribesmen. That was before the spell of Africa settled into me.

Two stars were finally signed, Elizabeth Montgomery and Robert Foxworth. I had
acted separately with each of them, on *Mod Squad* and *Storefront Lawyers* with Foxworth
and on *Bewitched* (in which I played a chimp) with Montgomery.

The story of *Face to Face*: Montgomery, a paleontologist, discovers an ancient skull in
her dig, takes it to Nairobi for evaluation, returns to her discovery site and finds Foxworth,
a British Meerschaum miner, shoveling away. They fight, fall in love, out of love, and end
up together. Not exactly Tracy-Hepburn, but enough to get us all to Africa. Foxworth
worked on the British accent with a coach in Los Angeles and became a convincing middle-
class Brit.

A small village of tents was put up in the bush for the cast and crew. I had a tent to
sleep in, a smaller tent with a two-gallon bag of warm water for the after-work shower, and
yet another tent, the smallest, contained a wooden box with a circle cut out of the top over
a hole in the ground. I was advised to always check for spiders or snakes before sitting on
that box.

Two Maasai and Robert Foxworth at his Meerschaum dig, on the set of *Face to Face*.

Above: **No telephone, no TV, no *New York Times*, none of the world's fright. *Left:* Elizabeth Montgomery with two Maasai tribesmen.**

The filming zipped along. Montgomery was a gift from Apollo. Under the most un–Hollywood of conditions, there was never a whimper or a complaint from her. A bit of makeup and hair in the morning and that was it.

The folks from Hallmark came from Kansas to visit. They were middle-aged middle Americans, and Mrs. Hall (as in Hall-mark) was among them. Nice Midwestern people. Too nice for a shot that would never be on a Hallmark card, Montgomery seeing Foxworth across the river taking an outdoor shower, buck naked. Halmi rushed over. "Put a bush over ... you know, hide his butt."

Maasai approving my set-up.

Above: **For my daughters, the choice between school or Africa wasn't a hard one.** *Right:* **Filming from high above the African plains. "Top of the world, Ma!"**

After the Halls left the set, I did another take that did not hide his ... butt. That's about all Halmi ever intruded. Well, one time a line of camels passed next to our set while I was shooting. "Film dem! Get da camels!"

"But, Robert, there's no caravan of camels in the script."

"We change da script. Get da camels!"

Well, sure, how often does a producer get free camels?

My two daughters, Elkin, 16, and Angelique, 15, arrived. They had their own tent, marveled at the quiet, the smog-free air, the needlessness of television. So happy experiencing our individual discoveries of Africa and ourselves with one another. To quote Brother Jim, "It's Africa, Lou. When will another offer like Africa come in?" Big brothers take care of little brothers.

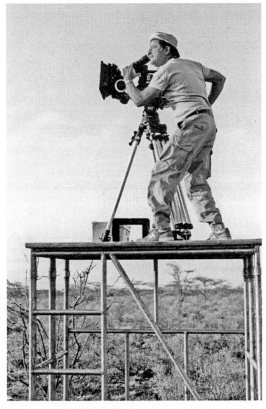

Correll's wife, Robin-the-Giddy, took them, my girls, to the Maasai Maura Game Reserve where they were enthralled by the herds of migrating zebras, wildebeest, gazelles, giraffes. Animals without walls or cages. We shared the wonder of Africa.

When I returned to the States, I fought to preserve and defend that serenity. Alas, the very act of fighting is contrary to serenity.

I was no longer in the midst of extended nature, I was surrounded by human nature, politics, guns, AIDS, traffic, riots, Wall Street, Congress, show business and post-production.

For a director, unlike Sisyphus, we hope there will always be a mountain to claw up, a problem to solve. Even after we take a tumble, we keep clawing. It's our nature.

43

Bean Balls, and Still at Bat

Passport to Terror (1989) was my third and last movie with Lee Remick. Previously I'd directed her in the romantic comedy, *A Good Sport* and the thriller, *Rearview Mirror*. She made a director look good. Talented, enthusiastic, her presence on a set elevated everyone's spirits, her good cheer and ability making the day's work, play. *Passport* was based on *Never Pass This Way Again*, a memoir by Gene LaPere, of the Joseph Hirschorn family. As a tourist in Turkey, Ms. LaPere paid $15 to a street merchant in the port town of Katay for what looked like a dirt-covered rock. As she was re-boarding her cruise ship, Turkish customs examined the rock, accused her of smuggling an antiquity out of Turkey, and threw her into prison for three months. She suffered harsh, demeaning treatment in filthy conditions. NBC was apprehensive about our teleplay adaptation and we were given strict guidelines regarding what we could *not* show in the prison. We weren't trying to make another *Midnight Express* for Heaven's sake, but they mandated we had to dilute or bypass some hard truths, thus diluting the drama.

While I was prepping in Los Angeles, I got a letter with an anonymous threat of "unexpected harm" because of the script's portrayal of the Turkish government's treatment of its prisoners. How this person got a copy of the script, I don't know. I was just thankful he didn't know I'm a Greek. So where did we shoot? Why Pasadena, California, of course. But we had to have one sequence among ancient ruins, which in the Los Angeles area can only be found in cosmetic surgeons' waiting rooms. Since I'd acted in and around Athens, I suggested to the producers, Bill Finnegan and his wife Pat, that we film that sequence in Greece, which ain't short on ruins.

"Oh, no," said Pat. "Greece is third world when it comes to filming."

"Third world? Hardly. *America, America, Never on Sunday* were filmed there quite nicely. Pat, they even produce their own movies and television shows in that third world country." We ended up in Arles, France. I discovered why. The Finnegans' yacht was anchored in Marseilles, less than a hundred miles from Arles.

Remick was running a low-grade fever during the filming, but her irrepressible energy and optimism got me through some hard times with the Finnegans, who appeared only to care about the money they could put in their pockets, not on the screen.

For instance, my first shot in France was to be a 100-foot dolly following Remick among the ruins. Finnegan tried to talk me into a 70-foot dolly. I said, "No. I stepped it out. A hundred."

"Lou, come on, I'll have to hire another grip for the extra 30 feet of track."

"Spend it, Bill. You wouldn't give the cast and crew a wrap party or tee shirts, both in the production budget, so blow a few francs on our *movie*." Grudgingly he ordered the extra track.

It doesn't get any better than Lee.

Van Gogh country, an amphitheater, the light, the air, the food, Lee Remick. A *bonne* shoot.

It's said that the president of NBC, Robert Wright, who never previewed his network's movies, watched ours before it was broadcast. Not a compliment. NBC was owned by General Electric, which did a ton of business with Turkey. He didn't cancel the broadcast, but out of my 28 television movies, *Passport to Terror* is the only one that has never been rerun on network television.

As I was doing my edit, Lee called to tell me that she was leaving for the National Institute of Health in Bethesda, Maryland, for treatment. The low-grade fever was caused by a cancer in her kidney.

44

Sonia Braga, Birthing
and Breeding

The Lifetime movie *The Last Prostitute* (1991) was the story of a pair of teenage boys looking to lose their virginity, using their summer vacation to search out an infamous prostitute to do the deed. Their journey leads them to Texas where, to their dismay, she's gone legit and is raising horses. She hires them as stable boys. The TV movie starred Sonia Braga as the former prostitute, with Wil Wheaton and David Kaufman as the horny boys.

Brenham, Texas, was our location. One would be hard put to find a sweeter place or people to film. Between Austin and Houston, it's a farm community of 14,000 with a town square complemented by a white Grecian-columned courthouse. The pickup trucks outnumber the cars, men in diners eat with their hats or John Deere caps on, youngsters address adults as "ma'am" or "sir."

Our living arrangements were not of Hollywood luxury. Because of a tight budget, our producer Peter Bogart had to put up cast and crew on the cheap, the *very* cheap. He found a defunct and abandoned motel outside of town, the only amenities being running water and electricity. It was a hot and muggy summer with no water in the pool, no maid service, no air conditioning or television, and a sheep farm next door with an appetite-numbing aroma blowing our way. Oh, the glamour of Hollywood. Though the accommodations were not first class, the cast and crew were.

Braga's first day of filming pumped my blood pressure up and my confidence down. The scene was a swiftly moving walk-and-talk dolly shot. Even though I knew the dialogue by heart, Braga's accent was so heavy I could not understand a word she was saying! I printed eight takes. In editing maybe I could grab an intelligible word here and there and make a sentence. Oh, woe. That night I met with the executive producer/writer Carmen Culver and with Bogart. We had to convey our dilemma to Tom Thayer, the Universal exec heading the project. Thayer was young and smart and had sold the project to Lifetime cable, Universal's first venture with them. From this movie, Universal was hoping to do more business with Lifetime.

"Tom, we can't understand a word Sonia is saying. We really should replace her."

"We could loop her in post."

"Yeah, but do you want Lifetime watching dailies and going, 'What? What language is that? Not English,' which is what our audience speaks!"

Thayer immediately saw the problems from Universal's point of view. "Make it work, Lou," he said. "If we fire her, Lifetime will think we don't know what we're doing and that could be the end of a promising relationship."

Heavy sigh.

I hired a college student from Southern Methodist University to run lines with Braga at night, diminish her Brazilian accent, and correct her diction. Smart actor that she is, Braga knew what the problem was and worked hours into the night on her diction until problem became no problem.

In the movie, Braga has to deliver a foal on camera. The delivery had been induced by a local veterinarian. who was going to give us a heads-up when the birth was imminent. Wheaton and Braga rehearsed the birthing business and dialogue and had the scene down cold. The due hour arrived, three cameras ready to roll. The vet led the mare in, the crew was quiet and we rolled the cameras. Show time. During the delivery, Wheaton is supposed to help Braga extract the foal during dialogue. I say "supposed to" because as the colt started to emerge, Wheaton became so slack-jawed his mouth could not form words, his limbs could not move. His lines went south along with every piece of business that we had so thoroughly rehearsed. Braga saw she had to go solo and without a blink she held the colt's legs, pulled and delivered the wet and glistening foal as if an everyday chore. Wheaton remained mute and wide-eyed after I called "Cut and print."

We also had to film that which precedes conception with a stand-in mare for the resting momma. The scene included our scripted hotshot antagonist watching his stud mount Braga's mare while talking with his sidekick. The actor, Woody Watson, was good, experienced, lived on his own Texas farm, and in a horseless rehearsal played the scene with a convincing arrogant bravado. "Horseless" because the stud had to be up for the filming. There were two cameras, one on Watson and his cohort and the other covering the activities of the horses. Another one-take-only deal.

We rolled cameras and with some help from the vet and a cowhand, the equine mating commenced. The stud reared up, put his front hooves on the mare's back, nipped her a quick kiss on the neck, the veterinarian and the cowhand guided his penis into place. The actual act is not of much duration, just long enough to accommodate the half dozen or so lines of dialogue that Watson had. Nature did its duty and I said cut. Watson rushed over to me, dread across his face. "Lou, did I say my lines??"

"Word perfect. What do you mean?"

"Well, I'd never seen horses breed before, and, uh, it kinda blew my mind. I don't even know if I did the scene or not."

I'm always interested in how other directors work and Braga had been directed by Robert Redford three years earlier in *The Milagro Beanfield War.* He was a first-class director; maybe I could pick up a trick or two.

"What's it like with Redford? How does he work?" I asked her.

She looked away for a moment and then answered quietly in her soft Brazilian accent, "Well, first, he make me fall in love with him, and then he break my heart."

Nothing I could put in *my* director's bag.

July 2, 1991: I was setting up a shot adjoining a thriving chest-high cornfield when Bogart ran up to me with his cell phone. "You'd better take this."

It was Kip Gowan, Lee Remick's husband: "Lee just died." The chemo, which I thought was winning, had failed. The cancer had spread to her brain. Her cousin Jonathan Reynolds got on and asked me if I would speak at her memorial. "I can't, Jonathan. I ... just can't."

I stumbled into the middle of the cornfield and dropped to my knees. Her smile, her eyes, her erect and confident stride, her laughter, cooking with her, drinking with her, walking with her, the moments of her infectious enthusiasm and appreciation of life. Smiling, radiating: "It doesn't get any better than this."

45

May the Pod People Perish

There was a popular Coca-Cola commercial in 1981 with a young kid and Mean Joe Greene, a renowned lineman for the Pittsburgh Steelers.

The commercial was expanded into a fluffy one-hour special called *The Steeler and the Pittsburgh Kid*. Greene lived in Dallas and that's where we had to shoot it. I insisted the original kid from the commercial come down to do a test. He was an experienced pro, but show biz and unlikable. Barbara Brinkley, our Texas casting woman, sent over local actors. Among them was this quiet sad-eyed ten-year-old boy who gave a sincere, simple reading. There was no doubt in anyone's mind that Henry Thomas was the boy for us. We thanked Kid Slick and sent him home.

Mean Joe was like a big (very big) brother to Thomas. The boy's deportment, concentration and talent made us grateful to be around this ten-year-old.

At the wrap party, I asked Thomas if that's what he wanted to do, be an actor. He said yes. I asked, "When did you know you wanted to be an actor?"

"All my life," answered the ten-year-old.

Within a year, he was filming *E.T.*

I had the chance to work with him 11 years later on the cable movie *A Taste for Killing*. Thomas was now an experienced and skilled 21-year-old professional, not just a dreamer, and there we were in Texas again. I was shooting a night scene in Houston. It was going well, but what's debilitating to a creative team?

Exterior night: Thomas' character drives up to a darkened house, parks and goes in. A 50-foot dolly shot, no dialogue. That's it. "Action." Thomas drives in. Me to dolly grip: "Slower, slower, Tom okay, Harry, now catch up with him. Good! Henry, turn out your lights this time! Okay, fine. Cut!"

Gary Griffen, my editor, called me the next night. "You're not gonna believe this. That drive up to the house? Randy, this new USA vice-president guy, turns to everybody and says the scene will have to be re-shot. Barbara [Barbara Fisher, prez of Universal USA] asks why, and he says, 'Well, Lou was talking all during the shot.'"

Randy, visit a set, watch an editor at work. Learn *something* about your business.

On that movie, I stumbled into my second Texas nugget. This one was Renée Zellweger, a 23-year-old from Katy, Texas. She auditioned, conquered and was cast. In her first scene, her character flirts with Jason Bateman at a party. Her inexperience and nervousness deadened her natural appeal. I joked with her, and mentioned some acting techniques that might help. She had not a clue as to what I was talking about. I switched to plain ol' Texas talk: What kinda girl is she? Why is she at the party? What about Bateman, does she like what she sees, and what does she want from him and what does she do about it? She relaxed, devastated me with her smile, and sparkled. When Barbara Fisher saw the rushes, she called from Los Angeles: "Who was that girl? She's wonderful."

Another location benefit.

After my seventeenth year of television movies and pilots, Alice West asked me to do an episode of *Picket Fences*, a 1992 series she was producing. In the '70s, a six-day shoot was customary for an hour episode. West told me nowadays the shows had eight-day shoots. I watched some episodes of her series. The scripts were outstanding and that cast: Tom Skerritt, Kathy Baker, Ray Walston, Fyvush Finkel, Costas Mandylor, Holly Marie Combs, Lauren Holly! Back to episodes? A one-hour episode of *Picket Fences* or another TV movie just offered, *Co-ed Call Girl*, with Tori Spelling?

I didn't get off to a good start with David E. Kelley, the creator and exec producer of *Picket Fences*. My assistant director informed me that there would be a tone meeting with Kelley and the other producer-writers. "*Other* producer-writers? And what the hell is a 'tone meeting'?"

She said that Kelley would go through the script telling me how the scenes should be played. "Gee, and here I thought that's what a director was hired to do."

In my very first "tone meeting," Kelley was quiet, almost shy, not wasting his time with small talk. About a half dozen of his minions were seated behind him. I mostly kept my mouth shut. If the script parentheses read (laughing), David would point that out to me. "So he sees the humor and laughs." And so on. Uh-huh, got it.

Then came my turn to give my script notes. Kelley had written a one-page speech for Skerritt that was flabby. "David," I began, "in this speech there's three references to the robbery when I think one, or at most two would suffice."

"I'm not making any cuts in the speech."

"The repetition dilutes the—"

"I'm not making any cuts in the speech."

My Bridge Burners have a mind of their own, "Oh, I see, you're one of those writers who thinks a thousand words is worth a single picture." I thought it was funny. The minions maintained grave expressions.

Kelley (deadpan), "Next note."

My first set-up for my episode was very Movie of the Week-ish, dolly shots, not much coverage. Michael Pressman, the series' producer-director, dropped in and watched a rehearsal. He nodded, smiled and smoothly moved me into the style *of Picket Fences*. Thank goodness I had always admired Pressman's work. One time his dad took over one of my Curt Conway acting classes. We were welded. DNA. I heeded his guidance on the "tone."

For the episode "The Dancing Bandit," there was an acting Emmy nomination for Marlee Matlin and a Directors Guild nomination for me. I thought, "Gee, that was easy. I don't have to fight the networks any more, David does it. The crew, the cast, a group of committed and highly talented people. And eight days! A snap."

In 1994 Kelley wrote "If It Pleases the Court," a *Picket Fences* episode with a strong Supreme Court story line. Whom did we cast as a lawyer? Alan Dershowitz, playing Alan Dershowitz. He was friendly, quiet, and did his scenes honestly and simply. A year later he was cast as the appellate adviser for the defense in the O.J. Simpson murder trial. Presently, in this era of political hubris, he is in front of the cameras again as a CNN contributor and as an active, respected political analyst. The Dershowitz Method works for him.

Back in 1971 I was directing like my fourth Hollywood episode and the female lead was to cry in a scene. She couldn't. I worked with her for three takes, but still she was dry. I was leading her into another take when my assistant director, a second generation old-timer, pulled me aside and tapped his wristwatch: "Let's move on."

"No, we don't have it yet."

"Oh, come on, Lou, it's only television."

More and more it's not "only television."

Not to Kelley. He was tough on his audience, made outlandish events believable. In case you saw some *Picket Fences*, remember when the mayor exploded? Or when the heavy wife unknowingly sat on her husband during his nap and killed him? Cable, web series and sometimes networks are producing offbeat concepts, material, characters, better photography and production values. To quote Steven Spielberg in a *New York Times* interview,

> The film business has always been competitive with television, and in the early age of television, some of the greatest writers worked in television. Paddy Chayefsky, Stirling Silliphant, Rod Serling. Then television went into the formulaic. But something has happened in the last seven or eight years. Some of the best screen writing today is for television. Look at *Transparent*, *Bloodline*, *Wolf Hall* and *Downton Abbey*. And a wonderful series I'm hooked on, *Homeland*.

Television is attracting all manners of talent: Spielberg, Scorsese, Bruckheimer, Pacino, Hoffman, Holly Hunter, Carl Franklin, Glenn Close, Alec Baldwin, David Fincher, Mamet, Drew Barrymore, Kevin Spacey. Jessica Lange. And they keep on coming. Welcome.

46

Sour Power

Mandy Patinkin says that for him, there is no fun in acting. I was directing my first *Chicago Hope* in which he plays Dr. Geiger, the chief surgeon. Geiger has to tell a patient that the new heart he was to get had been given to another patient. The patient's brother was played by Chris Penn. After a few bits of direction to Patinkin and Peter MacNichol, who played the hospital's lawyer, we did two takes and I printed them both.

"Okay, Tim," I told the cinematographer, "let's go to the two-shot of Mandy and Peter." The actors left the set, to return when we had reset the lights.

No one moved. Now this crew was easygoing, quiet and crackerjack fast. So when they just stood there, I went over to Tim and asked what was going on. He quietly said to just wait a minute. Two minutes later, Patinkin rushed back onto the set and said he wanted to do the scene again. No big deal, a good actor can always get another take out of me. It's not usually after he leaves the set and comes back two minutes later.

After too many of Patinkin's "one more" crises, we completed the scene. We were moving to a different set when I saw the executive producer Michael Dinner coming directly at me. He had that look. "Mandy complained about me," I said.

"Well, he says you're confusing him. Your direction confuses him."

"Michael, here's exactly the colors I thought he was missing. That it was not an easy decision for Geiger to have made, so be aware what it must mean to the man, his brother and how they react to it. That's it, Michael. Why is that confusing?"

"I don't know. He doesn't like direction."

Stars have the leverage *if* they are given it. An episode director? Piffle. His name's not even on his chair, it says "Director," and a different butt is going to be in it for the next episode. No producer is going to endanger their relationship with the star. It's called job security.

Other actors come to mind who took the power, but only because they were allowed to. Who is feared, rules.

William Shakespeare may have included us not that long ago when Hamlet lamented in 1603—"Fie on't! Ah, fie! 'tis an unweeded garden that grows to seed, things rank and gross in nature Possess it merely."

Or as Hunter S. Thompson wrote some years later, "The TV business is a Cruel and Shallow Money Trench, a long plastic hallway where thieves and pimps run free and Good Men Die Like Dogs."

47

They're Either Too Young
or Too Old

In 2000, Anne Hathaway, a beautiful 17-year-old in her first TV role, was playing the daughter in *Get Real*, one of those numbing series with three good-looking teenagers, handsome parents in an expensive house, driving a Mercedes. Is it any wonder reality shows invaded and conquered large territories in TV land?

In a scene with her father, played by Jon Tenney, Hathaway's line was, "I can't stand it when you're mad at me." She delivered it as fact, not with any sense of the open and loving relationship she has with her father. We tried it a few more times with my giving wrong directions, like "See *your* father, really see him." She tilted her head, not understanding. I tried another one.

"What if Jon were angry with you, has *Jon* ever been mad at you?" Useless. Though she may have understood what I was after, she didn't have the technique to call up the colors. I took her hand and knelt before her. "A few years ago, my mom was about 90, and we got into a disagreement and were very tense with each other, snappish. For two days I was miserable. I finally said to her, 'Mom, I can't take it when you're mad at me like this.'" The memory brought tears to my eyes. Hathaway looked at me, we shot it again. Tenney hugged her, Hathaway leaned her head onto her father's chest and her tears flowed. I don't know whence nor why. Sometimes a director simply stumbles into talent and lucks into sparking it. Her talent and beauty are now shining in good movies and good parts and she sure knows how to get there.

Another time I was directing a 13-year-old girl in my brother Jim's series *Amazing Grace*. The script called for some emotion in the scene. She wasn't getting it. I was gentle, I joked, I suggested, and in four takes nothing came of my sensitive, meaningless directions. Then the young actress turned to me, "Oh, you want me to cry?" I nodded. She nodded, "Okay."

Take five was a tearfest and we moved on. I had never once uttered to an actor, "And here you cry." A director never stops learning.

From the series *Get Real*, another example of misguided direction, and perhaps a sign of the times and the death of eras gone by. A scene with the 16-year-old son called for a simple sincerity, but knowing he was hired for being cute, the actor was doing cute, not the scene. I suggested, "Henry Fonda. Try Henry Fonda as an image for the scene."

"Who?" asked Jesse Eisenberg, age 16.

"Henry Fonda." Blank stare. "*Mister Roberts, Grapes of Wrath, On Golden Pond*?"

"Wait a minute, that one, the *Grapes* one. I think we did a clip from it on one of our episodes. Which one was he?"

"Tom Joad." Blank stare. "'Wherever there's injustice, I'll be there. Wherever there's—'"

"Yeah, I kinda remember that. So you want me to do it kinda dry, kinda boring."

"Well, maybe *understated* is what I was thinking."

Eisenberg is now well beyond his cute. As an actor he pursues challenging roles, he is a produced playwright, a published author.

It's not only the actors who come up short on history. Michael Gleason and I were before a cadre of young producers casting a one-hour pilot at MTM, not the MTM in its glory days of *The Mary Tyler Moore Show* and its comedies or *Remington Steele*, but after it had been sold and resold several times. We needed an actor to play the father to Bruce Boxleitner, our lead. I saw the list of actors to read that day and squirmed. "Cameron Mitchell? Cameron Mitchell has to *read* for you guys?"

New Boys: "Why shouldn't he? We don't know who he is."

"Okay, television, that should be easy for you. He starred in a series called *High Chaparral*."

New Boys: "Never heard of it."

"Ran four years, '67 to '71."

New Boys: "Nope."

"Okay, then, he was the original Happy on Broadway."

New Boys: "Happy? Wasn't that a rabbit?"

"That was *Harvey*. I'm talking about Arthur Miller's *Death of a Salesman*."

New Boys: "Is it still playing or on video?"

On an episode of *The West Wing*, the British actor Roger Rees and I got to talking. He was living in New York City and teaching a Shakespeare class to actors.

"In speaking of the great British actors, I can't use any of my former references now, Gielgud, Richardson, Newton, even Olivier. The students never heard of them. I've found I have to update my references to Fiennes, Branagh, Rylance, Beales and so forth, not even Finney."

There is an era-difference. Name a hot band or rock group and to my shame I've never heard them or of them. As the young today should be cognizant of the old, so should the older be hip to the new.

We must, as artists, and teachers (and parents), be current, irreverent, bold, and pass on our knowledge and experience to the younger. They may not take it, right, but the old and the new make a good mix. Age can be as arrogant as youth, but I hope the young'uns will be generous enough to spoon-feed their *Now* into the geezers' *Yesterday*. Yum. Feed me.

In the sacrificial speed of today, if while a scene were being filmed the ceiling crashed down, the director would be expected to look around, take a beat and then declare, "Okay, the camera goes here."

Case in point about falling—not ceilings, an actor. *Felicity* was a moderately successful Disney television series and I was hired to do an episode. My first day of prep, I walked into the production office not knowing anybody and no one offering a hello. The room was simmering with tension. A woman across the office waved me into her cubicle. She had a shock of gray in her black hair, early forties, British accent. "We've been doing the episodes in eight days, you'll have seven for your episode. Twelve hours and then I pull the plug. You're budgeted for three two-camera days."

"Hello. I am Lou Antonio. And you are…?"

During casting, I thought brother Jim would be right for the part of a judge. I showed his reel to J.J. Abrams, the producer, and he was impressed. "He's a very good actor," Abrams said. "You know, I've never had a director want his brother to play a part in one of my shows."

"Well, he's made a living at it for—"

"No, I think I want my dad to play the part."

Abrams Sr. has been active in television for probably longer than Jim, but as a *producer*, not an *actor*. Swell. Now with "You'll have seven for your episode," I'll have a brand new old guy. I got out-nepotismed. I wonder if Dad had roles in Abrams' *Mission: Impossible* or *Star Wars* films…?

The leading man, Scott Speedman, was to work every day of that seven-day schedule. A Canadian, he'd gone to Toronto to be at a friend's wedding, but all of his agents, lawyers, managers, publicists plus Scott himself had overlooked a visa requirement. He was banned from re-entering the United States. We quickly rearranged the schedule, confident that all those Disney lawyers easily would spring him in plenty of time. A bit of the Washington two-step was done and Canada and the United States of America ended the Speedman detente. He would be set free to be on set and ready to shoot Thursday. Instead of having him for seven days, I had him for four.

My first day of filming was dismal. The actress, a regular, was embarrassingly inexperienced, but at least I had Scott Foley, playing her paramour, to cut away to. I went home that night in a depressed funk. The next day I was having a great time with regulars Greg Grundberg and Amanda Foreman. They were hot and it looked as if I might make that seven-day cut-off. After lunch, Foreman came onto the sound stage, slipped, fell, cracked her wrist, cut her chin open and bruised her lip. Oh, what a fall that was. The medics came and I think the most pain Foreman felt was when the medic asked, "How old are you?" She was supposed to be a 22-year-old student. With cast and crew standing over her, the poor baby had to fess up for all to hear, "…Thirty-four…"

The medic leaned in, "Sorry, I couldn't hear you."

Painful pause, then: "*Thirty-four….*"

Bleeding and bruised actor or not, the Brit's "seven days" echoed coldly in the sound stage. Foreman's facial swelling would not recede enough to film until the following Monday, the sixth of the seven-day shoot. A wound-free cast hurriedly was called to fill what was left of our 12 hours. Every day the schedule was like throwing a jigsaw puzzle in the air and then trying to fit the pieces back together after they hit the sound stage floor.

Our leading man finally crossed the border. He and Keri Russell, who played Felicity, worked easily and efficiently, and thus with a jiggle here and a squiggle there we were on the Brit's "shedule." Hollywood crew, smart actors, experienced director, we again saved the British.

Episode television has the power to cloud men's minds. If there resides even a dying coal of a creative soul, one has to escape to fan it. As much as I love an all-expenses-paid job in New York City, it was either directing an anemic cop show episode in Manhattan or conjuring an experimental mixed media ballet under the auspices of the Atlanta Ballet. No per diem, no air fare. No salary. Every penny came out of my pocket. With no regrets.

Using a different set of creative muscles invigorated me. No formulaic series-styled masters, angles or close ups snarled my vision. Say bye-bye to all that episode pie. The stimuli were searched for and found in directing a ballerina who had never uttered a word on stage, guiding the choreographer to instill an inner life rather than cardboard poses. In an upstairs room, a *pas de deux* was being danced on camera while the downstairs audience watched it on a television monitor while two actors were playing a straight scene four feet in front of them. To emphasize changing moods and tone, I scuttled around in the dark re-setting lights and changing gels. After each performance I folded the chairs, took the drapes down. The next night I unfolded the chairs and put the drapes back up. My dancing Cousin Dick must have been grinning.

Far from being sleepy time down south, it refueled me for the remaining TV season. Detox is good.

48

Cassidy Catches Ledger

Shaun Cassidy, former star of the *Hardy Boys* series and writer-creator of the series *Cold Case* and the cult favorite *American Gothic*, sent me to Australia for his 1997 series *Roar*. The script about a young warrior in ancient Ireland was weak, but it *was* Australia. This time to avoid the brain-drain fog of jet lag, I negotiated a non-working arrival three days prior to prep. Though it helped some, three days are not enough to acclimatize my body clock after a 15-hour flight and a 12-hour time zone difference.

There are many stimuli in being on foreign soil, and also perils. On that first day location scout, I was looking at a possible battlefield and I asked the location man which way was south (for backlight) and he pointed south. Well, that wasn't hard, was it? Except when I held my hand up toward the south, it was front lit. No, no, I said, *south*. The guys thought I was daft. It finally penetrated my weary brain that I was "down under" and the backlight comes from the north. And then there's that water draining out of the bathtub thing. I still don't get that.

Another location peril the next day: With my group trudging through high grass, our location manager stopped and gestured for us to stop and stay. He found a sturdy limb in the grass and leaned over and fussed and strained with something out of our view. What was he doing? He raised the limb carefully and triumphantly; on it was an eight-foot, fully poisonous brown snake. In California the snakes, equally poisonous, are much shorter and usually found seated at the Polo Lounge in Beverly Hills or leaning into the steering wheel of a Ferrari.

We shot *Roar* in and around New South Wales and on sound stages on the outskirts of Surfers Paradise. There were eight sound stages with a big "WB" painted on them, as in Warner Brothers, as in investing the Yankee dollar into the cheaper union rates of Australia. As in the $200 million spent on *Superman Returns*, filmed there in 2005 by Warner Brothers.

Heath Ledger was the 18-year-old Cassidy snatched out of Perth, Australia. His character was a chieftain in ancient Ireland, fighting against a Roman invasion. Though a novice to television, he had trained and done stage work in Sydney, where he audaciously adapted and performed a one-hour version of *Hamlet*. An affable young man, fun to be with, and loaded with solid acting strengths.

There's lots of room for error in the early episodes of a new series and there were plenty of them on *Roar*. I did the second episode and while the actors were searching for their characters, Shaun was rewriting scenes and the crew was trying to figure out how to get the day's work done.

My third day of filming, the British production manager fired the top-level American cameraman, Levy Isaacs, and brought in a cheaper Aussie. They got what they paid for.

Series regular Vera Farmiga, who played a co-warrior of Ledger, had a life-threatening appendicitis attack during my episode and was rushed to the hospital. I was forced to shoot the principal actors' coverage over the shoulder of Farmiga's stand-in for the rest of my episode. Shoot, shoot, hurry up, hurry up, can't waste time, when you're racing with the clock, time is *money*.

Four years later I shot a segment of a lousy series with Farmiga in Canada, *UC-Undercover*, which

Left: **Bushes could not hide Heath Ledger's talent or charisma.** *Below:* **A great actor, taken from us far too soon.**

lasted as long as a cough. She has gone on to nominations for an Oscar, a Golden Globe, an Emmy and several "Best's" in film festivals. Her first film as a director, *Higher Ground*, was well reviewed. Heath Ledger. Ah. The youngest in the *Roar* cast, Ledger was a committed actor with a healthy curiosity. Even when he wasn't required to be on set, he stayed to observe, ask questions, learn what filmmaking was all about. Wish I could have seen his one-man version of *Hamlet*. Eighteen years old! Thirteen episodes were completed before *Roar*'s cancellation. As you know, the apotheoses of his successes were an Oscar nomination for *Brokeback Mountain*, an Oscar for *Batman Returns* and a daughter he profoundly loved. Ledger died while I was writing this. Personally and professionally, he is deeply mourned. Personally and professionally, his talent and self-effacing decency will be missed.

We shall not look upon his like again.

49

Shatner, Bergen, Fox—Doing It

It's a 32-mile drive from my house in Burbank to Manhattan Beach, California. At 5:45 a.m. it takes 50 minutes to an hour to drive there from Burbank, the return at seven or eight p.m. is 90 minutes to two hours. It was my commute each day for episodes of *Boston Legal*, and a return to excellence. David Kelley scripts, Candice Bergen, Bill Shatner, René Auberjonois, James Spader, talented beautiful actresses and A+ guests and crew. Worth every minute, worth every mile.

The punitive and infamous Blacklist of 1947 through the 1960s was an American disgrace. In the country today there is a Graylist. In many professions and jobs, gray hair means you're too old to be of much use, too old to cut the mustard so let's get a younger, cheaper one in. Dark hair dyes line the shelves. Not in the *Boston Legal* troop. ABC and producer-director Bill D'Elia were creatively color blind. When I worked with Shatner, he was 77 with untiring energy. He would bounce into work as if invited to a party, full of fun and ready to play. Shatner, Auberjonois and Bergen are in their seventh decade and still puppies in their enthusiasm for acting.

Each has a different way of working and each has to be worked with accordingly. Spader plans his performances and it's difficult to alter his concept. As the excellent director Jeff Bleckner said to me, "I just let him do what he's worked out. He knows what he's doing."

Shatner is the opposite, he will try anything. He seems to get a kick out of bringing a different shade to each take. His acting bursts with self-enjoyment, as if he's saying to himself, "This is *good*." Auberjonois is an immaculate actor. Always prepared, soaks up direction, always open to a suggestion. A few times when I've started a move in to whisper to him, he'll hold up his hand and say, "I know. Too actor-y." Bergen? A delicious laugher, a positive force on a set. Just like the good times we had on *Mayflower Madam*, she welcomes my lean-ins: "Yes, she is Hands' boss, but is she sure or unsure on his becoming a partner?" She'll dig into the question and on the next take pull my socks up with fresh nuances of her own. I just ask the questions, a good actor answers them.

Talk about hanging in there. I was a lucky man to direct the first of a four-episode arc on a *Boston Legal* with Michael J. Fox. While prepping, I read his book *Lucky Man*, an honest appraisal of his life. He has a second book out now, *Always Looking Up: The Adventures of an Incurable Optimist*. He is the youngest person on record to be diagnosed with Parkinson's disease. Fox has to take his meds to control its symptoms. His resolve got to me. We rehearsed a scene and his performance wasn't there yet. "Lou, it'll be better after I take my pills," he said. "I don't want to slow you down, but if you can give me ten minutes by myself…" Here's this man constantly in thrall to these symptoms and he doesn't want

Actors eat, crews hover. Shatner, Bergen and company on the set of *Boston Legal*.

Michael J. Fox. A paragon for us all.

to slow us down?! I took his arm, "Michael, this is the fastest crew in Hollywood. Take all the time you need."

This is what he deals with daily: Parkinson's, "a progressive disease of the nervous system marked by tremor, muscular rigidity and slow imprecise movement."

To have had the opportunity to work with Michael, *I'm* a lucky man. For a small person, well, he is immense.

50

In and Out of It,
Out and Into It

When I first started auditioning actors as a television director, I said to brother Jim that it's a wonder any actor ever gets hired. The odds seem lottery-like. Just walking from the door to the chair, an auditioning actor is evaluated and judged before they have read a word. It's all so damned subjective too. An actor might be handsome to one producer, plain to another. The same goes for sexy, which is a personal preference, oftentimes not revealed.

I was doing a guest teach at Tracey Roberts' Los Angeles acting group, and a good-looking man of 35 said, "I'm told I'm a pretty good actor and have a good look so if I just hang in there, I'll probably make it, won't I?"

"Make it" means different things to different actors. Commercially? Creatively? An actor must define what that means to him/her. I told him that when I was a young actor, I believed that talent would be all I needed to have a life as a professional actor. One of the most frightful phrases pounding my ears was, "It's all luck and timing." Yeah, you can name the stars who don't possess much talent or skill because that "indefinable something" keeps them employed. "Maybe you have that, too," I told him. "The right part might bring it out. But I have to tell you that in my experience, no matter how ready you are, no matter how long you hang in there, I'm sorry, but that doesn't guarantee anyone will make it."

If I may quote from an Arthur Penn interview conducted by James Grissom:

> So much of it is luck. Dumb fucking luck. There is so much talent out there—in every area—and it can't get a set of eyes to look at it or ears to hear it because it hasn't gotten into a magical circle yet. The magical circle of the right plays with the right directors with the right agents with the right reviews. No one escapes this, no one ever did. What I would like to do—and what we all should do, including you with your writing and recounting—is to persuade those with dreams and talent to keep at it, despite the odds and despite the fact that the luck hasn't noticed them yet. You have to believe that it will, and what you and I have to do is make some noise and wave some flags so that luck looks over and finally notices the mendicant that has kept up the work.

Work works hand in hand with making it.

I directed some early episodes of the series *Dawson's Creek*. It had a pride of talented young actors fed nourishing scripts by a young Kevin Williamson, the creator. Actors in their teens and 20s, writers in their 30s. Prominent in the series were James Van Der Beek, Katie Holmes, Joshua Jackson and Michelle Williams, all good actors who scored strongly in their roles. But Williams diverged a bit from the others. On a Sunday off during our initial episode together, she called and asked if we could get together and discuss her scenes. An unusual request. She was pumped and curious, and reading Uta Hagen's book on acting. She repeatedly kept asking me about "the craft," what technique I used as an actor, about the Actors Studio and the Method. Not one Hollywood question or piece of career advice was ever discussed. As we broke down her scenes, she confided intimate details of her young life, which at 16 she was still in. She was adventurous and I encouraged that attitude in her acting. Unafraid, she welcomed the laps ahead of her. During her hiatus, against the advice of "her people" (agents, managers, publicists), she replaced an actress leaving the Off Broadway hit *Dirty Joe*, the first produced play of Tracy Letts. What better classroom to explore and build an actor's craft than on a stage connecting with yourself and an audience, reaching them, losing them, controlling them? She started her second *Dawson* season with a better awareness of what she had and what she lacked. In one later episode, she told me, "I'm gonna kick the shit out of that scene tomorrow." Her character, leaving town, fills with emotion as she boards a bus saying goodbye to a friend. After each of three emotionless takes, Williams would whisper to me, "I'll get it, I'll get it." The sixth take she didn't get it and I had to move on. She was heartbroken. But that "failure" made her work even harder on how to reach her talent and use it. She has continued to explore access to her talent. It's been a Trip to Bountiful. Williams exemplifies a quote of Will Smith: "The reason I made it and some don't is because I worked harder than the others."

The employment goals of an actor are overwhelmed by the truth of unemployment. Though the acting vampire has sucked the blood of reason from the dedicated, they still explore, unknowing of their fate, that undiscovered country from whose bourn no traveler returns. Here's what was attributed to Edwin Booth, the most popular and admired actor of the 1800s: "I shall give you hunger and pain and sleepless nights, also beauty and satisfaction known to few, and glimpses of the heavenly life. None of these shall you have continually, and of their coming and going you shall not be foretold."

James Karen, acting roles much younger than his 94 years, is still doing guest shots and films. He hosts the Buster Keaton Festival in Kansas every year and is sought after yearly to much fan excitement at *Return of the Living Dead* conventions. When he was younger, 90, he was hired as a guest artist on a Turner Classic Movies cruise. He remembers every hour of every year of his fascinating life and career. His stories of his experiences in the original 1947 production of *A Streetcar Named Desire* still instruct me in the use of the unique skills and talents of that cast. He still gets casting calls.

Unlike some cultures that respect and revere their older generation.

Pat Hingle, a Broadway star and film veteran, at only 60-something, went to audition for two young movie producers.

Young Producer: "Tell us, Mr. Hingle, what have you done?"

Hingle: "Before or after you were born?"

Shelley Winters had this one: "So, Ms. Winters, tell us what you've done." Whereupon Ms. Winters reached into a large bag she had set on the floor, "Well, I've *done* this." One after the other, she extracted two Academy Awards.

Eli Wallach had an important role in *Wall Street: Money Never Sleeps*, when he was 94. He died at age 98.

Norman Lloyd, 102. We flock to him for his luncheon remembrances of the long-gone greats, e.g., Welles, Chaplin, Renoir, Hitchcock. Lloyd still does guest shots, plays tennis and does voice-overs. Connie Sawyer is 103 and in the movie *Trainwreck*, and guested on *Donovan*, a TV series. Cicely Tyson, 93, and James Earl Jones, 86, were recently on Broadway starring in a two-hander, *The Gin Game*. At 87, Lois Smith continues to grace the Broadway boards. And Norman Lear, 95, with a new book out and still politicizing.

Still on their feet directing: Clint Eastwood at 87, Ridley Scott at 80, John Badham at 77, Woody Allen at 82, Francis Ford Coppola at 78, Robert Redford at 81.

2014: Oklahoma City, Oklahoma, Coppola was fussing with filmmaking again. There he was delving into a new mode of shooting a movie with 115 film students and locals. He shot on a 7000-foot sound stage with 15 sets, 15 or 16 cameras, green screens, pre-taped segments, live scenes, filming all at the same time, sometimes not, and Lord knows what else. I wasn't there. I was told it was beamed from a satellite truck into two countries.

2016: UCLA, Los Angeles. Coppola is trying it again, learning and refining as he goes. We await.

Definitely hanging in there, and doing it.

In 1956, Gerald O'Loughlin, ballsy and strong, played Stanley to Tallulah Bankhead's Blanche. At age 89 with vision and hearing problems, he was still doing scenes at the Los Angeles Actors Studio. After a scene from *The Rose Tattoo*, I made a few observations of his work and of our admiration of his still being a curious, searching actor. That small room of fellow actors did something that is not encouraged at the Studio. With tears, smiles and applause, we expressed our appreciation and respect for a man devoted to his calling.

One of the younger actors, Holland Taylor, now 74, immersed herself for four years in researching and writing a one-woman show about Ann Richards, the ex-governor or Texas. She invested uncountable hours of her life and dollars into her obsession to portray Richards. At a young 67, pulling piles of cash from her pockets, Taylor acted and produced the play. While doing her TV series she moonlighted with a dialect coach, two alternating assistants to run lines with her, hired a wigmaker, costumer, line producer, scenic and lighting designers and stage crew, and held budget meetings. During one dress rehearsal, a stagehand suggested a way to save her money, though it would slow a set change. She responded strongly, "I climbed those whorehouse steps for eight years to do this. Spend the money!" (That house was her series *Two and a Half Men*.)

When someone screwed up, she did not accuse, berate or scream. She mended. My Bridge Burners would have remained closed had I known her earlier in my life. After observing one quiet mend, I said to her, "Holland, if only I'd worked with you early in my career, I wouldn't be in *Galveston* now!"

At the Actors Studio West, I teach a class for actors and moderate one for directors. As I remind the actors, "Pilates, gym, yoga, the beach, fine. *But have you acted today?*" Now it's, "*Act today!*"

Arguably the best acting teacher in the '70s and early '80s was Peggy Feury. She would say to the actors in her classes, "I can always tell you that you can make it. I could never tell you that you won't make it." I heard this from her and harkened back to my embryo days in New York when Paddy Chayevsky took over Curt Conway's acting class one session and splattered his bitter gloom all over us optimistic young actors. Chayevsky was a prominent playwright, television and Oscar-winning screenwriter. What he had gleaned over the

I'm back in a classroom again.

years, he dumped on us young hopefuls like a damp blanket of doom. "Show business is a bag of crap and only through luck will one or two of you possibly make a living in it. Your lives will be filled mostly with disappointments. Hardly any of you will be successful so get out of it now. Get a life, one based on reality, not on dreams."

At age 35, George Boyd left his reality for his dream. He was a successful Atlanta lawyer who longed to get away from what he had become as a lawyer, callous, deceitful and hypocritical. He moved to Los Angeles to become an actor. In scene after deadly scene in Peggy Feury's acting group, he was the actor no one wanted to work with. In his second year, fellow classmate Sean Penn heaped praise on Boyd's work and everyone in class wanted to do scenes with this gentleman from Georgia.

He popped around Los Angeles doing lots of 99-seat theater for seven dollars a performance, four musicals at the American Lyric Theatre, parts in short films for the American Film Institute, occasional television jobs. A highlight was playing the lead in *Night Must Fall* on stage opposite Frances Bergen, Candice's beautiful mom. I cast him in three or four of my television movies and he always gave a thoughtful and honest performance.

Though his years as an actor never supplied him a living wage, he said he was learning how to understand people and *himself* as he never had as a lawyer. In his 40s and wanting a more stable life, he returned to Atlanta after seven years as an actor. But you know what he said to me?

"I wouldn't trade those seven years for anything."

Some come back.

Ron Rifkin, 78, had seven years of envied employment as an actor. He had studied, done plays, television, films. Jobs. Most actors would have been satisfied with his employment record. The roles he was being offered, and accepting, had a sameness, a shallowness, a lack of challenge. "This is not why I became an actor." He went to work in his father's furrier firm in 1982. He and his lovely wife Iva formed a company and went into the clothing design business. He stopped going to the theater. Though the business was a success, he had lost himself, became deeply depressed. One evening Iva convinced him to go to the theater, Mandy Patinkin was doing his solo concert. Grudgingly Rifkin sat watching. After four or five songs, Patinkin stopped his concert and, looking out to the audience, said, "Ron? Ron Rifkin, is that you? I haven't seen you in such a long time." Somehow, and Rifkin can't explain it, that relit the fuse in him. After his seven-year hiatus ("The only three syllable word they know in Hollywood," say the Theatre Snobs), he went to his father and said he'd like to go back to acting. His dad said, "You are either in business or you're an actor. Not both." Rifkin is an actor.

Robin Baitz, a talented young playwright, wrote—in one day—*The Substance of Fire* and cast Rifkin. For this Off Broadway performance he won all kinds of awards, the Obie, the Drama Desk, the Lucille Lortel. Playing Herr Schultz in the 1998 Broadway revival of *Cabaret*, he snagged a Tony for Best Featured Actor. He is, these days, a respected and much employed actor with a potful of plays, TV series and movies behind him, and ahead of him. Dropping out, coming back and hanging in. Because he had to, his soul demanded it.

Each era goes with the times and, boy, it goes fast today. A director friend showed me episodes of his favorite TV series, *Breaking Bad*, on his Smart Phone. I could not share his excitement. "Rob, in your hand is now a radio show. With a screen that small, why bother with composition, lighting, interesting masters, a beauty shot? It's gonna be big head close-ups and words. Apple, give me the Silver Screen."

An actress at the Actors Studio said to me, "Lou, I just won best lead actress in a series!"

"Great. What series?"

"Oh, it's an Internet series, each episode is six to eight minutes long."

"Is there a SAG contract for those things?"

"Well, sort of, but not really. But if it gets a sponsor, we get paid."

We are warned early on, if anyone goes into acting to make a living, well... As Harold Hill warned us in Meredith Willson's *The Music Man*: "Either you're closing your eyes to a situation you do not wish to acknowledge, or you are not aware of the caliber of disaster.... Ya got trouble, my friend, you got trouble...."

But the territory keeps expanding. Prize-winning movies are shot on cell phones, there are thousands of digital motion pictures motionless on shelves across the world, many budgeted at $100, Big Ones at $6000. Employment opportunities are like little gopher holes popping up from the big city to single-stoplight towns. There can be even a bit of remuneration. Sometimes. Be it Internet or Waiver or Class or Auditions, failures and successes are Experience. On your feet doing it. Drill into it. Learn and practice your craft, whatever it is.

Here's a couple that Harold Hill would've gone green over. Rather than actors being paid for a job, *the actor pays for the job*. In the 99-seat waiver theaters of Los Angeles, plays can be properly produced for 10,000 to 30,000 dollars. Often the actor gets a part, but if the financing is not all there, more bucks are needed to open. Guess where it comes from. Yep, actors too often make up the difference to take a bow. No one makes any money, that's not what the actor or director is there for. You are not an actor if you are not acting. Nor a writer, nor a director if you are not testing and enjoying your talents.

Films have their cups on the sidewalk too. In those movie musicals of the '30s and '40s, there's usually some gray-haired angel (investor) giving money to the producer or director if he'll give a part to his cutie-pie girlfriend. Today the angel is your computer. Hustling has hit the Internet with the Kickstarter scramble. It is a media fund-raising concept open to all denominations of dollars, and, lo, sometimes it lands a biggie. A quote from Hillary Lewis' July 2012 *Hollywood Reporter* article about Steven Soderberg's donation of $10,000 for a Spike Lee project: "Spike Lee's Kickstarter for a movie that he describes as a 'funny,' 'sexy' and 'bloody' picture has so far raised $403,546 of its $1.25 million goal from 1,989 backers (including 21 at the $10,000 maximum level). There are 22 days left for the campaign to meet its fundraising target."

Conversely there's Michael Pressman. Like Spike Lee, he's an experienced and impressively talented director-producer who produced, directed and self-financed a movie about the hellish goings-on in a Los Angeles waiver theater production he directed of Terrence McNally's two-character play *Frankie and Johnny in the Claire de Lune*. Rehearsals were chaotic and tense. Lisa Chess, perfect as Frankie, the male actor awful, and fired after a preview. Pressman closed the show, re-opened weeks later with himself playing Johnny. Whew, the show drew excellent reviews. Pressman's movie of all the *sturm und drang*, *Frankie and Johnny Are Married*, is sweet, sad and hilarious. Money in mind, quality held, some juggling—digital camera for interiors, 16mm for exteriors, 35 mm for the scenes from McNally's play. Then why his out-of-pocket *Frankie and Johnny*, you ask? Pressman had *total control*.

Shakespeare thrived because of patronage of the royals, who were preceded by powerful patrons of the B.C. Greek boys, Aeschylus, Sophocles, Euripides *et al*. Today we bow to foundations, corporations and to the ever more caring Moms and Dads, Sugar Daddies and Cougar Mommas.

However achieved, Mr. Chayevsky, dreams can become a reality as more and more dream catchers float toward our stargaze. We battle, retreat, brook the losses, successes, humiliation, admiration, deprivation, and yet continue to endure the, if you will, thousand natural shocks that flesh is heir to. You gotta be a Tinkerbell. If you believe, applaud yourself, disregard those who don't. Step into batter's box as often as you can. You don't have to swing for the fences. A walk, a bunt, a looper to left. You can never tell when or where the ball will drop.

"Love it more than anything"? No. Enthralled and dedicated to it? Yes. Fascinated by its extraordinary possibilities and potential? Definitely.

Strasberg says it for all of us with this inscription in my copy of his book *Strasberg at the Actors Studio*: "For Lou, with high hopes for the future."

Here it is some five decades later, and as severely as some of this book illustrates the slings and arrows of life in theater, television and movies, yes, I still believe what my wise Greek Poppa used to say to his sons:

"We live in hopes."

Index